Golden Boy

Golden Boy

The Fame, Money, and Mystery of

Oscar De La Hoya

By Tim Kawakami

**Andrews McMeel
Publishing**

Kansas City

Golden Boy: The Fame, Money, and Mystery of Oscar De La Hoya copyright © 1999 by Tim Kawakami. All rights reserved. Printed in the United States of America. No part of this book may be used or reproduced in any manner whatsoever without written permission except in the case of reprints in the context of reviews. For information, write Andrews McMeel Publishing, an Andrews McMeel Universal company, 4520 Main Street, Kansas City, Missouri 64111.

www.andrewsmcmeel.com

99 00 01 02 03 RDH 10 9 8 7 6 5 4 3 2 1

Library of Congress Cataloging-in-Publication Data

Kawakami, Tim.
    Golden boy: the fame, money, and mystery of Oscar De La Hoya /
Tim Kawakami.
        p.   cm.
    ISBN: 0-8362-6941-1 (hardcover)
    1. De La Hoya, Oscar, 1973–   2. Boxers (Sports)—United States—
Biography.   I. Title.
GV1132.D37K39   1999
796.83'092—dc21
    [b]   98-45971
                                                                    CIP

Designed by Holly Camerlinck

Typeset by Steve Brooker at Just Your Type

Cover photo by Albert Sanchez/Outline

*To Allan Malamud and Jim Murray,
God rest their souls, and to the sport of boxing,
which enabled me to spend the best moments
of my career with the two of them. They were
my heroes, my teachers, and my friends. Jim
and Allan are irreplaceable, and every new day
since they left this world proves it more.*

Contents

Acknowledgments

It is a peculiar, and engaging, quality about boxing that it can produce the worst moments, and some of the best people.

This book could not have been written without the benevolence of the good people I met while writing about this conflicted, convoluted sport. I won't and can't name them all, but I especially thank Genaro and Rudy Hernandez for their integrity; Emanuel Steward, Joe Minjarez, Teddy Atlas, Jesus Rivero, Al Stankie, and Lou Duva for their honest expertise; Veronica Peralta and her husband, Art, for their friendship and faith; Bob Mittleman, Steve Nelson, and Shelly Finkel for their patience; and John Beyrooty for his insight.

I also am indebted to the great collection of boxing writers with whom I have shared tales, casino tables, and several arguments, among them: Ron Borges of the *Boston Globe,* Royce Feour of the *Las Vegas Review-Journal,* Tim Dahlberg and Ed Schuyler of the Associated Press, Richard Hoffer of *Sports Illustrated,* Robert Seltzer of the *El Paso Times,* Mike Katz and Bob Raissman of the *New York Daily News,* Norm Frauenheim of the *Arizona Republic,* Mike Rosenthal of the *Los Angeles Daily News,* Carlos Arias of the *Orange County Register,* Tom Friend of *ESPN: The Magazine,* Wally Matthews and Anthony Gargano of the *New York Post,* Fernando Paramo of *Deportes Hoy,* Greg Logan of *Newsday,* Jeff Schultz of the *Atlanta Constitution,* and Jon Saraceno of *USA Today*.

I owe gratitude to the editors of the *Los Angeles Times,* and mainly my sports editor, Bill Dwyre, who had the idea of putting me on the boxing beat in the first place; to my predecessor on boxing, Earl Gustkey, for all of his help; and to my friends Chris Dufresne, Lisa Dillman, and Mike Penner at the *Times,* and Michael Ventre and David Davis outside of it, who heard all these stories for years.

I thank my agent, Steve Delsohn, who ushered me through the hardest times, and his associate, Scott Waxman; my editor Chris Schillig and her assistant, Jean Zevnik.

Nora Donaghy, my first editor, deserves special acknowledgment for caring about this project, for making it better, and for understanding it sometimes better than I did myself. I thank her dad, too.

Lastly, and always, I thank my parents, who have shown me that with love and patience, almost everything does turn out for the best. See?

—Redondo Beach,
November 1998

Introduction

Every now and again over the years I wrote about him for my newspaper, and during the months I took to write this book, I kept thinking back to when Oscar was nineteen, and everything was just beginning. For him, for the boxing world, for his bank account, and for me. Though you knew things were going to get bigger for him, at that quiet moment in his mountaintop cabin, he was calm. He seemed to be just waiting. . . . Back then, I didn't quite know what for, but I do now.

We talked about a lot of things that first day. I asked him, not for the last time, Can you imagine what it would feel like to lose? And, for the only time, I think he answered from his heart that day.

"There was this guy, a real good fighter in the amateurs," he said, "Ivan Robinson. He was from Philadelphia, in my weight class, and he was always tough. But the guy always lost to me, or to somebody else. He was always finishing second, you know?" Then Oscar stopped, and looked at me, which he rarely does to any interviewer when he's talking. "Can you imagine that? Never winning? Man, I could never do that. I'd quit if that happened to me. You've got to win. Or else you go crazy." A moment of silence. "But I was born a winner. I *can't* lose."

Amid the rush of events and the flower of his particularly raucous flavor of fame, I keep thinking back to those words. And I think, even before I knew him, he was telling me all I ever really needed to know.

Maybe I should take it as a tribute that De La Hoya's handlers were so nervous about the writing of this book. They know what I know. But I never thought they should be worried; I always figured that Oscar knew that I was not in the business of selling scandal, or massaging minor incidents into tabloid headlines.

Anyway, he is too famous now, and too reckless at times, to avoid scandal, no matter what any one writer says or does. His handlers want and urge him to be painted as a Michael Jordan–style icon, as a beloved marketing brand name. But he'll never be that. That's not who he is. Just as this book was going to print, De La Hoya was hit with a $10 million civil suit by an unnamed eighteen-year-old girl from the L.A. area who alleges that De La Hoya raped her in June 1995, when she was fifteen. The alleged incident—which De La Hoya's handlers said was a blatant attempt to coerce money out of the fighter—supposedly occurred in Cabo San Lucas, in the weeks after De La Hoya's triumphant knock-out-victory over Julio Cesar Chavez.

That, interestingly and perhaps fatefully, was the period of time when Mike Hernandez and his wife, Cindy, were fervently pushing De La Hoya to break up with his longtime girlfriend, Veronica Peralta, worried that he was growing too attached to her. Peralta was originally scheduled to join Oscar at the Baja California resort, but did not. When he returned home, De La Hoya broke up with Peralta, forever.

And that the incident would be alleged to have taken place in Cabos, the bar, golf course, and strip-club studded playland for rich Mexicans and rowdy Americans, comes as no surprise to anyone who knows that De La Hoya feels freest there—at least unencumbered by promotional duties, familial pressures, the mistrust of East L.A. boxing fans, and, perhaps, the moral values of his upbringing. Stories of his binge drinking at Los Cabos (and wild gambling in Las Vegas) became public a few months before the lawsuit.

This book was not written to rain judgment down on De La Hoya, who, after all, is young, handsome, and luxuriously rich. He has a right, at times, to tiptoe toward the razor's edge. He has achieved great things, things to celebrate. And, though I do write about the baby boy he fathered with a woman who could barely even be called a girlfriend (and several other babies claimed to be his), this book was not written to detail every sordid moment of his life; I wouldn't want to write it, and I don't want to associate myself with those who would want to read it.

But I wasn't going to mislead anybody about his frailties, either. They help explain how and why he has had such a soaring career and unsteady life. And point to where he might end up.

We were around each other fairly continuously for more than four years. We spoke hundreds of times, we played golf, we pushed through crowds together. I saw great and messy things. I wrote about them, I think fairly, for more than four years in my newspaper. I talked to his friends, his enemies; I knew and interviewed just about everybody who was added to or fired from Team De La Hoya, and it was usually both. I talked to fighters who despised him, and those that only dreamed of fighting him. Oscar and I disagreed on some of the things I wrote, but most of the time, I was sure that Oscar appreciated sounding things out with me—testing the public waters, and thinking through some of his more revealing emotions. His handlers, the men who make money off of him and want him to be as bland a public figure as possible, did not fully enjoy it, but they had to tolerate it.

I have heard that they are afraid of this book. Which tells you much about their own channels of thought. They assume the darkest motives, because, as I have seen so many times from so many people who have come and gone, to be near De La Hoya is to lose your bearings. There is so much money involved, and so much attention, the people closest to him spend most of their time jealously guarding their positions, and suspecting the motives of all the others. Even his father and Mike Hernandez, his closest adviser—you could say *mostly* his father and Mike Hernandez—fall into this trap.

So I guess they think they know my motive for writing this book. Yes, I am making money—but I will not become rich. My life will not change by the publication of these pages. In many ways, I was much more comfortable writing about him every week, chuckling with the camp members I know and like, and having a front row seat in what already is a historic career. But instead, I went back and reinterviewed everyone I could, including Oscar. And I wrote this book. Then they started worrying.

If money wasn't the motive, then what? This is the best way I can explain it: Getting De La Hoya's story down right, if I could, was worth it. I've read previous attempts to tell readers who he is—and *why* he is —including my own, and I never was satisfied. Those articles didn't take the private, shy, and self-absorbed person I knew, and put him into a public perspective. They didn't explain why he can be so loved by the camera, and so cold to those closest to him; why he can be so dramatic and magnetic in the ring, but so meek in the face of any other confrontation; why he can find father figures by the handful, and walk away from them all, one by one except for his real father, whom has never fully embraced him; why he can be the most successful Latino athlete ever, and also the most vilified; why he can indulge himself with scores of women, and still complain that he is alone; why he can be one of the most exposed sports celebrities in America, and yet hardly utter a revealing word.

This book is my shot at getting it right. I'm sure Oscar's handlers will let me know whether they think I did.

chapter one

"Letting You Go Is Like Giving Up on Life"

He ran through clouds.

The fog hadn't vanished when Oscar De La Hoya got out to run, up on the masked mountain, and the gray-white gloom shrouded even the tallest trees. This was summertime, but the low clouds and cool wind surrounded him, hanging on the trees and covering the road. Usually, De La Hoya loved training for fights during summer, when he could close his eyes, taste the air, and feel like he was lifted by rock and dirt, high toward the sun and the heavens.

"And God is always smiling at me," he likes to say, with equal touches of humor and ego. "I know that He is always looking down and smiling when He sees me. Because I never fail at anything I do."

Which made Big Bear, his isolated training base, a special place to be.

In the summer on the mountaintop, 8,000 feet and 150 miles from Los Angeles below and to the west, De La Hoya was bathed by light, and unveiled. Above the clogged valley, below the sky. In summer, the mountains were always best, when the air was thin and sweet, and when De La Hoya trained to win championships.

But, aloft in the San Bernardino Mountains on this July morning, the clouds stuck to the peaks, dampening his mood and darkening the sky. He felt cold and invisible, left alone, brooding as he moved along the trail. De La Hoya ran his usual route, starting before six A.M., in the chill.

Out of his rented cabin, down fifty stairs, around familiar dirt roads, up into the forest again. Sometimes during this camp, De La Hoya ran with others—with his older brother, Joel, or with his oldest friend, Jose (Little Joe) Pajar. This morning, like most of the mornings, he ran by himself, with only his feet and memories to guide him.

He ran, and then he stopped at a familiar tree, carved with six letters, circled by a heart.

ODLH + VP

He felt like he was in a dream. De La Hoya ended up here, not just because he always made sure to pass by this tree and look at these initials, but because, on this morning, something was missing. Veronica, he thought, you should be here.

It was the most natural and the most disturbing feeling he had ever experienced, staring at that tree. She was down the mountain, refusing to speak to him, listening to her mother and brothers, finally. Veronica was down the mountain, back home in Norwalk, a two-hour drive and a heartbreak away.

It was his fault. He admitted that, and tried to walk away. He had walked away easily before, from so many other situations. But then he went up the mountain, and began the preparations to beat his rival, Genaro Hernandez, the most personal fight of his career. That was before he started thinking about Veronica Peralta again. Everything else faded away, hidden by clouds.

She was strikingly beautiful, a former Miss Mexico–Los Angeles. She was opinionated, set for college, a striver, sometimes too independent for his stubborn, cranky family. She was everything his family wasn't—and his family hated her for it. His father detested her, and called her a gold digger to her face. Despite that and because of that and due to so many other reasons, she was the most intimate friend he ever had.

They discovered each other when they were both nineteen years old, lost each other a few times, but always wound their way back together. In the face of his father's feelings, she was his first act of rebellion, his first taste of freedom from his father. And though he saw the tree and traced the initials again, on this foggy day, Veronica wasn't there.

De La Hoya was twenty-two years old.

It was 1995, and he was racing, inevitably, toward a kind of boundless athletic celebrity neither he nor anyone in the sport could quite yet understand. He knew it was out there, but it was all unscripted, it was all movement amid uncharted land, accelerating by the day.

Earlier in the year, De La Hoya was paid more than $2 million to destroy another rival, Rafael Ruelas, in a daunting display of showmanship and talent. That was the first time any lightweight fighter had earned as much as $1 million for a purse. The game but overwhelmed Ruelas earned $1 million himself, solely because he was fighting De La Hoya. But Ruelas was gone now, and it was just De La Hoya on the mountaintop. Everything led him back to the peak, looking back down.

At nineteen he had won a gold medal, hung it from his neck, and watched it glow even brighter in the reflection of everyone else's eyes. At seventeen his mother had died, and he had cried at her funeral, cried so hard that those who saw and heard him gulped back their own tears. Or they cried too, not for her, but for him. After the Olympics, fresh-faced and an instant celebrity in the fight-crazed East L.A. community, he had signed with two strangers who promised him $1 million. He never got all of the money, but he spent whatever he got wildly, spent it before he could even think of putting it in a bank. The offers kept pouring in, and the victories got bigger and bigger. This was not a career, this was a conquest. Everybody he faced in a boxing ring he beat. Dating back to his amateur days, he hadn't lost since 1991.

The sex appeal was electrifying.

"This is not the face of a fighter," his longtime trainer, Robert Alcazar, said half jokingly when De La Hoya was nineteen. Alcazar at times looked at De La Hoya like he, too, was consumed by him, that he would be lost without him. "Look at him, it shouldn't be wasted getting hit," Alcazar said. "He should be a movie star. That's the face of a movie star. It's too beautiful."

Already he was on magazine covers, and Hollywood producers told him he could be an actor whenever he gave them the word. He entered rooms, and girls sprinted to him, acted outrageously around him. Was he Elvis? Smart businessmen handed him money for nothing. De La Hoya's own nickname for himself was "the Magnet," and it was arrogantly apt. "Time to turn 'the Magnet' off," he said before he went to sleep, laughing. He was an eternal, relentless attractor.

This was, this could certainly be, an incredible life. This was a fantasy life. So why wasn't Veronica there with him?

He could have any girl in Los Angeles, almost any girl he ever looked at—actresses, models, virgins—and not the girl he loved? Is this why he ran in the mornings and trained and trained? He sat down by the tree. He looked at his own carving . . . ODLH + VP surrounded by a heart.

When he got back to the cabin, he went to his bedroom, and he started writing. Could he ever retrieve her? Once he started writing, he could not stop. He almost never read books, but now he was pushed to write, guided by a private compulsion. Except for his training, he ignored everything else up in Big Bear—the bowling alley and the blue-collar bars. With a cheap pen and a spiral notebook, over several days, in a rambling mood, De La Hoya wrote to Peralta, and opened up a piece of himself that maybe he had never opened before, and probably would never open again.

He wrote a love letter, he pleaded with her, he sounded bleak, he sounded frustrated. He freely admitted that something was wrong with his life, that he needed help. He wrote what he felt. Away from that cabin, down the mountain, they were already searching for the next Oscar De La Hoya, the next generation's boxing superstar.

The first one was searching for something, too.

"Veronica," he began, in his light, tight print—the writing of someone who still thought of himself as a future architect.

> *I sure hope things happen for a reason. What I mean is I know things for us aren't great, but I sure wish it's for the best. I said some foolish words to you and regret every word I said. When I said my feelings weren't there, I lied, of course. My feelings are there for you and I goofed up so bad. I have to confess. One night I called Cindy and expressed my feelings to her. I cannot explain why I didn't call you, but like I said, it's probably for the best.*

Veronica, I know you still love me and even if your life goes on and you find someone else who you can be silly with and goof around with, laugh together, cry on, and be very happy with, I am going to love you and not let go of you. We have broken up a few times and experienced different things and gone different places. And have been at our peak of our relationship too fast. I just hope I did the right thing by breaking up, Vero. I have been thinking so much about you and I know for a fact that you are the perfect woman for me. I swear to you, I am not going to see no one or date nobody.

I know you probably don't care, but I've made up my mind and I will wait for you. Please, Vero, understand my situation. I truly love you, and care for you. It is so tough for me right now, so many people to deal with and problems. . . . Please, please understand. I know for a fact that I will never love someone like you. Not that I'm confused.

I know what I want, Vero, and that's you. But it's hard to deal with at this moment. Not only my training and my family problems, but also in your part, like, right now I believe our relationship will work if we get engaged, but your mom will never agree. And that's tough to deal with. Please believe me, I want this to work out. It hurts me that I can't be with you by my side, cuddled up together. Every night I listen to a cassette from the Luis Miguel tape and I sit and wonder if you still think about me or if I should call you.

It is very painful to know that the only person I have ever loved with true feelings thinks really bad about me. Vero, it's not that love is not there, it's just that all these distractions are coming in between us, right now, at this moment.

Actually, since the last time I saw you, all I've been doing is thinking about you. I've realized that no woman can compare with you. I have been so immature about our past relationships and hopefully one day I will get professional help to deal and focus more on my personal life, other than just concentrating on my professional career.

You know you mentioned to me of how past boyfriends call you up and of how you feel sorry because you say you had a boyfriend. Well, if they can make you happier than I can and feel secure and loved, I think it will be time for us to move on with our lives. But, see, I will not accept that. I know I can make you feel loved more than anybody out there. I just need a little time to finish up my career and things will change, I promise you. Gosh, I need you. I really do miss you so much. I think of everything we have gone through and I pray that it's all for the best, even though it hurts.

Please, God help us is what I say.

I wish and pray to God that it can be us that can go the "retiro" that Joe says will change everything about me. Veronica, lonely I'm feeling at this moment, and if things don't work out, then lonely I will die. I love you.

Oscar

The letter does not stop there. Something inside him demanded that he keep writing in that notebook. Around him, as he wrote this letter, the events of his career and life swirled.

Recently, his most trusted advisers—businessman Mike Hernandez, De La Hoya's imperious father, Joel, and promoter Bob Arum, imperial in his own manner—hired a strange little man from the Yucatán, Jesus Rivero, with sleek white hair, thick black-framed glasses, and eyes that pop from his tiny head like Ping-Pong balls.

It was Rivero's appointed mission to make De La Hoya a professional, savvy fighter. But Rivero, true to his quirky nature, approached the assignment with larger goals. De La Hoya was an immense talent —with staggering potential to open up boxing to new audiences and a new era. De La Hoya was also, Rivero feared, dangerously sheltered, detached from real life, and headed for a plummet that matched the velocity, and drama, of his rise.

Oscar was emotionally stunted: He hardly spoke to his father, his brother was always in trouble, and the fighter himself barely if ever emerged from his own cold shell. He was being protected—and spoiled. He was still a little kid, in need of an enlightened authority figure. His mother was long gone.

"I looked at him," Rivero said, "and I saw a champion in trouble."

From his outsider's perspective, there was little doubt that De La Hoya was a boxing dilettante—all fists, no focus. The greatest fighters, Rivero knew, had complete minds and a quality of character that De La Hoya had never bothered to contemplate or cultivate.

So Rivero tried to mold him by badgering him, by demanding that the fighter address life outside of boxing, read literature, think about philosophy. By arguing over fighting and fighting over arguing. And, in a camp that was usually quiet and blank, suddenly, having Rivero around changed everything—the mood, the direction, the conversation.

The men who had preceded Rivero in De La Hoya's boxing life did not quite prepare him for the little man from the Yucatán. He had always worked with strictly boxing people, with Joe Minjarez in the baby days, with Manuel Montiel as a rising teenager, with idiosyncratic Al Stankie as an amateur star, and with Alcazar, who used to work with his father in a factory, late in his amateur days and into his professional career.

By example and experience, his father taught him, too. When he won, his father would talk to him sweetly. When he lost, his father would barely talk to him at all. Even in the professional days, that pattern was not altered in this strange family. With his mother gone, his father taught him how to be a warrior, fueled by fear and cold anger. And nothing else. Oscar knew this.

"I would never want to raise a child like he raised us," Oscar said of his father. "My dad was never a friend to us. Never."

Still, Oscar almost never argued with his father, even when he was making millions, even when his father got him into trouble by signing bad contracts and by fighting with his trainers. In truth, De La Hoya succeeded because of his father—and to spite him. Out of hatred and love, and nothing in between.

But Rivero, who had walked away from boxing fifteen years before returning for De La Hoya, was something complicated and nourishing for the young fighter. Rivero had spent the last decade at home in Mérida, tending to his ranch. He was a restless philosopher, a good-natured atheist, a man of music and letters, someone whose opinion seemed to matter about everything. By the time of the Genaro Hernandez preparations, his second training camp with De La Hoya, "the Professor," as De La Hoya called him, was teaching him defensive techniques he had never seen . . . and beginning to show him the world beyond boxing and East L.A. "Rivero has changed everything," a dazzled De La Hoya said at the time. Why are you who you are? Rivero asked De La Hoya. Who made you? Whom do you care for?

De La Hoya's answer, finally, was inevitable: Veronica. Though his father hated her and the rest of his family seemed to be organized to be rid of her, it was Veronica, he decided, she is the one I need. Always Veronica. The Professor helped him figure that out.

And De La Hoya kept writing.

I really don't know if you have heard much about "the Professor." I found out this morning after my run that the reason why they have brought him over was because Mike, my father and Bob found out I had lots of problems to deal with, not only in boxing, but personally.

Vero, this man has been helping me out so much. He has made me more aware about life. He's taught me to appreciate life and has guided me good so far about my love life. He tells me every morning about how something is bothering me and I always tell him that everything is fine.

Until one day, I couldn't take it and let all my emotions out to him. I told him of how stupid I have been of letting you go. He asked me, Why? And when he sensed that I was speechless, he

realized that you are the one I love. He saw how much I was
hurting. It was funny because he started telling me that if I was
sexually satisfied with you, and I said yes. And then I told him
that the only reason why we're not with each other is because I
was feeling pressured about everything in life. Not only you, but
I have so many things to deal with.

Well, I know all this doesn't really matter to you. But for once
in my life I feel more secure and in control about things. I am
very happy that the professor has guided me and telling me to go
after the person I really feel for and love very much. And the
last words to him this morning were "Don Chuy, yo la quiero
contoda mi alma. *[I love her with all my soul.]*" *And I do love*
you, Veronica.

May God bless you and your family. Take care . . .
        Oscar

De La Hoya was not done. He kept the pad by his bed, and he
kept writing.

This was an emotional fight for him, facing Genaro (Chicanito)
Hernandez, whose nickname means "little Chicano" and whose ring
savviness, successful title defenses, and low-key personality earned him
the respect and affection of the L.A. boxing community. Fans in L.A.
were intrigued by the talent and drama of De La Hoya . . . but most of
them *pulled* for Hernandez, whose career was far from a golden path.

Hernandez had talent, but not De La Hoya's power or speed or
magazine-cover looks. Hernandez had respect, because he so clearly
maximized his talent. De La Hoya drew obsessive interest, because he
so clearly struggled to harness his outrageous talent, because it over-
flowed, because maybe he would waste it, maybe he wouldn't, you just
didn't know. But De La Hoya had other things on his mind than his
upcoming fight.

He had six initials on a tree, a cheap, tiny, key-chain picture taken
of he and Peralta during a dinner at a Medieval restaurant. It was the

only picture he had left of her, after three years of the relationship. A few weeks earlier, she caught him in bed with another girl and tore out of his condominium with every picture of herself she could find. The key chain was the only one she neglected to take.

"You are probably wondering why I'm writing you so much," De La Hoya continues in his letter.

> *Well, I feel as if I have to, every night, to express my feelings to you, so you can know what's going on with my life. It's been so peaceful and relaxing to just focus on, concentrate on my upcoming fight with Chickenita. I hope you will be cheering for me. Anyway, today was a beautiful day. I woke up at 5:30 A.M. and ran to our spot. Yes, the tree where I engraved our initials. You know, those letters are forever, just like us. I'm right now laying in bed, just mesmerized by your picture. Ahh, you thought you took all of them. Haaa. Well, I still have the key chain from our special dinner we had, remember. Gosh, we have so many memories, and I want and need more from you, Veronica. It's hurting me not to have you by my side, holding you, telling you I love you with all my heart. Shit, I fucked up, excuse my language, but there is no other way of saying it. Every time I think about you, it hurts that you're not thinking about me. I did stupid things in my life, but letting you go is like giving up in life, not knowing where or in what direction my life will end up. I will never forgive myself for being so selfish and ignorant about a person who cared about me the way nobody else would care. I have let go of someone special and now regret every bad thing I did in my life.*

> *It is going to be a tough learning experience. But now I'm left with nothing to care for. My heart will never be able to love someone the way I love you, Veronica. There is a special feeling I have about you that nobody will ever erase, a scar for life is what I have left myself with.*

And now I hope it never heals, so I can only be left with my beautiful memories about the person I love.

Oscar

The relationship, De La Hoya knows as he writes, is fraying beyond recovery. In the future, as he can guess on this dark day, they will reconcile briefly, two or three different times. He will give her a "promise ring," looking toward a future engagement. He will plead to have a baby with her. She will say, Not until we're married. He will loan her a luxury car. He will shake his head at Mike Hernandez's pleas to stay single, and he will tell an angry Hernandez that he loves Veronica.

But, his premonition tells him, the devotion is gone—on both sides. The romance has passed. He wasn't ready to battle his family for her, or step away from his career long enough, or even stop cheating on her. He was only ready to ask for forgiveness.

Well, it's about 10:30 at night and I can only remember the times we would spend up all night talking to each other on the phone. If only I can turn back time, I would make myself a whole different person, with the same heart. What I mean is, if things were different for me, not having money, fame, etc. . . . our relationship would be such a wonderful one. I miss you. I don't want to live without you, Veronica. The feeling of pain is being away from you and hurt is all I can do now, hurt like never before. As time passes by, we will get older and I will realize that I have made the biggest mistake of my life. Letting you go is the last thing I am going to do, and whatever it takes, I'm going to do it to keep you, even though things have gone wrong in the past. I believe we're like a hand & glove, perfectly matching one another. Veronica, for some reason we have survived the battle, but the war will never end. Please do think about the whole picture, think about the good and the bad, think about the sad moments and the happy ones. Gather all your thoughts and at the end if you think we should move on with each other's lives, then let it be. But one thing, Vero, I love you forever.

Whoever you're with, wherever you are, I will always have you on my mind and in my heart.

Lots of love, God bless.

Oscar

P.S. All this that I wrote to you, I mean it with all my heart and would appreciate it if you can let me explain myself to you, in person.

Hi, well, it's been a while since the last time I wrote to you. But just a few minutes since I last thought about you. I'm going to be very honest with you. I have a really serious problem, and yes, you guessed it, it involves you. Well, here's the story. You, Vero . . .

Every minute of the day and night, I cannot stop thinking about you and my problem is that it's affecting my training so much. You know, between you and I, I don't think I'm going to be ready for my next opponent. For the first time, I'm scared to death that I might lose. But that's not your problem. And of course, I will deal with it the night of the fight, anyway. I am going to ask you for a big, big favor and I am really begging you on this one, please, let's just talk about the whole picture. All I want is for us to be at peace. I mean, if we can meet somewhere at a certain place and time and just talk to you, it would mean everything to me. I will go down the mountain and meet somewhere close to you, if that is possible. Please, Vero, this is very serious and I know that you don't probably care. But it is affecting me so bad. Please do think about it. I am not playing games with you or trying to do anything immature. I am asking this favor from you as a friend, putting everything aside, I am seriously asking you as a friend to please do this for me.

Oscar

In the end, the letter wasn't enough.

So, while his career catapults forward, something is left behind. There will be more.

His family has already long ago started spending his money for themselves, cousins and uncles that materialized as soon as he started making money—the very definition of "relative strangers." His father hates Rivero. His longtime trainer, Alcazar, has openly feuded with Rivero, and will continue to prove over and over again that his undeniable talent is not in boxing tactics, but in holding on, frantically, to his piece of the De La Hoya dream. He will not let go.

Within the sport, De La Hoya's parade of blowout victories fails to answer the hardest questions: Does he have the heart, the willingness to sacrifice his pretty-boy image for one magnificent, bloody fight? What, if anything, has he ever given up of himself to win a fight? Is he more of a marketing tool than a fighter?

In the barrio of East L.A. and in Mexico, die-hard fans angrily distrust his appeal to white America, his aloof personality, his soft looks and voice. The money is just starting to get gigantic. The pressures, the fissures, are starting, spreading, growing too obvious to ignore.

Less than two years after the writing of this letter, Veronica will marry someone else, even though De La Hoya once promised her that he would disrupt any wedding of hers that did not include him. Peralta is married on a fall day in 1997, and De La Hoya leaves her alone, though one TV camera is there, just in case.

After the writing of this letter, Rivero will be fired in less than a year. Emanuel Steward, another famous trainer brought in to guide Alcazar, will be hired, and he will be fired, too. Alcazar, of course, will remain by the fighter's side, smiling tightly and holding on. And De La Hoya's career will hurtle ahead, and he will keep winning big fights, keep earning gargantuan paydays. He will ask a seventeen-year-old girl, "a virgin," he says proudly, to marry him, then break up with her a few weeks later. He will father a son, with a woman he has known since the Olympic days.

He will, when the mood strikes him, remember this day and this letter. And know that that time is gone, the time when he would sit up and be driven to write a love letter to someone who won't take his calls. Years later, after their final breakup, Veronica will think about that letter, too, and wonder where it all came from. Because he's so different now from the boy she met, so much more protected, hidden, and lonely.

By the time he turned twenty-five—the age he once said he'd retire by—his career boxing earnings alone were almost $50 million. De La Hoya was a towering, mysterious matinee idol for the masses, and a lightning rod for an array of critics that stretched from his hometown to the contenders for his throne. His smile sold products, but the act of the sale was a form of protection, not revelation. He hid behind that smile.

From week to week, he had a new girlfriend, then another, then another. From fight to fight, practically, he had a new trainer.

"He has a disorder, because he is lonely," Rivero said. "It is a sexual disorder. He needs companionship, so he brings girls up. That's his disorder."

How did it all get this far? He was a shy child, then he was a rising star, and then he was a millionaire, one long *whoooosh,* and almost before he could catch his breath, he was an idol. Maybe boxing's last idol, as the sport shrinks into a mosh of controversy and ennui. De La Hoya blinks, and a room full of girls shrieks.

When every other fighter was struggling to sell tickets to fights, he went to El Paso in June 1998 to fight a cream puff named Patrick Charpentier, a nonentity compared to De La Hoya, and he sold 45,000 seats at the Sun Bowl, the fifth-largest crowd ever amassed for a fight on U.S. soil.

"It's just like Ali in the '60s," Arum said. "Oscar has become a symbol for the emergence of his people. In two or three years, there will be more Hispanic-Americans living in this country than African-Americans. By the year 2040, when Oscar De La Hoya is the president of the United States, 25 percent of all people living in this country will be of Hispanic heritage. The future is theirs, and Oscar symbolizes their dreams."

And what of his own? What *are* his own?

The answer lies in the story of his life, and in his letter to Peralta, with its tone of a confession. The girls dream of him, the opponents fall at his feet, and he stays on the mountaintop, colder, even when the sun is out.

chapter two

The Little Boy in the Ring

The Eastside Boxing Club was as good a place as any to be the cradle of Oscar De La Hoya's boxing life.

It could have happened any place, really, in East L.A., home to more than two million Latinos, and tens of thousands of proud fathers and tough little boys. It is a community of hopes and gyms cut out of garages or slapped into old storefronts—gyms carved, it seems, out of the very streets. If you want to be respected in East L.A., you want to be able to fight.

The Eastside Boxing Club in East Los Angeles was just another gym among dozens of gyms that served the area, not particularly famous, not particularly well equipped, not particularly anything. It was, as it still is, as serviceable as it could be, run on scraps of money and the energies of a few men: A ring, spare offices, room for shadowboxing and bag work tucked into the space of a large garage.

But out of all the boxing hot spots, this gym was, as fate would have it, only six blocks away from the small house of a family with a shy, skinny little kid who liked to skateboard through the streets of East L.A.

And so it would be the Eastside Boxing Club, and gym manager Joe Minjarez, who forged the fighter. How many other gyms claim to be De La Hoya's first? How many men say they were there at the beginning of the legend? Minjarez just shakes his head now. Twenty, maybe, he says. Thirty. How many people say that they were his first trainer, that they were the first ones who put his hands in gloves and pushed him into a ring? How many people raise their hands and swear they were the ones who saw him knock out his first opponent as a seven-year-old and knew they had witnessed the genesis of a future superstar?

"Seems like every other day I meet someone who says they started Oscar," Minjarez says with a tired grin. "Every other day. And I just smile and nod my head. I don't say anything. What are you going to tell them?"

You could tell them this: It was the Eastside Boxing Club, and it was trainer Joe Minjarez, at the beginning.

For eight years, De La Hoya headed over to the gym after school almost daily, sparred with other kids, went off to nearby competitions, and eventually made a name for himself as a little-boy assassin. By the time his father moved him to another gym, De La Hoya was a teenager, a rising figure in the L.A. boxing community, and, most important, a boxing commodity. Money changed hands because of him by the time he was ending his tenure at the Eastside Boxing Club with Joe Minjarez.

But he came to the gym as just another kid with another poor background and another immigrant father who wanted to see what would happen when his young son put the gloves on. Joel De La Hoya Sr., though, did not anticipate much from his youngest son. He did not send his son to box for glory. He sent him for self-defense.

Joel De La Hoya worried that Oscar was too soft, that other little boys were bullying him, that he depended on his mother for comfort. He cried more than he talked, simpered when he was surprised, and ran away from the first flicker of trouble. And in this community, whose heroes were the beaten-up and brawling survivors, Joel De La Hoya could not bear to see a son of his shake and shriek.

So, as likely as the gym was to produce a future star, De La Hoya, at six years old, was unlikely to be its proudest product.

At six, Oscar was no natural fighter, not in the usual, brawling way. The great fighters of Latino heritage were neither the quickest or the tallest or the flashiest. The legends, like Julio Cesar Chavez and the Panamanian Roberto Duran and Pipino Cuevas, all were blunt battering rams, willing to wade into an opponent and break him apart, one body shot at a time. For the Mexican-American community of East

L.A., that was machismo incarnate. Boxing was not art, it was survival. Winning was about persevering, and about ferociousness, and it translated to the street brawls and the boxing gyms and the six-year-old kids.

But De La Hoya, doted on by his mother, did not inherit the macho credo. He was a quiet boy who only on the rarest occasions engaged in what could seriously be called a street fight. He was, he admits it himself, a *madre*'s boy. Oscar had been tested young, and he thought he knew what he was: A crier and a runner.

Fighters' backgrounds are usually littered with bitter moments and excruciating escapes for survival on the mean streets. Mike Tyson beat up old ladies to make money. Others dealt drugs, slammed anyone who got in their way. Boxing was their way out of hell. But for Oscar De La Hoya, boxing became his way in.

This was not a little boy born to intimidate. The most vivid memories of his childhood are not of domination and triumph, but of tears, and his stories almost always end with him crying, in his room, afraid of something. Afraid of everything.

At his third birthday party, in 1975, his parents invited all of the cousins and friends over and put up a colorful piñata, tied to the ceiling. Little Oscar of course had seen piñatas before, seen plenty of them. But he still froze in panic at the sight of the colors and the prize, burst into tears, and rushed to his room and shut the door. His parents tried to get him out to his party, but he stayed in bed.

A few months later, his older brother, Joel Jr., put some huge gloves on Oscar's hands and pushed him at a young cousin. Oscar promptly got smacked in the face, immediately started crying, then ran home.

"Before I was a fighter," De La Hoya recalls, "I remember being put into a fight with my brother and little cousins. . . . I would just keep to myself. But I remember this one little bully in our block, he would beat everybody up and I was like the last one standing. Because I never fought him. They would throw me in all the time. And I would end up crying at the end. . . . I'd always lose."

Before I was a fighter . . . I'd always lose.

Who could imagine this nervous, timid child being any kind of fighter? Certainly not Oscar himself. The first, best candidate to carry on the family boxing tradition was his cocky brother, Joel, two years older, heavier, more aggressive, and fairly talented from an early age. Joel Jr. reminded his father of himself, when he was young and growing into his professional fighting days. Joel Sr.'s father, Vincente, had been a respected featherweight in the 1940s, and both Vincente and Joel Sr. had fought on cards at the legendary Olympic Auditorium in Los Angeles during their careers.

Vincente, who was five-foot-three, fought mostly near his hometown of Durango, Mexico, and moved most of his family to Los Angeles in 1956.

Joel came one year later, when he was sixteen years old. Joel, a lightweight fighter, was 9–3–1 with six knockouts as a professional, fighting both in Durango and in California. His first son he named after himself. His second, born February 4, 1972, he named Oscar.

Joel Sr. wanted to keep fighting—he considered himself a potential contender, and some who saw him say he could have fought for much longer—but the family needed money, and he had to quit to earn a steady income. For a while, he tried both.

"I had to support my family and then go to the gym," Joel Sr. once said. "It is not the same for Oscar, who has never had to work. . . . I didn't have anyone push me like I pushed my son. I could have been a champion like Oscar."

With that lineage, the De La Hoya men expected boxing in the souls of the boys, and, for a while, Joel Jr. seemed to have it. Oscar watched, without envy, as his brother started boxing.

"I didn't think I would be in boxing," Oscar says. "I thought my brother was going to be in boxing, like real big into it. But I never thought I would do it."

He would. He would have to. Even as Oscar was finding his way to the Eastside Boxing Club, Joel Jr., with his father bearing down hard, began to lose interest in boxing. Joel Jr. was a solid baseball player, with sharp hand-eye coordination, and he didn't take to the boxing regimen of morning runs and weight control.

"Joel Jr. was a better boxer than Oscar," Joel Sr. once said, "until he discovered girls."

By the time Joel Jr. was nine or ten, he was regularly skipping boxing training to play ball. His father, of course, did not understand how this could be happening.

"I was a damn good baseball player," Joel Jr. complained to his friends over the years, "and my father never cared. He never came to one of my games."

Recalls Oscar: "It wasn't his sport—he liked baseball actually more than boxing. It's funny, because to this day they say he was much better than I was. He just never liked it."

Once Joel Jr. quit boxing, the relationship between him and his father never was the same. As he grew up, it was the children's mother, Cecilia, who protected him, and Joel Sr. turned his focus elsewhere.

"I think he's hurt by it," Oscar says of his father's attitude toward his firstborn son. "A father always wants his first son to follow his footsteps. He has his name. He's hurt, but he's getting over it. He's hurt that his son didn't make it big."

Not the first one, anyway. Once Joel Jr. forsook boxing, Oscar was the favored child. Oscar, who never had a problem with baseball or rebellion, who never argued with his father or came close to disobeying his will.

Joel Jr., meanwhile, began scrambling even harder to get out from under his father's hand. He got into trouble. He hung around with wild friends. As a teenager, his father caught Joel with what looked to be marijuana, and hit one of his children for the first and only time.

"My dad slapped him across the face, and he still remembers it," Oscar says of his brother. "Till this day, they have that grudge. . . . My mom was the one always protecting my brother, always. Because my father would always be yelling at my brother."

But Oscar still idolized his funny, talkative brother. Since Oscar was so shy and didn't have many friends himself, he found himself tailing along with Joel aimlessly. And Joel could be aimless.

Oscar called him *"Callo,"* or "callus" in English, because, as he later said, giggling, "Joel drinks so much, he's got to have a callus on his stomach. Or else he'd be dead."

Joel had cool friends. He listened to rock 'n' roll. He hung out at downtown clubs, was in a band for a while, went to wild parties.

"I looked up to him, period," Oscar says. "I used to follow him wherever he went. With his friends, everywhere. Wear his clothes. . . . He used to get pissed off. He used to get pissed off I was wearing his clothes. He would always tell me, 'Hey, get the hell out of here! You small little punk, get out of here!'"

And Oscar would run back through the streets, back home, and maybe cry a little more.

One day, their father came upon them both in the park, playing baseball.

"What the hell are you doing in here, you stupid jerk?" Joel Sr. screamed at Oscar. "How many times have I told you not to play baseball? I don't want you to get hurt. You can get killed out here. Go to the gym and learn how to defend yourself!"

Which is just what Oscar dutifully did. And until he was introduced to golf a decade later, De La Hoya—who loved basketball—never again seriously attempted any other sport besides boxing. He could not even discuss it with Joel Sr. There was no question what the answer would be.

"You couldn't talk to my dad," Oscar says. "You couldn't go up to my dad and tell him, 'I love you, Dad.' Or, 'Dad, I got good grades in school.' Not that he didn't care, but too macho. . . . I'm going to be a more understanding father. Closer to my children, you know? Give them the opportunity to really talk to me, to be a good friend, you know? . . . Because of my father, I respect everybody. I am the way I am in public because of what my father did to me. I mean, I'm surprised he never laid a hand on us. Well, that he never hit me. Because of the way he used to yell at us. And the way he was strict.

"My mom, she was the one to talk to. It's like we have her side, and we have my dad's side, too. There's times I thank my father, and I thank my mom—for having their two sides, you know?"

The mother's side was the cheery side, the laughing side. The boys inherited their mother's high voices, and her gentleness. When Joel Sr. yelled at them or scared them, she took them and stopped their crying. She would cook them something. She would maybe sing for them.

"When his mother was alive," says local boxing figure Marty Denkin, who became a sponsor of De La Hoya's amateur career, "it was a different atmosphere. Cecilia was something. She was one of the few Hispanic women that truly ran her family. It wasn't the father, it was her. She was quiet, she would listen a lot. She was very gentle. But she had a tremendous amount of respect from the children, especially Oscar."

Amid the storm, Cecilia was the safe place for the boys. And as long as she was there, they would never be as hard as their father. If you ask the father, they had it easy. Their father told them that when he was a child in Durango he would be punished by whip and chained to walls. That was not the case in Cecilia De La Hoya's household.

Hit them? She'd try maybe, but mostly the punishment would produce only laughter and scurrying around the house.

"My mom was the one to hit us," Oscar recalls. "But it was funny to us because it never hurt. We would always laugh at her and stuff. She would always throw stuff at us. Anything she could see she'd throw at us when she was mad."

Cecilia was a singer when she was a child, with a personality to match, then worked as a neighborhood seamstress. Joel met her in East L.A. when he drove past her on the street. She was seventeen, he was ten years older. And though she ignored him on their first meeting, there never was a question in Joel's mind that he was going to marry her.

"You should've seen Joel when he was young," one old friend says. "You think Oscar's gorgeous now? Joel was a knockout."

The boys remember playing with their mother, because she was around. Their father?

"My dad would always work," Oscar says. "Of course, he had time for her, but they weren't very loving, not really. And my dad was never a friend to us. Never. We would fear him. Man, we would fear him. If my dad says something, to this day, I'll do it. I mean, he'll tell me what to do."

Though the De La Hoya family struggled financially, the boys never really noticed it. Joel Sr. had so many brothers and sisters living nearby, there was always food available. Grandfather Vincente had sixteen children from two marriages, and most of them lived within a mile or two.

It was enough to get by. Plus, before he moved back to Mexico, Vincente owned a neighborhood restaurant called Virginia's Place that served as a family gathering place. Nobody around them thought they were any poorer or richer than anybody else in the neighborhood.

"We never ever felt poor," De La Hoya remembers. "I mean, even though we were. I know there were times it was tough for us to even have food on the table. We used to borrow it from neighbors or somebody. Luckily, one of my aunts lived next door. So they did us a lot of favors. But we never felt poor. We always felt like we had everything."

Joel Sr. worked as a dispatcher for a City of Industry company that made industrial heating and air-conditioning systems, and the family lived in a two-bedroom house on South McDonnell Avenue, just a few blocks from the merging point of the Long Beach and Golden State freeways, on the south border of East L.A.

It was Cecilia De La Hoya's dream to move the family not far away, but at least to the hills of Montebello, close enough to East L.A. to be a part of community but middle class enough to be considered "the Beverly Hills of East L.A." She told her children that they would save enough, one day, to live in Montebello. While they waited, the house on South McDonnell Avenue was far from luxurious, but it was not poverty.

"I'd say it was one step above *really* bad," De La Hoya says of the house, which got crowded when little Ceci was born, nine years after

Oscar. "We had water, electricity. Oh, there were rats and the cockroaches and all that. That was bad. Oh, yeah…we used to put traps everywhere, corners…and at night, I'd be asleep and hear 'clack-clack-clack!' That's scary. To this day, I can't stand rats."

His family's dependence on food stamps, however, affected De La Hoya the most. For almost twenty years he has kept an old one dollar food stamp in his wallet, as a reminder.

"There's times I forget," De La Hoya says. "Looking at that food stamp, man, it brings back those times. It brings back times. . . ."

The De La Hoyas lived six houses down from a corner liquor store, where Cecilia would sometimes send her boys to buy groceries with their allotment of food stamps. One day, when he was six, she told Oscar to go. Instead, he stood still and cried.

But she insisted, "Go."

"I was crying like crazy," Oscar says. "But she forced me to go. So I went, and there was like, five or six people in the grocery store."

Oscar stayed in the back, refusing to go up to the cashier, until the store was empty of customers. For twenty, thirty, finally forty-five minutes, the little boy crouched in the back, ashamed that he would have to pay with food stamps.

"I got the milk right away, the eggs, put them on the table," Oscar says. "The lady found me crying, with red eyes."

The woman at the register asked him why he waited so long to buy the milk.

"Because I have these little food stamps," Oscar said then.

"You shouldn't be embarrassed by that," she said.

But he was.

Look back now, sift through the tears and the hiding from his father and the idolization of his brother, and you can see: All these things shaped him into the prizefighter he would become. He was raised to respect and fear authority. He had the temperament that avoided bumpy spots. And, by the grace of genes and savviness, he was born to throw punches.

Oscar De La Hoya, at age six, at fifteen, at twenty-one, for his whole life, was always the same: A lightning flash of raw talent, masked by a cautious soul. It just had to be nurtured, and it would come alive in the ring—only when he had an opponent in front of him, and gloves on his hands. Then, and only then, he could spring forward and act out his emotions.

"I learned long ago to live with fear—controlled fear," De La Hoya once said. "All I know is that fear is always with me."

His brother, most of all, knew it. "Oscar hated physical confrontations," Joel Jr. says. "He never had a street fight."

But when his father told him to go to the gym, Oscar went. And, really, once he got there, he never left. Before De La Hoya came into his own, a handful of talented athletes emerged from the teeming East L.A. streets, and they were scrappers, hustlers, and battlers. Paul Gonzales, only eight years older than Oscar, came from East L.A. to represent the United States in Los Angeles at the 1984 Olympics, and won a gold medal for his country, his city, and the people of East L.A. Gonzales, bubbly and full of braggadocio, was a true child of the barrio, a street fighter, and proud of it. If you could train hard enough and win a gold medal, every kid in East L.A. knew, you could be famous.

So Oscar wandered over to the Eastside Boxing Club as kind of a lark, curious to at least see what might happen. He was six. His father was still mostly concentrating on Joel. And Oscar began to box. The first day he came, De La Hoya rolled off of Olympic Avenue on his skateboard, through the gym's garage door.

The kid was scrawny, Minjarez remembers. Not particularly tall for his age, but bony, sharp-edged, and long-armed. He was definitely quiet, almost silent. And he was left-handed. Wrote with his left, threw a baseball with his left, swung a bat from the left side. But Minjarez had four other kids he was working with, all right-handers, and he didn't want the complication of tossing a lefty into the batch. De La Hoya stuck to his left-handed stance for a little while before he figured things out.

"There was a little kid that was beating him up for about two months," Minjarez recalls. De La Hoya awkwardly tried to lead with his right hand, and blast away with his left. Then came the move that would unleash De La Hoya's talent on the boxing world.

"I turned Oscar around to right-handed," Minjarez says, "and within a few days, the kid wouldn't spar with Oscar anymore. I turned him around, and he caught on *like that*. I mean, the left hand was just too strong."

Lining up his stronger hand out front, Oscar could throw the left either as a stinging jab or a hard hook with accuracy and power. Minjarez set him loose. Instantly, Oscar started to dominate sparring sessions, walloping the other kids with his piercing left hand and incredible force. Because he was so skinny and, eventually, a little taller than some of the others, De La Hoya had a leverage advantage that, when he moved forward, could take his opponent's breath away. His right hand wasn't much of a factor, but it didn't need to be.

Not with that left, coming hard.

"By the time he was twelve, he could push a grown man back just with a jab to the body," Minjarez says. "I made the jab. I used to embarrass him. I'd call the kids over. . . . 'Look at this—Oscar, throw a jab.' *Pow!* He'd knock people back about two steps. When you get a jab like that, then you're a boxer."

Early on, Oscar's father even got into the ring to get a feel for the weight of his little boy's left hand. For the first time, Oscar had a chance to show his father something. And he did. Joel Sr. was startled.

"He took a step backward when Oscar hit," Minjarez says. "Man, it looked like they hooked him with a broomstick."

It was the punch that would make Oscar a superstar—a hard, hard left hand, used either as a straight jab or, if he dipped his shoulder, a lashing hook. And, as a boy, it was the first sign of his boxing genius. Not only did Oscar have power, he had style. Maybe because he had never been a street fighter, Oscar could be patient, dancing on his toes, staring in at his opponent, until the precise moment when he would take a half step in, bounce, and rocket a combination to the chin, and take over the fight. He wasn't sloppy or foolish. He would pounce with his punches, and they almost never missed the mark.

"I worked on the jab for two years, probably," Minjarez says. "But that's the weapon. That's basics. In Spanish, they call it *la mano mayerto*. The master hand. And that's what it is. The jab and the hook are my favorite punches. And Oscar's got those two things down perfect. The hook and the jab."

Little De La Hoya had something beyond technique, power, and a right-handed stance. Once he was in the ring and throwing fists, something clicked inside of him. The polite boy got angry. He took offense at someone trying to hit him. He hit back.

And you saw it first in his eyes. Wide, soft eyes. Then he got into the ring and they were wild.

"He was fierce," Minjarez says. "He had a real small voice. . . . He was one of those kids that didn't say hardly anything. But he worked hard. And once he got in the ring, he was fierce. His eyes, man, he was like an eagle, you know? He'd pin his eyes on the kid and just go."

Early in his boxing career, his father would rarely come to his workouts. But his mother came by often, and was stunned by the son she saw in the ring and in the peewee boxing tournaments around the neighborhood. He was raw, but he was scary.

This was her shy little boy?

"She used to say she didn't recognize me, her own son, when I went into the ring," De La Hoya says. "She said she saw red in my eyes. She said she saw a beast."

About two months into it, De La Hoya registered his first knockout in sparring, making another little boy cry. It was a euphoric feeling. Making somebody else cry, that was a revelation. A few months later, he had his first official fight, before a crowd, at a real event. It was at the nearby Pico Rivera Sports Arena, and he weighed fifty-one pounds. He was seven.

Here was an introduction.

"It was against this kid who had four or five fights," Minjarez says. "I said, 'Well, I'll put him in and see.' Stopped him. Made him cry in the third round. I mean, he was only about seven years old. Skinny little kid. But he could hit. He dug to the body with that left hook, man, it knocked the wind out of that kid and he just started crying."

It was enough to send Joel Sr., with several of his buddies in tow, into near hysterics. His timid son suddenly was a killer.

"I was laughing so hard," Joel Sr. said of that fight. "I thought, 'Maybe I got something here.'"

Right after that fight, Oscar ran to his father and told him, "Poppy, I like it!" And Joel Sr. began thinking about the big picture. If you keep training hard, Joel told his son, you can keep boxing. But if you ever slip up, that'll end it.

Joel kept to his word . . . and his warning. And Oscar became a boxer, basically, twenty-four hours a day. The gym wasn't a refuge, it was a five-days-a-week release. It was where he belonged.

By the time he was nine, De La Hoya was becoming famous in the neighborhood and attracting his father to most of his fights—along with a few uncles, who wanted to see the miracle transformation from crying kid to future champion. It was a show.

"Before the fight, there was nothing, nothing on his face," Minjarez says. "But his eyes . . . he'd sit on his stool and his eyes were just fierce darts."

Remembers Oscar: "I loved fighting . . . well, I loved winning. Getting that reward at the end. It's amazing. Amazing. I will never forget, I had this awesome fight, awesome fight, this guy was perfect for me. There was blood everywhere and I think I stopped him like in the last seconds of the final round, the third round. . . . My father had taken friends from his work to go see me fight and they rewarded me with like fifty cents, a dollar. I'm thinking, 'Shit, this is awesome!' I must've been around eleven. I ended up probably with four bucks, and *happy!* I used to fight like every week. Sometimes, fight Saturday and then go to another show on Sunday. Man, I could keep this up and make a living out of it!"

In very little time, Minjarez had to go searching for opponents for the little kid. Anybody who had fought him once before—or even watched him—would find a reason not to get into the ring with him to see up close his flashing eyes and his flying hands.

Back in Mexicali, Mexico, where Vincente lived, the patriarch of the family heard about his fighting grandson.

"I think Vincente was a little suspicious when we started telling him Oscar was a good boxer," said Adrian Pasten, an older cousin who lived next door to Oscar on South McDonnell. "Oscar didn't look like a fighter to him, I don't think."

By the time Oscar was an Olympic hopeful, Vincente wanted to see how he fought.

"We've shown videos of Oscar to Vincente. He looks and always says 'That's how I used to look,'" Pasten said in 1992. "But he smiles when he says it."

The taller Oscar got, the harder he hit. And he kept getting taller ... taller than most of the kids around him ... tall enough for everyone around him to wonder if he really was set to become the Latino dream of a big, athletic welterweight or middleweight—weight divisions that the smaller-framed Mexicans were usually too small to succeed in—a fighter like Sugar Ray Leonard or Thomas Hearns. De La Hoya had a skinny little waist—he was no bigger than twenty-eight inches late into his teenage years—and sharp, broad shoulders. He had the body of an athlete.

Nobody remembers who the first one to say it was, but by his twelfth birthday, Oscar De La Hoya was obviously headed toward professional boxing. He was too phenomenal not to. In a town that was, at that point, loaded with an incredible assortment of young talent—twelve- and thirteen-year-olds beating everybody and on their way to eventual world titles in a decade or so—De La Hoya was the name at the top of the list. Even then, De La Hoya was the star.

"You know, I've had hundreds of kids in my thirty-some-odd years. He was better than most kids," Minjarez says. "Because he fought everybody and anybody. And he never said no. The guys that beat him, like [future pros] Shane Mosley, Larry Loy... they beat him when Oscar was eleven, they were thirteen. They were two years older, heavier, more experienced. And he had to fight those kids because nobody else would fight him. By the time he was eleven or twelve, he was already known around here, baby face and all. Nobody wanted to fight him."

De La Hoya kept winning and winning, mostly by knockout. When he didn't fight, he had one regular sparring partner. Alfred Garcia, another boy of the neighborhood, has melted away from boxing. But when he was eleven and Oscar was nine, they went into pitched battle just about every day in the gym. Alfred was older and stronger. Oscar was faster and more ferocious. Minjarez is not the only one who suspects that Garcia is the toughest opponent De La Hoya has ever had to face.

Another longtime opponent, but not in the ring, was Joel Jr., who continued to torment his little brother and occasionally make him cry. Until one time, at the age of eleven or twelve, Oscar finally said something back to Joel, saw Joel charge him. Instead of ducking, Oscar landed a hard left straight to Joel's stomach. And that was that. "That sure changed our relationship," Joel Jr. said later, only half in jest.

Then, an eleven-year-old De La Hoya ran into Mosley, two years older, a swift, powerful fighter from nearby Pomona. Mosley was a star, too. A few years after their meeting he would become a two-time national amateur champion, and eventually a professional world champion when he was twenty-six.

In their amateur showdown, De La Hoya stayed in there with the older, faster fighter. But he wasn't given the decision.

"Didn't register nothing on his face," Minjarez says of the loss, De La Hoya's first ever. "He was one of these kids who shrugs his shoulders and says, 'It happens.'"

He never got to fight Mosley again, but the loss didn't derail his youthful rise. He fought over a hundred times before he was fourteen, and had two losses. Minjarez took him to tournaments, and he won almost all of them.

In one tournament when he was twelve, he faced another famous amateur—Rafael Ruelas, from Sylmar, who was a year older, and who also would go on to win a professional world title. And who also would go on to fight De La Hoya when both were professionals.

In their first meeting, De La Hoya knocked Ruelas out. They would fight again, and Ruelas would win. They were evenly matched. There was some money to made off of these two when they were professionals, knowledgeable observers knew.

Oscar was the star. But away from boxing, Oscar was still the retreating, hidden kid. He didn't have girlfriends, and he mostly just stuck around with the other kids who worked out at the Eastside gym, or played with his cousins.

"One time we went to the beach, that's the first time I found out he couldn't swim," Minjarez says. "Couldn't swim. All the kids were out there, and Oscar was only up to his waist. He was jumping up and down. . . . Everybody was out there. I kept looking at him, thinking, 'That sucker don't know how to swim!'"

He didn't need to swim. In fact, he never learned. He had boxing.

Sometimes De La Hoya allowed himself to think that, once the novelty of winning ended, he could leave boxing, take off, and just be a quiet little kid. Sometimes, he thought about just playing. He learned, viscerally, that those ideas were best left unpursued.

One day when he was ten, he came home from school tired and plopped on his couch to watch TV. He made no move to get ready to head over to the gym. His father got home from work and stared at his son.

Oh, you *think* you're going to skip training? Think again. And swiftly.

"That's when I realized my dad really wanted me to be a fighter," Oscar recalls. "He actually got pissed off that I didn't go. I was just tired from school, and I didn't want to go. I was just fed up with it. I was laying on the couch and my father saw that I wasn't getting ready to go the gym. All of the time, he would come back from work, and I would always be ready to go to the gym. Always. This time, I was just watching TV. And he got pissed off. Real pissed off. And I ended up going. And I was like, 'Shit, I'm in this for life.'"

For better or worse—mostly better—it was true. Oscar loved to draw, and he dreamed of being an architect from a very young age, but he didn't get very good grades. Too much time was spent on boxing—training, traveling, and fighting. The prodigy had to practice. His father made sure of it.

"My dad probably gave me the . . . probably, uh, gave me the strength to never give up," Oscar says. "All the times he would force me to the gym and the times he told me, 'Don't miss a day of training.' It made me strong, made me always believe in myself."

Eventually, Oscar would come to believe that it was his destiny to be a great boxer. All the work had to lead to something, didn't it? By that time, it was not far-fetched at all. Knockouts draw attention, and Oscar was knocking everybody out. Eleven in a row. Fourteen out of fifteen.

The word was out, and with that came the usual boxing complications. Other would-be trainers found ways to hover near him during his workouts, or whisper things in his father's ear during fights. De La Hoya's fights were happenings, where the local fight crowd would size up his latest show and extrapolate his worth into the next dozen or so years. This kid was going to make somebody some money.

In 1988, when Oscar was fifteen, he stamped himself as a national contender—a definite 1992 Olympic hopeful—with a single, destructive performance. He was in his first local Golden Gloves tournament, held in nearby Lynnwood, matched up against Manuel Nava, considered at that time one of the most formidable amateurs in the nation.

"And he just cleaned him out," says Minjarez. "Knocked him down three times. Stopped him. Wow. It was a clean knockout. He'd stopped a lot of kids, but not like he knocked this guy out. He hit him with a left hook and he was *out*."

In the same tournament, De La Hoya faced an older fighter from the navy. Robert Alcazar, who worked with Oscar's father at the factory and was a former fighter himself, was helping out in Oscar's corner that night. Alcazar, who would hang around the periphery of De La Hoya's career for a few years before taking over the training duties, says that Lynnwood night is burned in his mind forever.

Not the fight so much as the eyes.

"That was the first time I was working officially with him," Alcazar recalls. "He was fighting that night with this twenty-four-year-old man. So when the fight starts, Oscar got hit on the face. And in the twenty-seven years I've been involved in boxing, I've never seen anything like the expression he had after getting hit. I've never seen that from nobody. It was like a sign from an assassin."

In the corner, Alcazar had only one thought: "What's going on with this kid?" It was like watching a lion attack. Something natural, violent, and beautiful. Unnerving, too.

"He really scared me," Alcazar says. "And in the second round, he knocked the guy out flat. The guy was out. For five minutes he was laying down in the ring. Right from the beginning, I knew he was special. That night, everybody knew."

Minjarez, his first teacher, his first man of boxing, knew, of course. He had known for a while.

He also knew then that his part in De La Hoya's career was over. Minjarez is nearing seventy now, retired from his days running the gym. Now he just hangs around the gym, watching the kids fight, yelling at them when they cuss, slipping away to go fishing when he likes. And sometimes he thinks he sees something that reminds him of a little shy kid who used to skateboard into the gym every afternoon.

"Yeah, I've seen a few. But not like Oscar. There's only a few like Oscar," Minjarez says. "Every fifteen years a fighter like that comes around, that's got everything, and the luck. See, Oscar had a lot of luck, too. He came in, with the skill that he's had. He listens. Kids like that come rarely. You see a lot of them who have everything except discipline."

Even when Oscar was becoming a big name, bragging to friends, he had to get home before curfew or else face his father. It was never pretty when he disobeyed. When he was sixteen, he tried to ignore him, and he paid for it. It was nine P.M., curfew time, and Oscar was half a block away, with his cousins and friends. He heard his mother yell for him, and he did not move. Then he heard his father, and he did not move. Why should he be treated like a child? he thought. He was sixteen. He was a tremendous fighter. He could ignore curfew one time.

A few minutes passed, and Oscar thought he might have proven his point. Suddenly, his father charged up, wearing only an old robe, screaming and, as Oscar describes it, partially exposing himself to the other kids. It was time to go.

"I was never more embarrassed in my life," Oscar says. "Which was the reason why he did it."

What could Oscar do? Except head back to the gym the next day and batter his opponent. And then do it again. That seemed to fulfill something inside of him, something that he couldn't ever fulfill with his father. Where did those fierce eyes come from? What was it that drove him to violence in the ring?

De La Hoya knows the answer is obvious.

"Man, it's like inside the ring is where I used to unleash all my frustrations," he says. "If I was mad at my father that day or anything, I used to go crazy. I used to be crazy inside the ring. Back then, it used to be all anger. I mean, I still feel that anger inside, but it's more controlled. Back then, I used to go wild."

And he became a star—seething at his father, but a star. When he wanted to quit, his father would not allow it, and he would not challenge his father. When he felt sorry for himself, his father barked him back to reality. Quitting was not a possibility.

"Sometimes I get down thinking about the things I missed," De La Hoya said then, before the Olympics. "I feel like I'm almost in a prison.

Like I'm in a camp where if I go to a party, I would lose everything. But it's really going to pay off. I believe I'm going to have more fun than anyone's ever had."

Years and $50 million later, De La Hoya looked back and verified the prediction: "I thank my father. If he wasn't around, if he wasn't forcing me to go, I wouldn't be here. I would be doing something else."

Sometimes, his mother would make a little intervention. "If he doesn't want to go, why force him?" Cecilia would say to her husband. "If he's tired, he's tired."

Why force him?

But when it came to boxing and the boys, Joel Sr.'s opinion was not reversible and no appeal was ever granted. A carefree childhood was worth sacrificing. . . . How can anyone look at De La Hoya now and say it wasn't? Certainly the fighter himself wouldn't.

"I mean, I was a kid back then, you know?" Oscar says. "It wasn't that big of a deal. I'd get angry at myself for listening to him too much and letting him take over my life. Angry at him for yelling at me, and forcing me. But, hey, it paid off."

And everything was fine, because Cecilia De La Hoya was in the middle of it, laughing and hugging her children and calming down her husband, making everyone smile.

chapter three

Gold for My Mother

Cecilia De La Hoya could keep a secret from her boys.

She was in her late thirties when the cancer attacked her body, and the disease coursed through her system, weakened her, and finally made her blind. Her children had no idea. She wore a scarf, but there were no other clues, at least for a while. She tried to stay cheerful around her children. But hiding it could not stop it.

The breast cancer came, and she could not beat it back. She tried, Lord knows, but there was no answer. She was wracked with pain, she endured chemotherapy that ripped her apart and left her sobbing in bed, begging her husband to comfort her with only one promise.

"Please take care of my babies," Cecilia pleaded to her weeping husband. "Don't ever let anything happen to them."

He promised. He prayed. She kept getting sicker.

But to her children, like the rest of the world, she told nothing, until her hair started falling out because of the chemotherapy. Little Ceci was not yet ten. The boys were still in the house. Cecilia had only months to live.

By this time, Oscar was bigger than a neighborhood phenom, he was a bona fide Olympic hopeful. He won the U.S. Junior Olympic 119-pound title in 1988 at age fifteen, and the next year won the national Golden Gloves. Then he moved up to 125 pounds, and won the U.S. amateur title in 1990, and followed that up with the gold medal in the Goodwill Games in Seattle that same year.

Joel Jr., though, won none of those awards, and none of his father's praise. If the brothers ever really were competing for their father's attention, the competition was over. Joel Jr. stayed in the background, stewing.

"Oh yeah, I feel that. And my brother knows it. You ever see *La Bamba*?" Oscar says, referring to the life story of Richie Valens and the older brother who brooded in the background of his singing sibling. "You see that movie, it's the exact same story."

Years later, Joel Jr. would repeat that he never felt jealous of his little brother. How could he say he was jealous when Oscar was the one who had the family's fortune tied to his fists? Joel Jr. said he enjoyed his brother's boxing triumphs and was proud of his success.

But in private moments, Joel Jr. didn't deny that he was hurt when his father ignored him once Oscar's boxing career took off. Oscar, always watching, knew that from the beginning.

"When I was winning tournaments, growing up, fourteen or fifteen, everybody would put all the attention to me, you know?" Oscar says. "Uncles and aunts and our parents. And I would feel bad, because my brother wouldn't really get much attention. I would feel real bad. He was never there with us. Never."

The family couldn't help it, really. Oscar was the one, suddenly, who was about to make them all rich, or at least all of them who could stick close to him. Oscar was making them all a little bit famous. He was their gold mine. They all had something invested in him. At times, it seemed like the whole community had something invested in the teenage Oscar De La Hoya.

Everybody in the neighborhood knew the path.

From the days of Cassius Clay in the 1960 Games to Sugar Ray Leonard in 1976 to Paul Gonzales, Pernell Whitaker, and Mark Breland in 1984, the Olympics were boxing's proven road to fame and a ready-made pro career. Boxing wasn't like gymnastics or running the hundred meters or even basketball. The Olympics made fighters into names, made them marketable, launched them as professionals. No Olympics, and the road was tough.

In East L.A., everyone knew the drill: Get to the Olympics. Win a gold medal for America. Come home, and the promoters will be throwing money at you.

Paul Gonzales had done it—but had seen his pro career smashed up by prickly, time-consuming business disputes and his own fragile hands. Also, Gonzales was a little man—a flyweight—and De La Hoya clearly was tall enough to develop into the richer, heavier weight divisions as a professional. The next one from East L.A., if he could keep his hands and mind intact, would be bigger, and richer. The next one, if things broke right, could be East L.A.'s dream athlete.

De La Hoya already was glowing gold to everybody who looked at him before he was even a teenager. De La Hoya was eleven when Gonzales draped gold around his neck, and the taller, better-looking, more powerful eleven-year-old was already etching his own path toward the same result. He knew Gonzales. Everybody in town knew Gonzales.

It was possible.

A year after Gonzales's gold, even as Gonzales's career was stalling and in litigation, De La Hoya grabbed an Olympic poster and inscribed a message to himself and whoever wanted to see it. The message was a cocky promise, from a child to himself: "92 Champ."

He still has that poster, and he still smiles when he tells the tale.

"I knew I was going to do something, even then," he says. "That was my goal, my dream."

He was not the only one dreaming, of course. The family was not blind to his rise, and to his professional promise. Joel hadn't turned out to be a moneymaker, but what could young Oscar deliver? Thousands? Millions? Tens of millions? Nothing was certain, but Oscar was too precious to screw up. And changes had to be made to ensure that he would not falter.

The first to go was the one who was there at the beginning. Joe Minjarez's departure started a relentless pattern, repeated over and over again throughout De La Hoya's career, but Minjarez couldn't know that. Joe Minjarez was the first official De La Hoya discard, and the sloppy handling of the situation would be repeated constantly and chaotically throughout the rest of his career.

De La Hoya, Minjarez says, did not leave well.

"It wasn't in good graces," Minjarez says now, quietly. His success, by the time he was fourteen, had already made Oscar a hot property among those boxing minimavens who scour the amateur ranks for prospects. He was a sure-thing amateur star with the power for a good pro career. Whether or not he actually made it through the Olympic gauntlet—tournaments, the Olympic Trials, the politics, and, finally, the box-offs—De La Hoya was going to make money as a pro.

Plus, most importantly, his slamming left hook and spindly body frame projected greater things when he made his move into the pro ranks. Minjarez saw the other trainers maneuver their way into the gym whenever De La Hoya was working out. Minjarez threw them out when it became obvious they were trying to poach De La Hoya away from him. But you couldn't throw them all out, or else Minjarez would practically have had to hire a bouncer.

One day, Minjarez saw George Payan, who would later train De La Hoya for a time and who was close to De La Hoya's father, work a little too obviously with De La Hoya, right before Minjarez's eyes. As always, Oscar was listening. Which was part of the problem: Oscar would listen to whoever was talking to him, and loyalty was something that did not seem to emanate from his soul. Oscar would stay quiet, nod his head, and keep working. That's what he always did with his father, and he'd follow the same pattern with any other authority figure. His father taught him not to do anything but pay attention, or else there would be hell to pay. Didn't really matter who was talking, as long as sensible advice was being dispensed. Even if it angered the real trainer.

"You better leave," Minjarez told Payan. And De La Hoya, according to Minjarez, left with Payan.

Payan took over De La Hoya's training, but that did not last long. There were always others whispering into Joel Sr.'s ears, and others young De La Hoya followed. De La Hoya started working with Manuel Montiel, a respected trainer who worked at Resurrection Gym, a run-down boxing facility housed in an abandoned Catholic church a few miles from downtown L.A. Over the dark wood floors and the chipped-away paint, a giant painting of Christ stared down over the main ring. The setting was atmospheric enough to draw the crew from *Rocky,* which filmed some early scenes at Resurrection.

But when the cameras weren't rolling, the gym wasn't just atmosphere. Resurrection smelled bad, it was dark and cramped. But the boxing was fierce, the potential sparring partners—pro and amateur—were plentiful, and Montiel and De La Hoya, it turned out, were an unbeatable team. De La Hoya was fifteen.

"When I took Oscar, right away you could tell he was going to be an Olympic gold medalist," Montiel recalls. "Because he had that look, in his eyes, you know. A lot different than other fighters."

Under Montiel's tutelage, De La Hoya roared through his Resurrection days—registering more than twenty knockouts in a row, blasting through everybody his age and many that were older. There are rules against amateurs sparring with professionals, but with De La Hoya's size and power, and all those pros lingering around the gym, it was impossible to resist the temptation.

When fighters came through from Mexico to train for fights at the Forum, they stopped by Resurrection, and De La Hoya climbed in against many of them. This was serious stuff for someone still in high school. So serious that he was away from classes almost as often as he was at school, off to tournaments, and up to U.S. Olympic headquarters in Colorado Springs, Colorado.

At Garfield High, famous as the school that inspired *Stand and Deliver,* De La Hoya was famous, too—but also isolated by all his training. If people expected a fighter to be brash and out of control, De La Hoya was completely the opposite with his peers. He had his best friend, Jose Pajar. He had a few girlfriends—girls were always attracted to him. But what people remember most of his high school days is his dedication to boxing and his gold-medal goal.

"He was so humble, he was so quiet," said Maria Elena Tostado, the former nun who was the principal at Garfield when De La Hoya attended the school. "He never looked for trouble. He just did his work. . . . He was just so single-minded, preparing for his fights. He knew what he wanted and he wanted it from day one. I never would've picked him out as a fighter. When I first met him, someone told me he was going to the Olympics, and I thought it was a joke. He was the most quiet, unassuming young man you'd ever want to meet. Super nice. Super humble."

Everything was focused on the run to the Olympics, and it was a fast-paced sprint by the time Oscar was a teenager.

At fifteen, and 119 pounds, De La Hoya alerted the U.S. national coaches with a blazing, title-winning performance in the 1988 Junior Olympics at Michigan and was named the competition's outstanding fighter. Quickly, officials for the U.S. team sought to get him experience and started booking him into international competitions, and his star rose even faster.

In Mesa, Arizona, De La Hoya, sixteen years old at the time, won his first U.S. national title in 1989 at 125 pounds. To win it, he had to take a tough decision from Lamar Murphy, considered the favorite to win the title. His other fights in the competition were all knockout victories. But De La Hoya couldn't blast through the much more experienced Murphy, who would go on to a successful professional career.

De La Hoya, his family, and the U.S. coaches considered the Murphy fight a milestone because De La Hoya had to outthink him, move, and feint. He had to make adjustments. He was forced to do all the things he'd have to do if he was going to be an Olympic gold medalist.

"I never saw him nervous in the ring or anything," Montiel says. "He always was 100 percent sure he was going to win. He had that in his mind that he was going to go in there and do the job and get out, you know?"

That same year, De La Hoya won the national Golden Gloves tournament in Biloxi, Mississippi, and as the run continued, Alcazar stayed nearby, earning the trust of De La Hoya the most direct way—through his father. The first time Alcazar met Oscar, Joel Sr. told him to come by the gym when Oscar was twelve to look at some boxing equipment. Joel had spent countless lunch breaks at the factory telling Robert about his son's young career, and Alcazar was curious—and he also needed to buy some boxing equipment at the gym.

"I just came, got my equipment, met the kid, and went back home," Alcazar recalls. "Then his father came to me and asked me, 'Would you like to help my son on this particular weekend? We're going to be competing in this very hard tournament.' So I said, 'Yes, sure, why not?' I brought all my stuff and I paid five dollars to get into the place and I was looking for him....Finally I found him in one of the rooms and we just started talking to each other and I started wrapping his hands. And that's the first night I worked officially with him."

Alcazar, who had come to America from Guadalajara when he was thirteen, fought professionally in the United States for five years, running up a 29–5 record as a lightweight. After he retired he became a mechanic, which landed him in the same factory as Joel.

And in the De La Hoya world, forever.

Even though he wasn't De La Hoya's official lead trainer (Alcazar was the lead trainer for a few other fighters, including Lalo Velasquez, a pro from Baldwin Park), he was passionate about the boy, especially about the wrapping of his hands before he put on the gloves. Oscar, like almost all fighters, especially fighters who have great hand speed, had tender hands from all the ring work, and a good hand-wrapper was always welcome. For Alcazar, it was always about attention. Alcazar threw himself into wrapping Oscar's hands, barely speaking as he carefully folded the wrap, measuring his movements in an almost artistic way. It was like he was worshipping those hands, and protecting them.

"Manuel would ask Robert to help me out, to wrap my hands or something," De La Hoya says. "My father always loved the way Robert wrapped my hands."

Explained Alcazar: "I told him, 'I will not talk to you about your personal life. That you are responsible for. But I will be responsible for your hands.' And he agreed."

Alcazar stuck around, even after Montiel was bounced. This time, the De La Hoya departure was all about money, and the real offers for real money that were rolling in by the time he was climbing the high amateur ranks. Joel Sr. needed money, and he was looking for "sponsors," a code word for businessmen who would provide money without a contract (thus keeping the fighter eligible for the Olympics as an amateur) with the understanding that he would sign with them as a professional.

Johnny Flores, one of the key figures in local amateur boxing, knew that Joel was ready for some money. And he was being paid by Marty Denkin to refer fighters to a gym Denkin was organizing around trainer Albert Davilla, a famous retired fighter himself. Denkin moved in quickly.

Joel wanted some money and a car. In exchange, Oscar would leave Montiel and move over to Denkin's gym, which was being funded by a construction company, and to Davilla. Nobody had told Montiel anything. But Denkin says that after he agreed to terms with Joel Sr., he made a point of speaking to Montiel and offering him about $5,000 to walk away. When asked about the circumstances that led to De La Hoya leaving his training, Montiel now says, "Things didn't work out."

"The reason why me and Manuel got split up," De La Hoya explains, "there were these lawyers that got interested in me. And I remember that they wanted to sign me up when I turned pro—for life. I was like, 'Man!' They offered Manuel $5,000 to walk away. I remember that, $5,000. And they promised me, 'We'll sign you up for $50,000.' I was like, 'Shit, let's sign!'"

Very quickly, though, things got tense, as USA Boxing fretted about De La Hoya's amateur status, Joel Sr. kept asking for extra cash, and Denkin and Davilla wondered if it was all worth it. USA Boxing put De La Hoya in the ultraprestigious Operation: Gold program, which meant that the organization believed he was an odds-on bet to win an American gold medal in the Barcelona Games. With that came a stipend that was about $500 a week, and a relatively undemanding job at a Budweiser plant for more money. In return, De La Hoya had to go to the U.S Olympic Committee headquarters in Colorado Springs for frequent training sessions and was on the list for international competitions.

At one tournament in Las Vegas, the triheaded relationship imploded. Joel Sr. went to the Denkin group and asked for twenty-five dollars to cover expenses that he had already received. "If he was double-dipping for that much," said one person involved in the situation, "what was he going to do when it got to be big money?"

After paying the De La Hoyas about $10,000, the Denkin group called Oscar and his father in and terminated the relationship. It was going to be too much trouble. They'd let somebody else deal with the escalating cash and demands. Oscar was talented, but he and his father were a headache.

"We were criticized, but we knew what we were doing," says Denkin, a longtime referee in California, pointing out that they were not the last ones to lose a grip on De La Hoya. "We were right."

The episode made De La Hoya a free agent again, looking for a trainer and sponsors, with only two years to go before the Olympics. "I don't know what happened [with the Denkin group]," De La Hoya says. "All I know is after that is when my father brought me to Al Stankie."

Actually, Joel De La Hoya had enlisted Stankie's help years earlier, just to take a look at his son, to be an adviser on the ways of big-time amateur boxing. Even while Payan and Montiel trained him, Joel consulted with Stankie.

When De La Hoya left Montiel, then Davilla, he needed a trainer who could get him ready for the Olympic Trials and the Games themselves. Someone who had been through it all before. And there was Stankie, who had been there all along.

Al Stankie was and is a minor legend in Los Angeles boxing, a wild-living, irresponsible, hyper, retired lightweight fighter, a motivational specialist who shepherded Paul Gonzales to the 1984 Olympic gold medal. Stankie was a former vice cop, known to spend a bit too much time with the criminals he chased, and had more than his share of adventures with alcohol. But he was a proven amateur trainer. And he was available. Who better to grab hold of De La Hoya for the Olympic spit and polish than Al Stankie?

"Al, help me make Oscar a gold medalist," Joel De La Hoya told Stankie.

What could Stankie, struggling with Gonzales's dimming pro career at the time, do but welcome the opportunity? Stankie wasn't sure he wanted to be a full-time De La Hoya trainer—there had already been at least three full-time trainers hired and fired, and De La Hoya wasn't sixteen yet—but he agreed to help. De La Hoya was too interesting an opportunity to turn down.

"This kid has more tools, more natural ability, than anyone I ever saw," Stankie said then. "There just isn't any limit to his future. He can be as good as anyone ever was."

From the beginning, it was an odd pairing—the still-shy, extremely focused fighter with the crazy former vice cop. With the garrulous Gonzales, Stankie was a perfect, hysterical match. The two old associates screamed at each other, hugged each other, went to war together, hated and loved each other every minute they were together. They became known as "the Kop and the Kid," and it was a pairing everybody could understand.

But De La Hoya and Stankie? The wildly talented introvert with the wildly extroverted coach?

"That guy was a nutcase," Oscar says about Stankie. "Oh man, we had some good times. We had some real good times. He trained me pretty good. He showed me a few things, you know? And I think I needed it."

Stankie, always chock-full of ideas and newfound innovations, fixed his sights on getting De La Hoya ready for the mental grind of the Olympic experience.

"I said, 'Oscar, in 1992, Barcelona, Spain, Olympic gold medal time! Oscar De La Hoya!'" Stankie recalls. "Every day, I'd make him say those things. Think it, eat it, feel it, taste it. That's the mind repertoire.... And he was receptive-plus."

De La Hoya's talent was electrifying, and Stankie basked in it for a while. So what if the kid kept to himself? He was listening, he had to be listening. But as Oscar kept moving toward the Olympics, Stankie knew that he wasn't guaranteed a long stay with De La Hoya.

"Al, what are you working so hard with that kid?" someone once yelled to him. "Alcazar, he's going to train him after the Olympics. Don't you know that?"

Stankie thought about that, and kept going. How do you let go of a kid so talented, even if you know what's coming?

"Honest to God, I thought, 'Okay, that might happen. But I want him to get the gold,'" Stankie says. "But it was the truth. They were talking the truth."

It would take some time, though. In 1990, under Stankie's tutelage, De La Hoya won a gold medal in the Goodwill Games in Seattle, beating Ivan Robinson in a blistering gold-medal match.

"The thing is, no one could stop him," Stankie says. "He was just too strong. I'm not the greatest coach in the world. But I'm a great motivator. I'd tell him, 'Oh man, you're lucky! This guy is nothing. You're going to go right through him. You're too fast, you're too strong.' I'm pumping him up. I'm making him feel like a bantam rooster. Yeah, you're going to win!"

While De La Hoya worked with Stankie—usually at the Hollenbeck Youth Center in East L.A.—he got an up-close view of Gonzales, who was struggling with his hand injuries and his motivation as his pro career ran aground.

"I would see him changing his attitude, because he'd win fights," De La Hoya says of Gonzales. "He'd come back the next day thinking he was all that, and I would study the mistakes he made."

The most important connection Stankie made for the De La Hoyas, though, was not to a fighter. He brought them to their first serious boxing moneyman, New York agent Shelly Finkel, a former rock 'n' roll manager and now a major player in the boxing world. After the 1984 Olympics, which created a host of new American boxing stars, Finkel signed and adroitly guided Pernell Whitaker, Evander Holyfield, and Mark Breland to successful professional careers.

Finkel flew Joel Sr., Oscar, and Stankie to the East Coast for a Breland fight, and there was an immediate connection: Finkel would pay, and the De La Hoyas would take it. This was all part of the intricate dance of Olympic fighters eyeing the professional ranks—they can't sign anything official, or risk their amateur status, but they all make arrangements, some more seamy than others, to accept money from "sponsors," as De La Hoya already had from Denkin. Now it was Finkel, who was associated with the powerful Duva family (Lou Duva ended up training most of Finkel's fighters, and Dan Duva, the head of the Main Events Monitor company, did the promoting), who controlled much of boxing on the East Coast.

Recalls Finkel: "I knew how the father was. I wasn't kidding myself. . . . There was always something. 'Oh, can you give me this, you've got to get that. . . . I'm only a poor worker.' It was always something more."

But the fighter was too good to resist.

The Goodwill Games triumph was De La Hoya's last in the 125-pound division, where he was ranked No. 1 in the world. Oscar was growing too much to stick at 125 pounds—keeping his weight down was taking too much out of him.

He headed into the last eighteen months before the Olympics as a 132-pounder, and with wild momentum. By November 1991, when he went to the 1991 World Championships in Sydney, Australia, De La Hoya had never lost an international match, and hadn't lost any match since 1987, when he had been beaten in the Junior Olympics by Ruben Espinoza, 3–2. In national boxing circles, as he grew to almost six feet tall, and as the knockout victories continued, De La Hoya was the talk of the amateur ranks.

"He reminds me of a professional fighter," none other than Sugar Ray Leonard said of De La Hoya in 1991. "He's very poised. And when he punches, he punches with such conviction."

At the 1991 U.S. Olympic Festival, held in Los Angeles, De La Hoya was feted by the national media and the assembled officials, who recognized him as a local star ready to make the stretch run to a gold medal in the Barcelona Games of 1992. For De La Hoya, it was the perfect launch, both athletically—he won the competition—and symbolically.

The national media loved his story, his soft voice, and, of course, his striking looks. He wasn't squat like so many other Mexican and Mexican-American fighters. He was lean and sharp-shouldered. His feet were light, and his hands were lightning. Here was a pro prospect, gleaming bright.

And De La Hoya swiftly learned what made the media happy: Don't be surly, smile, be respectful, and answer each question with a wink. It was a dazzling contrast—from the gang-infested barrio, here came a thoughtful hero, with a heartwarming background and an appreciation for boxing's rich history.

De La Hoya's hero in boxing always was Alexis Arguello, the stylish Nicaraguan who was a three-time world champion in the late 1970s and early '80s. Arguello, like De La Hoya, was almost six feet tall and dominated fights with his lightning lead left hand.

It was a strange choice for a Mexican-American fighter. Though the great Mexican Julio Cesar Chavez was in his prime in 1991, and Pipino Cuevas had only recently retired, and Salvador Sanchez had the respect of the whole sport during his brief but brilliant career, De La Hoya loved Arguello's rhythm and precision. Arguello wasn't a bull. In fact, he lost two devastating, bloody fights to the rampaging Aaron Pryor, in the signature fights of both boxers' careers. But Arguello fought like a master. Like an artist, with venom in his hands.

"Alexis Arguello was beautiful," De La Hoya said. "He threw straight punches. He didn't waste punches. He was beautiful. And he had a presence outside of the ring."

With the national media documenting his every punch, De La Hoya easily won the Olympic Festival 132-pound title, including a dominant 44–15 triumph over Patrice Brooks of St. Louis.

At the festival, organizers cautioned athletes not to wear their sweat suits away from the sites, for fear the outfits would be mistaken for gang "colors." But De La Hoya was a walking example of how to survive and flourish amid the gangs. The infamous MMV—or *Mariana Marivilla* —gang dominated his neighborhood. But, because he was known as a fighter with a promising future, he had never joined, or been pressured to join, he said.

Instead, gang members would yell across the street to him, "Yo, Adrian!" in a strange homage to the *Rocky* movies and to his future. "I've been asked to join gangs, but I've never wanted to," De La Hoya once said. "I've always had something else."

De La Hoya, the budding public speaker, also was careful to include a warning that life in the barrio did not come without trouble, even for him. Recently, he told the national media, he was walking with his girl-friend late at night, when three gang members jumped out of a passing car and pulled a gun on him. De La Hoya offered no resistance, and they stole his wallet, with $150 in it, and an expensive camera.

"They were amateurs," De La Hoya said, noting that they stole neither his new leather jacket nor several rings. But apparently the gang members went through his wallet and discovered whom they had mugged. De La Hoya returned home a few hours later and found his wallet returned with the $150 still inside.

"They kept the camera, though," De La Hoya said with a laugh. And the moral of the story? "Don't walk at night in East L.A."

A few months before the Olympic Festival, it came time for his senior prom, May 1991, and De La Hoya wasn't even in town. He was at Fort Bragg, North Carolina, for a major dual-country meet against the Cubans, the perennial power in international boxing.

There he had to face Julio Gonzales, who was one of the most renowned amateur fighters in the world. De La Hoya was the up-and-comer. Gonzales was the establishment, a two-time Pan American Games winner, a two-time amateur world champion, and, unless De La Hoya upset him, the favorite to win the gold medal in Barcelona. Gonzales, also, had never lost to an American before.

If De La Hoya, who hadn't lost a fight since 1987—four years earlier—could beat Gonzales, he would be the No. 1–ranked 132-pounder in the world. Already, amateur boxing experts figured this could be a preview of the Olympic gold-medal match in 1992. De La Hoya played to that angle, without a doubt, when asked to look toward Barcelona, fifteen months away. "The only one I'm going to worry about is the Cuban," De La Hoya said.

At the Fort Bragg meet, De La Hoya started a little tentatively against his Cuban rival. "At first, I was a little intimidated by his name, by his experience, and by the fact he'd never lost to an American," De La Hoya said. And Gonzales was a right-handed counterpuncher who could shoot his right straight over De La Hoya's left jab and throw off his rhythm.

But Gonzales, too, seemed cautious against De La Hoya. Gonzales threw flurries, but with very little effect. De La Hoya hunted for a big left, and it never came. In the end, the scoring system gave him a 3–2 victory, though most observers said it was hard to pick a winner.

In a broader perspective, for De La Hoya, facing down the Cuban legend was a mental hurdle. "In the second round, I realized he wasn't even the toughest guy I'd fought," De La Hoya said.

Though he was the clear No. 1 in the world at 132 pounds, there was still some trouble for him to survive.

Stankie was good for Oscar, but he was constant controversy. It was like a clichéd fighter-trainer relationship turned upside down: The trainer was the reckless soul, and the fighter was cool and calm and knew exactly the path he had to take. At the 1990 U.S. Nationals in Colorado Springs, Stankie showed up stumbling drunk at the training center and was immediately thrown off the grounds of the Olympic complex.

"I had a few beers, so what?" Stankie said.

But USA Boxing was less than amused by his self-destructive nature. He was suspended for a year, which meant he wasn't supposed to train anybody associated with USA Boxing, which, of course, only really referred to De La Hoya. There was no real way to police his training of De La Hoya, so as long as the fighter stayed in L.A., Stankie was with him. He just couldn't be with him at meets or when he went to Colorado Springs. But the episode only heightened the De La Hoyas' sense that Stankie was just a short-term option.

"When he's got his act together, he's the greatest trainer in the world," Gonzales once said of Stankie. "But he's got that other side to him. And you don't even want to be around him then."

Stankie was always on the brink, and Oscar, for the most part, seemed to enjoy that. It gave him a little edge, a sense of unpredictability. But everybody, except for maybe Stankie, understood that one more embarrassment and he would be dispatched, like all the other trainers before him. There now was a De La Hoya image to uphold. And it did not take Stankie long to run afoul again—this time far more seriously.

In April 1991—a month before De La Hoya's victory against the Cuban—Stankie, who was fifty then, made an illegal left turn in front of the Broadway Gym in L.A. He was pulled over for a routine stop. But somehow Stankie had forgotten or ignored two earlier drunk-driving warrants for his arrest. When those came up on the computer during the pullover, Stankie was hauled to jail and given an eighty-four-day sentence.

It was while he was in Los Angeles County Central Jail, dressed in a prison-blue denim jumpsuit, that Stankie greeted a visitor—*Los Angeles Times* reporter Earl Gustkey. After getting into a fight in jail, Stankie was in lockdown, so he couldn't take off his handcuffs, even to speak to a visitor. He had to talk through a window, with a prison guard looking on.

"Handsome!" Stankie called out to Gustkey, because he called everybody "handsome."

"I'm just going to do my time, then get back out, jump back in," Stankie said then. "I've got Oscar, I've got the Olympics to look at."

Which is when Gustkey told him: He had just talked to Joel Sr. Stankie was "out of the picture."

"When I heard that, it stabbed me right in the heart," Stankie recalled years later. "He said, 'You're out of the picture.' I'll probably never forget those words. I knew he was telling the truth. I knew it was solid. But it hurt."

Stankie at the time only had one answer for Gustkey: "I'll believe it when I hear it from Oscar."

He never heard from the De La Hoyas, but it was true. He still hasn't heard a word from Joel De La Hoya, seven years later.

At the time of the firing, Oscar was sanguine: "It was very hard, but I had to let him go. I don't think I let him down. He let me down."

"To be very truthful, he threw me away," Stankie says of Joel De La Hoya. "For the money. I was thrown away. It kind of hurts me because I spent a lot of time with the kid. I loved him. And I still love him. He's a good kid. We had a great relationship. I feel so badly because I was thrown away like an old shoe. I'm sure the father probably did what he thought best for his family. That's the way I can rationalize it. The other way, I've got a lot of venom built up. How many times do you get a chance with an opportunity to be financially secure, and then when you lose that chance, how many more chances do we get, no matter who we are? That's the part that hurts. . . . You tell yourself, 'Well, I'll just make another one.'

"But I've had the opportunity to help Paul Gonzales, [1988 Olympic silver medalist for Mexico] Hector Lopez, and Oscar De La Hoya. And I'm saying, you know, it's hard. A lot of time, a lot of effort. You can't just turn around and make another one."

Once Stankie was gone, no search needed to be conducted for his replacement. He'd been there the whole time, wrapping Oscar's hands when he could. Whispering in Joel Sr.'s ear. Watching from the sidelines.

A year from the Olympics—less than that to the Olympic Trials and box-offs—there was no other choice but to turn over De La Hoya's training to the man who wanted it most, who had stayed patient the longest, and who was burning to show the world he could be a major league fight man. Robert Alcazar.

"He was a gift," Alcazar says. "He never lost a fight with me. He was a tall kid, with a hard punch. Oh my God. A spectacular punch."

And Alcazar was going to do everything in his power to make sure the natural talent of the fighter was nourished, and that meant making him into boxing's greatest knockout star.

"The majority of the trainers, they don't have success in boxing for one simple reason: The trainers try to teach the fighters how to fight their way," Alcazar says. "They try to duplicate their old experiences, especially the fighters they've had in the past. They try to teach a kid the same way they used to fight. And that's a big mistake. They forget about the talent of the kid. So now they're turning these kids into actors. But they never discover their own talents. That's part of my success with Oscar. I worked with him on his own exclusive style. How to throw his jab better, help him how to hit harder, how to make his defense better. Basically, try to improve the things he already has naturally."

By November 1991, De La Hoya was a glorious 36–0 in world competition. He had already beaten Cuba's Gonzales. The World Championships in Sydney, Australia, looked like the perfect way to end a perfect year as Barcelona beckoned.

De La Hoya got a bye in the first round, then faced Germany's Marco Rudolph, a respected fighter, but not considered one of the elite. But, in a technical battle, the savvier Rudolph kept De La Hoya at bay with a long jab and worked the international scoring system brilliantly with clean outside shots.

De La Hoya never was in the fight, and didn't complain when the score went up: Rudolph 17, De La Hoya 13, De La Hoya's first loss since 1987.

"The guy is nothing," De La Hoya said soon afterward. "I didn't train well enough for the tournament. My timing was off. I learned a lot from that. I wasn't able to get my punches off. His style was really awkward. I've never seen anything like it. It woke me up."

That night, as he brooded on his first defeat in four years, he called up his cousin Adrian back in L.A. and figured out that this was a piercing lesson going into an Olympic year.

"Adrian, I think this is the best thing that's ever happened to me," Oscar told his cousin. "I was actually getting bored with boxing. I was in a rut. This really woke me up. I'm coming home and work harder than I ever did, and I hope I get this guy in the Olympics, because I'm going to beat him."

Despite the defeat, USA Boxing clearly didn't lose faith in him: He was named the organization's 1991 amateur boxer of the year. "The kid has all the tools," said Pat Nappi, a two-time former U.S. team coach. "Right now, based on what I've seen, he has the gold medal."

During this period, De La Hoya's best and only friend in amateur boxing circles was Raul Marquez, a rough-and-tumble middleweight from Texas who was De La Hoya's apparent polar opposite.

Marquez was emotional and honest, a constant talker and somebody who liked to wrestle with his friends and laugh the night away. He was already established on the scene, a gold-medal hopeful by 1989. De La Hoya came more quietly into the amateur ranks, barely said a word, just hung next to Marquez and stayed in his shadow.

"I'm the one who introduced him to amateur boxing. I think it was 1990 when Oscar first won the Nationals," Marquez recalled. "We were in the Olympic Training Center [in Colorado Springs]; I was in the dorms. I didn't have to fight in the Nationals that year because I was already a top national champion from '89 and I was getting ready to fight in the World Challenge in Germany against the world champion. I was the No. 1 ranked guy in the world. And I ran into Oscar in the dorms, a quiet little shy guy. And he's like, 'Oh, you're Raul Marquez.' I said, 'Yeah, what's your name?' We just clicked and we started hanging out together. He won the Nationals that year, and we were roommates everywhere we went. We were in Australia together, Italy together, everywhere.

"He was always the lighter guy, 125 pounds. I've always been in the same weight class, 154. . . . I was the one who would take care of him. I remember one time, we were in training camp in Lake Placid, New York, and we were running and this dog came after us. Oscar gets behind me, 'Get him! Get him!' Stuff like that."

Once the Olympics were over, Marquez tried calling De La Hoya, but rarely got any calls back. Now, Marquez just writes off the friendship as a thing of the past.

"Oscar was born with a star and it's just shining and shining," Marquez said. "That's great for him. We were together everywhere. Then we went on to the Olympics and he won the gold medal and it was history."

With Marquez, he went to work out with the Duva stable in Virginia Beach, sparring with Pernell Whitaker and John John Molina—both of whom would be future De La Hoya opponents in the professional ranks.

To get to the Olympics, De La Hoya had to get through the Trials. And that turned out to be more difficult than anticipated.

De La Hoya, with the chance of a lifetime in front of him, started slowly in the June Olympic Trials in Worchester, Massachusetts, struggling through two unimpressive bouts to get to the final round. But in the final, he burst out quickly, carefully stayed on the outside, and cruised to an easy decision over Anthony Christodoulou of Syracuse.

The last step to Barcelona was in two weeks, when USA Boxing anointed Patrice Brooks, the same fighter whom De La Hoya had dominated in the Olympic Festival, as his opponent in the final box-offs in Phoenix. De La Hoya, meanwhile, cautioned observers not to judge him on his tentative showing.

"You haven't seen the real Oscar yet," he said at the Trials. "Foreign judges want to see power shots, so I'll make them happy at the Olympics. The key for me here was to use the jab and make the team. I'm being very careful here."

On Saturday, June 27, De La Hoya took apart Brooks in Phoenix, walking away with a 50–16 victory and an Olympic berth. He was almost there.

"I never thought I would screw it up," De La Hoya says. "I always thought other people would screw it up, not me."

The family had suffered its most tragic loss, though, a few years earlier, in October 1990, when Cecilia, after her painful battle, died of cancer. Though she was undergoing chemotherapy and radiation treatments, she didn't want Oscar to know until the latest possible moment, because she didn't want to disrupt his training.

But she was definitely dying.

In order to watch her son in the Goodwill Games in August—in what would be the final fights she ever saw—Cecilia skipped a week of radiation treatments. A few days after winning the Goodwill gold, Oscar was finally told about her cancer.

There's no way she can die, Oscar thought. Not his mother.

"I felt she was going to be okay... because she's strong, she's strong," De La Hoya recalls. "She was very strong. And she never told us she felt bad or anything. But then I found out she was real sick when they would give her that therapy and that stuff and her hair would fall out— that's when I found out she was real sick."

De La Hoya did not cry then. He just watched and accepted fate without outward storms.

"I always felt that she was going to be okay," he says. "I always felt she was going to be okay."

She was going to be okay. . . .

The De La Hoya boys were in denial.

"Don't worry about me," Cecilia De La Hoya told her sons. "I'll be okay. Don't worry."

And because they wanted to believe it, they did. But there were hints that Cecilia knew there was no avoiding reality.

"She would always tell us, take care of your little sister," De La Hoya remembers. "And I would never think, 'Wow, shit, why is she saying that?' I never thought that she would go."

What was that household like? The beloved mother was dying, trying to hide her pain, the boys were silently hoping for her to get better, without daring to discuss it. And little Ceci, seven years old, was watching it all.

"My little sister knew," Oscar says. "My mom would talk to my little sister, my father would talk to her . . . saying that she has cancer and this and that."

There was an unspoken dread in the house. And through the eyes of his sister is how Oscar felt it most.

One night, near the end, the movie *Beaches* was on television, and Oscar was watching it with a girlfriend and Ceci. Before it was over, he walked his friend back home quickly, knowing that he wanted to get back home before the emotional dying scene at the end of the movie.

"I said to myself, 'I'm going to make it back home before that scene comes up,' you know?" De La Hoya says. "I came back, and the scene had already passed. And I saw my little sister, she turned around and she was in tears. Oh, man, that hurt big time. Whew. She knew, she understood. That broke my heart there, that really broke my heart."

Still, the family kept its solemn silence. She was not going to die. She *couldn't* die.

Meanwhile, Cecilia's treatment expenses were piling up, and Joel turned to Finkel again and again for help.

Finkel gave him money several times, he says up to $100,000. At the October 25, 1990, Evander Holyfield–Buster Douglas heavyweight title fight at the Mirage in Las Vegas, Joel made one more fervent request for cash. He pulled Finkel, who managed Holyfield, underneath the Mirage stands and begged him for more money. He cried.

"You know my son is with you," Joel De La Hoya said, according to Finkel. "My wife is dying. I need help."

"You've got it," Finkel said.

No contracts were signed, no agreement was forged. It was understood. You give money for a man to pay for his wife's chemotherapy, and maybe nothing needs to be written and signed. Maybe.

Three days after that conversation in Las Vegas, Cecilia De La Hoya, at age thirty-nine, died. And the world began to fall in on her boys.

"I never thought that, never, ever. . . . I never thought she would go," Oscar remembers. "Even when she was in the hospital, I always thought she would be okay."

Oscar was not even there when she died. He arrived at the hospital for a visit, and nobody looked at him as he walked into his mother's room.

"What happened, what's wrong?" Oscar asked. His mother was dead. But he didn't cry then. His brother, Joel, who had ignored her sickness, the better to make it go away, had a harsher reaction.

"Joel, not once did he visit her in the hospital," Oscar says. "And he went like two hours after she passed away. And it hit him hard, man, it hit him hard. He didn't want to believe that she was sick. He didn't want to face it. He couldn't face it. I don't think my brother ever did tell my mother that he loved her. Not once. And he regrets it, bad. Oh, he feels bad. Whew, he feels bad."

There wasn't a real way to prepare the family for her loss, or repair it after the death. Cecilia, by the time she knew she was dying, didn't have the strength.

On one of her last lucid days, she talked with Oscar. "She told me she was very confident after watching me win the Goodwill Games," De La Hoya said then. "She told me, 'I want you to win the gold medal.'"

And Oscar promised that he would. For you, Mom, I will win the gold. And then Cecilia lapsed into the worst stages.

"The last conversation with my mom, the very, very last conversation, she didn't know who I was," Oscar says. "Man, that crushed me big time. Because I would visit her in the hospital, and we would like say, 'Aw, you're going to be okay.' She would even laugh about it. And then one day, I walked inside the room, I remember it was like my dad and my sister was there and I walked in and she didn't recognize me."

"Who is that?" Cecilia De La Hoya said, nodding to her second son.

"She recognized my dad, but she didn't recognize me," Oscar says. "Oh, man, that crushed me. I started crying. . . . But I don't think she was hurting. I believe that she was happy that we were going to grow up to be good kids."

Oscar and Joel were already almost men when she died, at least. Ceci was devastated.

"My little sister's taken it hard, you know?" Oscar says. "She's very strong like my mom, but inside she has all this hurt and pain. She didn't cry. My sister didn't cry. She couldn't cry. It's still all inside of her."

Years later, when Oscar got into a serious car accident, only by luck avoiding injury, Ceci ran to him as soon as she could, and in a panic hugged him hard enough to cut off some air.

"She was crying like crazy," Oscar says. "She hugged me, she didn't want to let me go. It would hurt her so much if she lost somebody else. It would crush her. To think that she had to even think that she was close to losing me. . . ."

When Cecilia died, Joel Sr., desperate and alone, once again asked Finkel for $5,000 to pay for her funeral. At the funeral, Oscar was the only De La Hoya child to cry, and he did that throughout the ceremony, loudly and stirringly. He mourned her hard. For the first time anyone could remember, the pensive little boy was letting the world see how he felt, exposing himself as he broke into pieces. For his mother.

"His mother was everything to him," his former principal, Maria Elena Tostado, said. "She was paramount. He still misses her a whole lot. And she had all her faith in him. She encouraged him from day one. She was concerned about him, concerned about his education. She must have seen he had special qualities. He really is a single-minded young man. There's not many like him. One thought in his mind. Never, ever complained once about what he was doing or how much it was taking of his life. He didn't have much of a youth. I can remember him always trying to keep his weight down. He's a tall kid.... I can remember him eating apples, when I'm sure he would've liked to have eaten more. He always had that plan."

But, for at least a moment, the focus wavered. The plan seemed senseless without his mother. And, to himself, he said he was quitting boxing.

"That's it," he told himself, "I'm going to retire from boxing. Why fight anymore?"

But it lasted a week.

"I just had to go back. I said to myself, 'If my mom was here, this is what she would want, for her son to keep on training and working harder.'"

If he was dangerous in the ring before his mother's death, after it he was incandescent. Pent-up anger turned into rage, into frenzy, into destruction. His first sparring session back, he faced Rudy Zavala, a solid professional fighter. It was not a fair match.

"Man, I was going at him," De La Hoya recalls. "I had so much anger in me, I was going off at him. I tried to just get rid of him. I was going crazy on him."

Was he insane? Those in the gym who didn't know his mother had died didn't know what was happening. They tried to stop him, but he was a torrent of punishment. Zavala was broken apart.

Then De La Hoya stopped.

"I just started crying," De La Hoya says quietly. "It was crazy."

Years later, with time to put the experience in perspective, De La Hoya says he knows his mother prepared him for his future as well as she could. He just wishes he could have returned the favor.

"Even though we had a small home and it was run-down and everything, she would always keep it clean," Oscar says. "My mom would always be talking about having the best in life and always being clean. We used to struggle to wear some nice clothes. My mom used to buy herself a dress once a month or something. . . .

"My mom would be window shopping and saying, 'Oh, I want this.' Couldn't have it. And it hurts me to know that now I could buy her whatever she wants, she's not here. . . ."

Though she is not with him literally, too many things have gone right with his life—too many missteps narrowly avoided—for De La Hoya not to believe that his mother is watching over him, even now.

"I know for a fact that she's taking care of me," he says. "I know for a fact. Everything. I know she's there. I know. She has to be. I know she is. Everything I do always comes out good. Even if I'm in a hole. For some reason I come out of that hole and it turns out good."

During their four-year relationship, which started after his mother died, Veronica Peralta says that sometimes De La Hoya would go to her grave at Resurrection Cemetery on a hill in Montebello, and just sit. Veronica would wonder, Is he speaking to her? What is he saying?

"Nobody will ever be able to replace the loss of his mother," Peralta said while they were together. "He says sometimes . . . he has so much now that he wishes his mom had just a tiny part of it. If his mom was around she would be his . . . counselor, helper, friend. She was everything to him."

In every victory after her death leading up to the Olympics, De La Hoya dropped to his knees when the fight was won and blew a kiss to heaven.

"It's just a way of saying, 'For you,'" De La Hoya said then.

And soon after she died, he went to her fresh grave site, and repeated the golden promise: I will come back here and show it to you.

chapter four
Golden Boy

When the day came to leave for Barcelona to fight for gold, De La Hoya felt like he was carrying more than 132 pounds, like the gravity of it all finally was wearing on his shoulders. It was the whole rest of his life in the balance, really, coming down to a five-fight tournament.

Win the gold, or go home disappointed, empty, with no mother to comfort you when the quest was finished. Win gold, or start your professional career off in the dullest way, as a would-be instead of a star. Win gold, or be just another fighter. Win gold, or support your family with ... what?

They had all come to expect glory in Spain, domination in his last amateur showing, and then a quick leap into all the cash he could draw. Once his mother died, that was about the only thing that tied the family together. Alongside Joel Sr. and Oscar's brother and sister, a dozen or so family members scrambled on board during the Olympic journey, and they were in Barcelona, too, to cheer, and hope, and wonder how much treasure there would be to split up when it was over.

Oscar had been preparing for these Olympics in his mind since he was ten, or earlier, and it was hard to picture a future without a Barcelona gold medal. He had been counted on to win since he was twelve or thirteen. He had promised his mother twenty months ago. So it was no real surprise that he arrived in Spain edgy, distracted, and full of anticipation.

Five fights to gold. How much pressure is there when you've only given up most of your life for this?

"There's a lot of pressure when you're favored to win the gold," De La Hoya said right before the tournament started. "Some guys are coming into this with nothing to lose. They're just here for respect. But the pressure is on me. I'm expected to win. That pushes me harder in training. I'm only nineteen, though, and it's tough sometimes. I've been thinking about winning a gold medal for six years. I put everything on hold for this."

On hold, and holding his breath.

"When I won the box-offs in Phoenix and made the team, I felt all the coaches in the corner helped me, but I owed it all to my father," De La Hoya said. "Now I'm in Barcelona to win the gold medal for my mother. . . . My father, he's always telling me what to do, what I'm doing wrong. Definitely, I think the most pressure's on me. Sometimes, it affects the way I fight. If I don't look right, everybody starts talking about me. The pressure's been building and building. It'll be a relief when it's over."

Those in his camp worried a little that the responsibility was too much. What had happened to the teenager who threw his heart into fighting? Though De La Hoya hadn't lost any of them, his performances heading into Barcelona were joyless and mechanical.

That was not the way to win a gold medal—or to make yourself a star on the worldwide Olympic stage.

"I know he's better than he's looked in recent fights," Finkel said then. "He reminds me a lot of Mark Breland before the 1984 Olympics, coming in with so many expectations. It's something Oscar will have to deal with."

There was plenty to deal with at the time. Days before the Olympics began, De La Hoya finally started thinking past this tournament, to the rest of his life. Once the Olympic Games were over, he would still be nineteen. His mother would still be gone. Then what? At a time when most fighters were just starting to deal with the business of boxing, De La Hoya had already been through three or four trainers, several sponsors, and a handful of family members ready to guide him into the professional ranks. For a cut, of course.

"A medal could set me up for life," De La Hoya said. "It's kind of scary, because my life will change. There's a lot of crooks, people who just want to use you. Pro boxing is very dangerous, not only up in the ring, but outside."

Despite his gaudy amateur record (217–4 with 152 knockouts entering the Olympics), De La Hoya was only one of many U.S. team members projected to contend for a gold medal in this tournament. And, because of his relative youth and the less-than-roaring last few performances, he wasn't the top pick, either.

"I'm aware of what people are saying," De La Hoya said. "But I have things inside me—secrets—that people don't know what I'm feeling. That's okay. People can talk all they want. I'll show them. I'm going to take that gold medal home."

Experienced light-flyweight Eric Griffin was the team captain, probably the most talented, and expected to cruise to a gold. Junior-middleweight Raul Marquez, De La Hoya's best friend on the team, was probably the most powerful fighter in the tournament. Middle-weight Chris Byrd, bantamweight Sergio Reyes, and light-heavyweight Montell Griffin all were considered possible gold medalists.

Not that De La Hoya wasn't considered, along with Eric Griffin and Marquez, part of the team's elite. He clearly was a pro prospect. But at 132 pounds, De La Hoya was in the most talented division in the tournament. To win the gold, he probably had to beat both Cuba's Gonzales and Marco Rudolph, who had beaten De La Hoya in their only meeting.

Yes, he said, he was nervous. But De La Hoya said that he had matured as an international fighter since his loss to Rudolph, and that the loss had given him a lesson about the quirks of the new international scoring system.

Typical of the Byzantine Olympic rule-making process, it was a quirky system. Five judges with computer keypads sat around the ring, pressing a key when they saw a scoring blow land. If at least three of the judges credited one of the fighters with landing a scoring blow within a one-second window, that fighter was awarded a point.

The quirk: If three of the judges missed the one-second time frame, even if all five saw the scoring blow and pressed the button for that fighter, no point was awarded. Hesitant fingers, quick fingers, political leanings . . . they all heavily influenced the scoring, and already had produced wildly controversial results in international competition.

The system rewarded fighters who stayed outside, landing long, clean jabs, one at a time, easy to see and tally. In contrast, the inside brawlers, whose body shots can be obscured and whose strongest shots are difficult to separate from punches that are blocked, consistently suffered at the hands of the scoring system.

Under the system, it was feasible, and indeed not at all rare, that fighters could get knocked down with huge inside punches that did not register as points. De La Hoya, like Marquez, enjoyed brawling inside, jumping in to wound his opponent with body shots and tough uppercuts.

But as the Olympics arrived, De La Hoya proved how quick-witted he could be. With Alcazar's help, he concentrated on landing hard, loud shots from the outside—easy to see and more likely to draw a score. He was less likely to fly off on one of his gigantic, violent flurries, but more likely to win.

"I changed my training habits around after I lost in Sydney [to Rudolph]," De La Hoya said then. "The new scoring changed my style for now. I think of throwing the jab more and I don't go to the body the way I used to because I know they won't count those punches. So why throw them? I have a whole different game plan now when I go into a fight. People think I've lost something because I haven't been showing the same power, but it's better to win than to lose looking good. I'm only here for one thing. I'm here to win the gold medal."

The boxing competition was held just outside of Barcelona, in Batalona, Spain, at Joventut Pavilion, a converted basketball arena. There was a low-slung balcony where twenty of De La Hoya's family members and friends always sat, unofficially called "Oscar's Corner." From that perch his father sat for every one of his fights, leaning forward over a sign that read: GOOD LUCK OSCAR—WE LOVE YOU!

As usual, De La Hoya roomed with Marquez, who was also aligned with the Duvas, in an Olympic Village dorm suite that housed nine members of the team altogether. De La Hoya saw so much of Alcazar and Lou Duva, it's a wonder he ever made it to the official U.S. team training sessions with Coach Joe Byrd.

Privately, but insistently, De La Hoya complained about the U.S. coaches, silently seethed at their practice drills, and broke away from the Village as often as he could to work with Alcazar at the trainer's nearby hotel. De La Hoya loved working the hand pads with Alcazar, firing his rocket punches into red leather pads strapped to Alcazar's hands. The workout was De La Hoya's favorite, part cardiovascular, part pure power, as he cut loose, faster, faster, faster, and Alcazar whistled with pain and pleasure.

Along the way, the Duvas were doing what they do best: operating a loud P.R. crusade to get ink for both De La Hoya and Marquez, unabashedly exerting the family's influence over the judging, and running off would-be interlopers. Lou Duva, the potbellied family patriarch and one of the most famous trainers in the world, dispensed advice, introduced reporters, and generally made himself the cantankerous center of all things.

Alcazar and De La Hoya may have thought Duva was over the top, but Olympic boxing was always a political minefield, and the Duvas were good enough and brazen enough to act as effective buffers. You stood with them, and you stood at least an even chance of escaping a disastrously wrongheaded decision.

And it was clear early, after Eric Griffin, who was not tied to any of the major professional promoters, lost an outrageously bad decision to Spain's Rafael Lozano, that anybody wearing red, white, and blue could use some political juice to survive. If you were with him, as De La Hoya said he was, Duva was glad to provide.

"Let me tell you something, I was instrumental for him to be good enough to win the gold medal over there," Duva recalls. "I used to take him out to run, I made sure he was okay, you know what I'm saying? Every judge, every referee knew that he was associated with me. I made sure. At that time, it was a lot of controversy with these other countries. I wanted to make sure he didn't get robbed. Everybody got robbed. It was outrageous what they did to Griffin. But he didn't have the connections that Oscar had at that time. And the connection he had at that time was me.

"I had the 'in' with NBC, with the Olympics . . . even though I couldn't work in the corner. I was there to make sure that everything was okay. And all we wanted was a square shot. And if it was close, I wanted it. There was a couple fights there that could've gone either way."

Yes, there were.

First, there was the tournament draw, on Saturday before the Barcelona Games opening ceremonies, which put De La Hoya in the same half of the bracket as Gonzales—and ensured that he would not face Rudolph until the final match, if both fighters got there. De La Hoya's first-round fight wasn't until Thursday—after every other American had debuted in the Games, except for light-welterweight Vernon Forrest.

As De La Hoya waited his turn, there was a fast example for anyone looking for scary signs: Marquez opened things up on Monday, and, stunningly, almost lost to Nigeria's David Defiagbon. Marquez, who rampaged through the U.S. Trials, averaging almost thirty points a fight, was hesitant against the taller Defiagbon, and needed a late scoring blow to squeak out a chilling 8–7 victory.

U.S. coach Joe Byrd said this was the best collection of U.S. talent in more than a decade. But, after Marquez's tentative debut, even Byrd seemed to be backpedaling. They were talented. But it was a high-strung team, easily bumped off course by a surprise or two. Could they win?

"I've been saying all along that this was the best team since 1976, when Sugar Ray Leonard, Howard Davis Jr., Michael and Leon Spinks, and Leo Randolph won gold medals," Byrd said. "And if they lose, they let me down, and they let down the whole United States."

"If I had lost," Marquez said after his narrow escape, "I don't know what I would have done. I've been working for this my whole life. . . . I'm on my way to the gold. I'll get better from here. The first fight is always the hardest fight."

De La Hoya had to wait four more days—until July 30—for his debut, against Brazilian Adilson Silva, who was not expected to test him. Then again, Defiagbon wasn't supposed to test Marquez the way he did.

"All this waiting, waiting . . . all the training," De La Hoya said. "I just wanted to hit somebody."

In the ring against Silva, De La Hoya, not for the last time, showed that he was not Marquez, and not subject to the same nerves and limitations of other fighters. On the big stage for the first time in his life, De La Hoya was dominant from the opening bell, pressing Silva with his heavy left jab and knocking the Brazilian flat on his back with a left hook only thirty-five seconds into the bout.

Silva got up and continued fighting, and caught De La Hoya in his tracks with a counter-right when De La Hoya rushed him after the knockdown. But by the end of the first round, Silva had a bloody nose and the wobbly look of a man just trying to hang on. De La Hoya led on the computer scoreboard 9–2 after the first.

Though Silva never seriously threatened De La Hoya, the second round did produce a worrying moment: A scraping shot opened a cut beneath De La Hoya's left eye, producing a trickle of blood that would flow the rest of the fight.

"At first I was worried, because when I closed my eye, I could feel it swelling," De La Hoya said after the bout.

But instead of panic, the flow of his own blood only triggered more De La Hoya thunder. Moments after the cut opened, De La Hoya slammed Silva with a ferocious left hook to the body, then followed up with several hard lefts to the head.

There was enough blood pouring from the cut to induce the referee to stop the bout in the third to have the ringside doctor examine it—with De La Hoya's family peering on, worried—but it wasn't deemed serious enough to end the fight. A few moments later, De La Hoya ended it on his own with a swarm of shots against the dazed Brazilian, and referee Ryszard Redo waved off the fight with seven seconds left in the third and final round.

At the time of the knockout, De La Hoya led Silva 24–9. "I said all along that I would use my power shots in the Olympics," De La Hoya said. "I felt energized tonight. I felt great."

Then, right after De La Hoya's victory, Vernon Forrest became the first U.S. medal prospect to lose. There would be more to come.

But, even though his right thumb was a little sore afterward because of an awkward punch, De La Hoya got a double victory that day. Not only did he win impressively, but Gonzales was upset the same day by Bulgarian Dimitrov Tontchev. Meanwhile, in the other half of the light-weight bracket, Rudolph marched through the first round, beating Romanian Vasile Nistor 10–5.

De La Hoya felt good, and in better shape than he had been in a long while. Since he'd moved up to 132 pounds, he had been planning to make his pro debut at 135—thinking that he could no longer make a weight anything close to 130. But as he was weighed before each fight in Barcelona, he felt strong—and light.

"You know, I'm thinking of turning pro at 130 pounds instead of lightweight," De La Hoya said. "In five weigh-ins at this tournament, I weighed 128 three times and 131 twice. I was 131 this morning."

Two days later, on August 1, the sky fell in on the U.S. team. And it was left up to De La Hoya to avoid a total day's failure. Earlier in the day, Eric Griffin suffered his loss to Lozano—throwing an easily shaken U.S. team into fulminations and conspiracy theories—followed by the more deserving departures of Pepe Reilly and medal hopeful

Sergio Reyes. The tension had taken its toll, and Reilly felt it after watching Griffin lose.

"I put it on myself after seeing Eric and Sergio get beat," said Reilly. "I wanted to pick up the team again. It all got to me a little bit."

De La Hoya faced awkward left-hander Moses Odion of Nigeria, fully aware that the United States absolutely could not afford another loss this early in the tournament. With Griffin gone and Marquez struggling, De La Hoya was suddenly the top gun. But by now he was used to carrying the weight.

"I knew I had to win tonight, plus I was worried about the judges," De La Hoya said after his victory. "There's no trust in the scoring system." De La Hoya wasn't as dramatically dominant as he had been in the first fight, but he controlled Odion and scored easily, coasting to a 16–4 victory. And the United States had at least some reason to plug on after the triple losses. But, as would be proven only two days later in the third round, De La Hoya would not be immune from scoring controversy— and brushes with elimination.

At the same time, Marquez moved into the third round with a more impressive defeat of Rival Cadeau from Seychelles. Aggressive, and perhaps smarting from the reviews of his first fight, Marquez overwhelmed Cadeau 20–3 and looked like he was buzzing toward a medal.

Then came Monday, August 3. Medal elimination day: A victory guaranteed at least a bronze medal, and the chance to grab gold. It was when Marquez and De La Hoya were first and forever separated in the boxing mindset—one was a star, and one was not.

Marquez had to beat the lightly regarded Orhan Delibas of the Netherlands. And he couldn't, losing 16–12 in a bout where even the Americans couldn't find reason to complain about the scoring. Marquez blamed himself for looking ahead, and for listening too hard to Duva, the professional trainer. "I was never the same fighter I was in the Trials," Marquez said after his loss. "I don't know why. Maybe I was looking ahead to the pros. I tried looking forward to these amateur matches, but I'm really a pro. I'm glad this is over with."

It was over for Marquez, short of gold.

The opponent for De La Hoya was Tontchev, the shifty, under-appreciated Bulgarian who had toppled Gonzales in the first round. Tontchev trailed Gonzales early in their bout, but, in a bit of De La Hoya–like dramatics, exploded in the third round, almost knocking Gonzales out, to take the victory.

Against Tontchev, De La Hoya was aggressive from the outset—active and sharp, throwing bombs against the seemingly overmatched Bulgarian. But when the round was over, De La Hoya's lead, surprisingly, was only 2–1, even though De La Hoya appeared to land at least ten clean—and clearly visible—scoring shots. Glancing up at the scoreboard from his corner in between rounds, De La Hoya was visibly upset.

"The words I wanted to say, I can't say on television," De La Hoya said after the fight. "Everyone says, 'You got to start off fast, use your jab, snap your opponent's head back to please these judges.' I did all that, and got nothing for it. I thought maybe I had a 20–1 lead or something. I guess the little zero must have faded away."

After the second round, dominated again by De La Hoya's long, thudding jab and left hooks to the body and chin, he looked up at the scoreboard and wondered if the judges were signaling that he was about to be beat, regardless of what he did. He led only 7–6, and he couldn't fight much better than he had in the previous two rounds. Would this be another Eric Griffin–style theft? Would he leave the Olympics as yet another aggrieved American fighter, disgusted and demeaned?

"I was worried," De La Hoya said. "I thought they were trying to get me, too."

In the American corner after the second round, Byrd told De La Hoya to switch gears. He wasn't winning doing it the standard way, so he had to start going in and trying to hurt Tontchev. Let the Bulgarian feel his power. Up on the balcony, the De La Hoya family sweated.

"It was incredible," Joel Sr. said later. "When I saw the 2–1 after the first, and then the 7–6, I wondered, 'What's going on here?' Those jabs, Oscar was snapping the guy's head back. How could the judges not see those punches?"

They saw them in the third round, though, because De La Hoya would not let them see anything else. This was a signature moment for the young fighter and man. What separates great fighters from the rest? The great ones, the special fighters, exert their will exactly when they have to, for as long and as frantically as they have to.

De La Hoya attacked Tontchev for the entire three minutes, hit him so hard that the judges—from Sri Lanka, Nigeria, Argentina, Ireland, and Canada—couldn't help but start pushing the button in unison. De La Hoya took the round 9–1 and the bout 16–7, but seemed exhausted by the drama.

He was into the medal rounds, but was he spent?

"Oh, my God," recalls Alcazar when asked about that fight, "it was tough. That was the toughest one." It got tougher.

Korea's Hong Sung Sik was a short, thick fighter, exactly the kind of little man that the five-foot-ten De La Hoya had regularly faced and feasted upon throughout his amateur career. When the little fighters charged him—what option did they have, stay still and get pummeled?—he stepped quickly aside, landed a few rocking lefts, and the bout was over. If they stayed away, he stalked them, stung them with jabs, and won that way.

So nobody thought Sung Sik, five-foot-two at most, was a troubling foe. The sights were set on Rudolph, and the gold-medal match only a few days away. Sung Sik, who had upset his way into the medal rounds by knocking out Ronald Chavez of the Philippines, was an afterthought.

"I wasn't too impressed," De La Hoya said of Sung Sik's Chavez knockout.

After the Tontchev tightrope, this unheralded Korean wasn't going to be a problem, was he? "This may have been a gold-medal bout for me," De La Hoya said after beating Tontchev. "I don't expect the Korean will be as tough as the Bulgarian. I've knocked out two Koreans before, so I'm confident going into it."

The bout was on Thursday, August 6. By Thursday night, a sore, relieved De La Hoya was calling his experience against Sung Sik "a nightmare." Years later, after facing and beating Julio Cesar Chavez, Rafael Ruelas, and a handful of other famous fighters, De La Hoya would still call this fight one of the toughest of his life.

Was he tense or just looking past the little Korean? Was he feeling the weight of the entire team—only two other U.S. fighters had made it to the medal rounds—and crumbling?

Whatever the reason, Sung Sik came out with his head down and his body flying into De La Hoya, ignoring the taller fighter's hard shots and burying his forehead deep into De La Hoya's chest. All De La Hoya could do was try to push the Korean off. And De La Hoya had come to the Olympics to box, not wrestle.

If De La Hoya was going for style points, it wasn't going to happen against Sung Sik. And instead of embracing the wrestling match, De La Hoya seemed to shy away, to lose interest at times, to let Sung Sik's intensity dictate the bout.

"He did not box well, and I don't know why," Joel Sr. said of his son after the bout. "I want to have a talk with Oscar."

De La Hoya, for his part, blamed his showing squarely on Sung Sik, saying that he did not come to Spain to win a wrestling medal. De La Hoya ended up winning 11–10, but not without almost losing it in the late going by drawing a three-point penalty for ducking too low. He needed—and landed—a clean shot in the final seconds to get the victory.

"It was a terrible experience, a nightmare," De La Hoya said afterward. Even his supporters indicated that De La Hoya, who for some reason was wearing headgear that obviously was too big for him (he fiddled with it throughout the scrum), made it more difficult than it needed to be by refusing to throw his usual hard left jab. That could have kept the Korean a little less interested in charging him, but it rarely happened.

Sung Sik was able to ignore De La Hoya's right, and did so effectively, because De La Hoya seemed either unable or unwilling to throw his right hand with any sizzle. Later, it was discovered that De La Hoya hurt his right hand again during the fight.

In the first round, Sung Sik controlled the fight, but, typical of the inside fighting style, did not get rewarded in the scoring. After the opening round, De La Hoya led 4–2. Sung Sik also was warned twice for holding De La Hoya's head down with his left and hitting him with his right. But Sung Sik wasn't trying to light up the scoreboard, he was trying to confuse De La Hoya. Trying to erase his will.

Then, midway through the second, Yugoslavian referee Streten Yabucanin nailed Sung Sik with a three-point penalty for holding, and suddenly the confused and lethargic De La Hoya had an 8–4 lead after two rounds. Though Sung Sik appeared to score frequently, he was not credited with a single point in the round. Had the U.S. team's bleating complaints about the Griffin decision finally helped gain some tactical edge for an American fighter?

De La Hoya was leading but impressing nobody. No power, no intensity, no charisma. The charging style had him flustered.

"I told Oscar to use straight right hands with the guy, but when he comes flying at you and tackles you, what are you going to do?" Byrd said after the fight. "I was afraid he might break Oscar's neck. You can't hold a man's head down, then hit him. The referee let the fight get out of hand. He should have disqualified the kid in the first round."

Marquez, sticking around to watch, just shook his head after the bout.

"I don't know what was wrong with him," Marquez said. "The guy was holding him a lot, but Oscar wasn't throwing any good punches. Those right hands had nothing on them."

Despite the penalty, Sung Sik stuck to his game plan and kept grabbing at De La Hoya. Though he was warned several more times by Yabucanin—which, by Olympic rules could have led to a disqualification—

Sung Sik never stopped the tactic, and De La Hoya had no successful answer for it. "I can't explain his style," De La Hoya said dryly. "He has no style."

The wrangling continued until the final moments, until De La Hoya himself was penalized the three points for ducking too low to avoid a punch. Finally and fatefully, he landed the last crucial shot to push him into the gold-medal match. Finally.

"I knew it would be a wrestling match," De La Hoya said afterward. "I'd watched him earlier. I know how to box a guy who's in there to box, but I don't know how to box a wrestler. Based on just his boxing, the guy was no better than a JO [Junior Olympics] boxer."

De La Hoya hadn't done anything to boost his stock, he admitted. But he didn't blame himself for it.

"My performance was terrible," he said. "I feel kind of bad because I enjoy impressing people. But it was his fault, not mine. And one bad performance isn't going to hurt me."

More pressingly, De La Hoya's right hand was sore after the fight. The injury was slight enough not to be serious, but painful enough to bother him for the following fight. Which was only the one he had been waiting for all his life. De La Hoya, however, was not focused on bad omens. Where the other U.S. stars had faltered, he had escaped.

He was special. The mission continued.

"The day I really believed I would win the gold medal is when I fought the Korean in the bronze round," De La Hoya later recalled. "He was beating me, I thought, and we were going into the third round and he was still beating me, and I needed a miracle. And I landed one punch to give me the win, seconds before the final bell rang, even though they penalized me three points. During that, I was scared, thinking, 'My dream is not going to come true.' When I won, I'm like, 'Oh shit, somebody's looking over me.'"

Later that day, the coach's son, middleweight Chris Byrd, also won his match, joining De La Hoya as the only two Americans with a chance at gold. Earlier, flyweight Tim Austin, the only other U.S. team member to get to the medal rounds, suffered a first-round knockout loss at the hands of Cuban Raul Gonzales. That meant that the U.S. team, by far the most medaled boxing unit in the history of the Games, which had boasted Cassius Clay, Joe Frazier, and countless other heroes in the past, had as many in the gold round as Ireland.

Already, this was the worst U.S. Olympic boxing performance since 1972, when only Sugar Ray Seales made it to the last round. Also, in 1964, Frazier was the only one in the finals. Both won gold.

If neither De La Hoya nor Byrd won their gold-medal matches, it would mark the first time the U.S. team, which had won nine golds in 1984, five in 1976, and three as recently as 1988, had ever gone gold-free.

"Well, we've got to go with what we have," Coach Byrd said. "We have just the two of them left, and we've got to hope we come out with something. They got to give us 100 percent. I must admit, this is a big disappointment to me."

As his teammates disappeared from the tournament and drifted out of the Village back to the United States or to hotel rooms to enjoy the rest of the Games with friends and family, the American boxing quarters took on a silent, tense atmosphere. The stakes were reinforced by the empty rooms: Everybody else had failed.

Even in the early stages of the Games, many of the U.S. team fighters spent late evenings wandering through the streets of Barcelona, hitting the clubs, soaking up the warm Olympic mood, hanging out with Charles Barkley and other members of the U.S. basketball "Dream Team." De La Hoya and Marquez went out a few times, but for the most part, De La Hoya preferred to stay inside.

Some of the other fighters started calling him "the Spoiled Brat," because he didn't speak to them much, and because he seemed to hold himself above the others. For De La Hoya, it was just a matter of staying true to the only thing that mattered: winning gold.

"I would stay in my bed," De La Hoya recalled later. "I didn't want to blow it. Everything had to be perfect."

And as all the others disappeared, one by one, loss by loss, De La Hoya's solitary sensibilities took on a literal meaning: He *was* alone.

"It was loud . . . and long," De La Hoya says of the experience. "Especially when all the fighters on the U.S. team were losing, and I didn't get the support from them. At the end, there was nobody there for me, just my family. I don't even think Marquez was there."

By this time NBC had decided that De La Hoya was good TV. NBC wasn't particularly fond of boxing—it had gotten its fill during its first big Olympic Games coverage in 1988, when the Seoul boxing competition was laughably corrupt, filled with outrageous decisions, arrogant officials, ring riots, and backroom politicking. Viewers were sickened by it all.

In the old days, ABC glorified boxing in the Olympics, launching the careers and reveling in the charisma of Cassius Clay, Joe Frazier, Sugar Ray Leonard, and Mark Breland. But NBC for the most part kept boxing from its airwaves, and, given the struggles of the U.S. team in Barcelona, who really cared? The one face, the one storyline that NBC saw in boxing, was sweet-featured Oscar De La Hoya, from the East L.A. barrio, winning fights destructively and blowing kisses to heaven.

This wasn't a boxing story, it was a family tragedy turned hagiography. It was the way NBC wanted the Olympics to be. Women wanted to see it, boosting the ratings. NBC broadcast all of De La Hoya's later fights, and told and retold his story every time, to slow music, focusing in on his sad eyes and supermodel cheekbones.

This was a star. And another pattern of De La Hoya's career emerged: When every other fighter is marginalized, he is lifted. When the sport of boxing is degraded, he is unscathed. De La Hoya, by talent and attitude and charisma, is somehow separate from the workaday business of boxing; and the worse it gets, the better he seems.

If he could win the gold medal, De La Hoya would be an American hero. The only hurdle: Marco Rudolph, the only fighter who had beaten him in five years.

After beating the Korean, De La Hoya peered hungrily ahead two days to his gold-medal bout with Rudolph, who had moved into the final round a day before De La Hoya.

"I was kind of glad he didn't fight today," De La Hoya said then. "His timing's going to be a little off. It's going to be good for me."

Less time for De La Hoya to get stale, less time to relive the burden all over again.

"I know people will talk a little about me today, but I'm in the gold-medal round and I'm happy for me," De La Hoya said. "Now I'm going to take home the gold medal and fulfill the promise I made to my mother."

Losing to Rudolph the first time was not about being a poorer fighter, De La Hoya told himself, it was about being inexperienced internationally. If anything, the scrambling victories over Tontchev and the Korean were the best tests for facing Rudolph, who, like Song Sik, was smaller and bulkier than De La Hoya.

Again, things were breaking right.

"I want to fight Rudolph again," De La Hoya said. "He can't beat me. He didn't beat me in Australia."

It wouldn't happen again.

So it was, on the first day of the gold-medal round, in the 323rd bout of the tournament. De La Hoya stepped into the ring calmly and lifted ten years of hope and promise from his shoulders. Measured against what De La Hoya had to beat just to get there, Rudolph was nothing.

In a strangely scored first round, De La Hoya obviously dominated Rudolph with sizzling outside shots, but it ended only tied, 1–1. De La Hoya, though, was not distracted by anything. His father, rigid with anxiety, was only part of the background. Rudolph was inconsequential. The only thing that mattered was De La Hoya, in rhythm, relaxed, and crackling.

A hard shot from Rudolph startled De La Hoya in the second round, but that only seemed to settle De La Hoya in. With fifty-five seconds left in the second, De La Hoya rocked Rudolph with a left hook to the chin and followed immediately with a left to the ribs—two of his best punches of the tournament. De La Hoya's right hand hurt, and he barely used it. But with the left hand alone—like his hero Arguello—he was dominating Rudolph. It was only a 3–2 De La Hoya lead on the scoreboard after two rounds, but the pace and control of the bout was his, clearly.

"He fought his kind of fight today," Joel Sr. said later. "And he wasn't tight, like he was against the Korean. But those judges, they didn't give him anything. These judges, they don't like the U.S.A."

The third round was De La Hoya's showcase. After about a minute of exchanges, the two fighters met in the middle of the ring. Rudolph tried a right and never saw the counter-left that De La Hoya bounced off of the German's jaw. Rudolph swooned to his knees with 1:10 left in the fight, but did get back up at the eight count. He was not the same, though, after his knees met the canvas.

As the count was progressing, De La Hoya snuck a look to the balcony and gave a tiny nod.

"I really didn't throw it with a lot of power," De La Hoya said of the knockdown punch. "If I did, he probably wouldn't have gotten up. But it felt pretty good against his chin."

De La Hoya tried for the knockout, but Rudolph wisely kept away from the attack, which was the only way the German stayed standing until the final bell. As soon as it rang, the decision was so obvious that Rudolph himself hugged De La Hoya in cordial congratulations. De La Hoya chose to wait for the announcement, and when the 7–2 decision was flashed on the scoreboard, when he knew he had won the gold medal, he dropped to one knee, made the sign of the cross, and pointed to the sky.

"I've been carrying this for many years now," De La Hoya said right after the bout. "I'm very relieved now. All this pressure is finally off of my back. I was putting pressure on myself. 'I have to win the gold, I have to do it.' It's like a load off my back. Finally it's over and I'm happy."

Later, in a harkening back to George Foreman waving the U.S. flag to celebrate his 1968 Olympic victory, De La Hoya was handed two miniature flags—the U.S. and the Mexican—and he danced around the ring, cannily catering to two audiences. Actually, it was his mother's idea, back in 1990, her way to make sure Oscar saluted both of his heritages.

NBC loved it. During the flag-raising ceremonies, De La Hoya blinked back tears during the playing of "The Star-Spangled Banner." He didn't want to cry, as he thought about his mother, and his promise.

"I was afraid I might start to cry," De La Hoya said. "But then I figured my mom would say: 'Don't cry, be happy. You won the gold medal.' Then I realized she wasn't there to hug me, and I started feeling sad all over again."

In the stands, his father was crying, too. "He has made us all so happy," Joel Jr. said.

Hours later, at a party thrown by the Duvas and Finkel, De La Hoya was surrounded by his family, by various members of the Duva-Finkel stable, including Pernell Whitaker, and by the media.

De La Hoya picked at his lemon chicken at Restaurante Chino, a Chinese restaurant across the street from the boxing venue.

"It hasn't sunk in yet," De La Hoya said. "I don't think it will for several days. That I actually did it, that it's all over. Maybe it'll hit me when I get home."

De La Hoya walked into the restaurant wearing his gold medal and held it high over his head for the rest of the diners, drawing a standing ovation. Nearby was a party of Thais, celebrating the bronze medal of welterweight Akram Chenglai.

Earlier in the day, Chris Byrd lost his gold-medal match to Cuban Ariel Hernandez. De La Hoya was America's only golden fighter. He, alone, had launched himself from amateur stardom to Olympic gold.

The Golden Boy. It wasn't yet officially his nickname—that would come a few months later, when Forum publicist John Beyrooty introduced him with the golden name at a press conference. But it was what he was.

De La Hoya enjoyed the rest of his time in Spain—including an interlude with a girl who years later would have his baby—then boarded the plane back to Los Angeles. At the airport, he was met by scores of fans, one holding a sign that read: OSCAR, YOUR MOM MUST BE SO PROUD . . . OSCAR DE LA GOLD. He arrived home to a constant, weeklong party, jammed with distant cousins and half-brothers and nieces and nephews he never knew he had.

He was the pride of East L.A. And he was home. "In my dreams, I dreamed something like this," Joel Sr. said.

There would be more, of course. "He's going to be a millionaire," Alcazar said. "He's going to be a world champ in no longer than two years. I know that."

De La Hoya was so giddy, he wore his gold medal everywhere—to meals, to parties, even to bed. He cherished it like a magic talisman: It made him a hero. "He even wore it to IHOP," Joel Jr. said.

Somewhere in the din, Oscar escaped from the revelry and went back to the grave site of his mother. The family hadn't yet put a headstone on the grave, but she was there.

Quietly, he laid the gold medal on the grave, and whispered to her that he had done it for her. It was magic. But it wasn't magic enough to bring her back.

chapter five

What a Million Dollars Can Buy

It was an arrival, all right.

Oscar De La Hoya's life, until the Olympics were over, had been an act of repression—push back the temptations, look past the lazy impulses, and keep the focus on the goal ahead. Only the gold medal, and boxing, meant anything. Oscar was a shy kid, so, at least when he was young, he wasn't presented with overwhelming choices.

Everything he ever avoided, every vice he ignored, every groping groupie he never knew existed, every schemer with a handful of cash, every businessman with an eye toward the future, every carefree, feckless thing he ever sacrificed for the sake of training... from the moment De La Hoya got back from Barcelona, it was all there for him.

Most of the time, just waiting for him at the apartment, at the nightclubs, at the auto dealerships, was anything he wanted. It was a permanent party. And he did not abstain, not this time.

"Too much too soon," his cousin Adrian Pasten said later. "He believes people who tell him he's the greatest. One fool was comparing him to Michael Jordan, telling him that Mexicans consider him a god. Not true. Someone's got to bring him down and put his feet on the ground. The family doesn't like the changes in him. He says he's the same kid, but he's not."

One day, De La Hoya eagerly showed someone a message he had received on his text pager: "I want to lick your body all over like an ice cream cone." Then he said, with a giant leer, "I've gotta call this one back!"

The Arsenio Hall Show wanted him for an appearance, and there he was. He showed up on *The Tonight Show with Jay Leno* for the first of what would be dozens of national TV chats with Leno, and actually, perhaps naturally, seemed far more at ease smiling out to Leno's Middle America audience than he did yapping with Hall's urban crowd.

He could tell cute stories, and just gleam. At a recent visit to the White House, he told Leno, he went to use a bathroom. "I thought, 'Wow, to sit here where George Bush sits is a real honor,'" De La Hoya said, to roaring laughter.

He was nineteen, he was famous, and there was a lot of fun to catch up on.

"It felt good, going out there, spending money like crazy, buying stuff that doesn't even matter to me," De La Hoya recalls. "I bought a pool table that was worth, like, $20,000. I remember the pool table, all marble. It was priced at $20,000, and I told the guy, 'Come on, I'll give you $12,000 cash.' And I called one of my people, 'Yeah, bring twelve down in cash, right now.' And he came with a little bag, full of cash. I didn't care, you know? That went on for a while."

Hucksters walked into the apartment offering easy cash for strange schemes, and Joel De La Hoya Sr. signed up, pocketed some money, and conveniently forgot about the deals. Oscar went out to clubs, danced, drank, and savored the sweet taste of fame. Everybody else just kind of hung around.

"I didn't think I'd be here, you know?" De La Hoya says of that time in his life. "World champion. I never thought I would do that. I said, 'Yeah, I'm going to make the best of it. Hey, let's live the happy life, why not?'"

Publicly, De La Hoya knew enough to try to keep his clean-cut image in tact. And his cannier family members helped out.

"Oscar said to me once, 'I don't want anyone in the family to change if I get famous in boxing. Never treat me like a star. I just want to be Oscar to you,'" Pasten told a reporter in 1992.

Pasten, by then acting as Oscar's publicist, made sure to remind the media that Oscar had forbidden only one thing: There would never be pictures of him at his mother's grave site. Ever.

It was at a club one night soon after the Olympics that De La Hoya met Veronica Peralta, a former Miss Mexico contestant. De La Hoya's outfit was typical for his night prowling: jacket, slacks, no shirt. Peralta, hired occasionally by the clubs to dance in special areas by herself, wore knee-high boots. They talked, they exchanged numbers, and neither forgot the other. In a few weeks, they were a couple, and De La Hoya was telling people he was in love for the first time. He missed his mother, but now he had Veronica.

"I got to know this Oscar who was kind and he was sweet," Peralta recalls. "He was really naive, he was really innocent. He was gullible. It was like a child. It was like, Oh, my God, sometimes I felt I had to mother him or nurture him in some way."

Meanwhile, De La Hoya's professional life was growing increasingly chaotic.

Though De La Hoya liked to tease himself at times with the thought that he would retire from boxing after the Olympics, that never was seriously considered. How else was his family going to make money if not from his professional fights?

Plus, the family had already taken close to $100,000 from Finkel, and that was not simply because Finkel was softhearted. As the summer ended, Finkel prepared to finalize his assumed deal to become De La Hoya's manager.

It had all worked out well for Finkel, it seemed. He had spotted De La Hoya early, he had befriended the father through troubled times, he had paid for a funeral. De La Hoya had won a gold medal, and become a fighter people remembered and would probably follow into his professional career. Finkel was there, and he would take De La Hoya to Main Events. He was going to be De La Hoya's manager. He had to be.

But despite Finkel's efforts, there was a disconcerting unclarity about De La Hoya's future. The De La Hoya family might have been looking for cash, but they knew how to keep their options open.

"We still haven't made a decision," De La Hoya said the day he won gold, with the solid bids beginning to roll in. "It's mainly my decision and my father's. We have to find people we really trust, who really deserve to be with us. There's only one more thing I want now. That is for my father to able to retire from his job. He's been working hard his whole life, and now I want to take care of him."

The only American to win a gold medal—there was a tremendous marketing potential in that. The fact that he was always considered a strong pro prospect, that he was fluent in Spanish and English, and that he was probably the best-looking fighter to enter the pro ranks in decades—that suddenly put De La Hoya into the middle of a boxing bidding war.

Yes, Finkel had provided support, including paying for twenty of De La Hoya's friends and family to fly to the Olympics. But he was not the only sponsor. Mat Tinley, a midlevel promoter-manager with deep family pockets, had also apparently been providing support, including the purchasing of airline tickets. ("It turns out," Finkel recalls with a laugh, "that three or four of us all bought the same twenty people tickets to Barcelona.")

Other supporters included two relatively unknown men from New York, both of whom had been involved in boxing but at nowhere near the level of Finkel. Robert Mittleman and Steve Nelson jumped into the picture a little late, without a lot of P.R. cachet or major influence. It was hard to imagine that these two low-rung operators would land the Golden Boy of boxing.

At first, they couldn't imagine it, either. Mittleman made the first contact. He was a huge fight fan who had quit his music-management business (he had once managed the funk band Parliament). He had managed heavyweight contender James "Bonecrusher" Smith for a while with Nelson, and both were actively scouring the world for fighters to manage. Nelson had his own mortgage company in New York and wasn't as heavily involved in the details of the boxing business, but wanted to continue the partnership.

A few months before the Olympics, Obdullio Muñoz, a well-connected friend of Mittleman's who ran the popular Brooklyn Gym in Boyle Heights, called to tell him that he had just witnessed a nineteen-year-old amateur get the best of Genaro Hernandez, a world champion, in a sparring session.

"You should've seen Oscar De La Hoya here today beating up Genaro Hernandez!" said Muñoz, who was partners with Mittleman on a few L.A.-area and Mexican fighters.

"A nineteen-year-old beating up a world champion? Get out of here," Mittleman said. "And even if it's true, what good does that do me? He's going with Finkel and Duva, anyway, everybody knows that."

But Muñoz knew better, and told Mittleman so. Finkel had sprinkled money into the De La Hoya household, but that did not mean he was guaranteed to be there when Oscar turned pro. Robert Alcazar, De La Hoya's trainer, wasn't dumb. If Finkel was the manager, that meant the Duvas would be the promoters, and that Lou Duva would be the head trainer. That's the way it always worked with the Main Events–Finkel operation, and there was no reason to think it would be different this time, not with such a valuable property. That meant Alcazar had to be pushed out the door if De La Hoya signed with Finkel. And Alcazar knew it.

"I knew that if Alcazar had half a brain," Mittleman recalls, "he didn't want to go with the Duvas. He'd have to leave the corner completely. First, they'll shunt him down to third man down [assisting Duva], then they'll just throw him out."

So Muñoz gave Mittleman a phone number for Alcazar, and a dialogue began. Has De La Hoya committed to Finkel and the Duvas? Mittleman asked. "No, no, no," Alcazar replied. "We're definitely not committed to them."

"That's a very smart thing on your part," Mittleman told Alcazar, reminding him of what was obvious about Finkel and the Duvas. "They're in, you're out."

Alcazar was immediately intrigued. Joel Sr., for once, was being careful—although he had a tacit agreement with Finkel, there was nothing signed before the Olympics. There was and is still a sort of unwritten rule with high-profile fighters preparing for the Olympics—everybody knows that they need and take money from managers and promoters who want their services once they turn pro.

Training costs money. Flying families all over the world costs money. But as long as you don't sign anything, you are not violating the amateur rules that govern the Games. Or so goes the unwritten understanding. Plus, if you happen to hit gold in the Games, you suddenly are a very eligible free agent, with no ties. Unless you've signed something binding. For instance, by this time, Mittleman and Nelson already were "working with" U.S. Olympic team super-heavyweight Larry Donald, but signed nothing.

By the time the Olympics started, Mittleman was feverishly working to put together a group to support a big offer to De La Hoya. For a while, he didn't know if the mercurial Nelson would be with him or not on this deal. "Steve, being Steve, disappeared from me for three or four months before the Olympics," Mittleman says. "He disappeared until after the gold medal, then he magically reappeared again. I hadn't put anybody together yet. I said fine."

A few weeks after the Olympics, Finkel flew out to L.A. It was time to get the now red-hot fighter officially signed. At a meeting with Oscar and his father, Finkel says the two agreed that he was their man. But they didn't sign anything. Finkel had heard that Mittleman and Nelson might be emerging as factors in the bidding, but he had a sterling reputation, connections to the Duvas, and the two De La Hoyas standing in front of him.

"Shelly, I want you to handle me," Oscar said, according to Finkel. "Fine," Joel Sr. said.

And Finkel didn't press it, didn't ask them to sign right then and there. He should have.

"At the time—no offense to Mittleman or Nelson—they weren't in the same league, you know?" Finkel recalls.

Whenever Finkel had doubts during these few weeks, he thought back to the dinner at Restaurante Chino, and Oscar posing for pictures with Finkel and Duva, and figured he was being paranoid. Surely that soft-voiced kid remembered who paid for his mother's funeral? Oscar never seemed to have a duplicitous bone in his body.

Weeks went by, and the De La Hoyas were still listening to other offers. Actually, Finkel didn't really make an initial offer—he was perhaps waiting for Tinley and Mittleman-Nelson and whatever other offers might surface. He didn't want to be bidding against himself. The De La Hoyas, though, took the lack of an immediate bid as a sign of arrogance and slackening enthusiasm—Oscar was the only fighter on the U.S. team to win a gold, shouldn't he be worth big numbers, on the table, right now? Did Finkel take the De La Hoyas for granted?

"I told them I'd match any deal they were offered," Finkel recalls.

But the De La Hoyas' interest in other options was obvious. Mittleman and Nelson picked up on it immediately.

"We knew there was something wrong with his relationship with Shelly," Nelson recalls. "We didn't know what it was. But the fact that Shelly had been there for years and the fact that he was even talking to other people, there had to be some kind of relationship problem. Otherwise why not take the deal from Main Events right away, the more established group and the person that obviously had paid for his mother's funeral?

"There had to be some type of relationship problem that was blocking that deal, because I think they were really looking for a way not to make a deal with Shelly. We were actually of the belief after the Olympic Games not that we were going to sign him, but that Shelly *wasn't* going to sign him."

The magic number, the De La Hoyas made it clear, was $1 million. Put a package like that together, and they'd sign. Finkel was nowhere near that number, preferring to keep it strictly safe and sane, no wild promises and strange clauses for future performances. He was offering about $250,000, with the $100,000 already paid out. And he also was busy with his other big fighters, Evander Holyfield, Pernell Whitaker, and many others.

"I think the money was a major issue," Nelson says. "But we spent more time with him and his father and with Robert Alcazar than anybody else. I mean, this was not just being done on the phone. We were flying out to Los Angeles every week. And we did have time to develop a relationship with his family. I think that they saw that this was going to become our major project, whereas everybody else I think would not give them top priority."

The texture of the deal was not complicated. The De La Hoyas wanted a new house, in Montebello—only Montebello, because that was where Cecilia dreamed of owning a nice home. Oscar wanted an Acura NSX. Alcazar needed a piece—about $25,000, and a contract to receive the standard 10 percent trainer's fee. And Joel Sr., obviously, needed a slice—about $50,000. They wanted a van for training use.

"Those were the basic ingredients," Nelson remembers. "So the deal was set up where all those parts were taken care of. The numbers grew dramatically as we sat down. In fact, one of the early conversations, we thought we had pretty much a deal . . . and then while sitting at the table, the numbers basically doubled from our starting point."

The Mittleman-Nelson offer, finally, was in several tiers—an up-front chunk of about $425,000 (including the car, a van, and a four-bedroom house), several bonuses paid over time, and chunks of cash tied to certain events, such as a world title bout.

This was the richest contract ever offered to an amateur, by leaps and bounds. Strung together, it was a five-year, $1 million management deal. As Finkel pointed out, the deal was back-loaded, "with most of it on the come"—not due to be paid out unless things worked out well. Unless De La Hoya was successful as a pro, the whole deal fell apart.

At last informed of the Mittleman-Nelson offer, Finkel told the De La Hoyas he'd match the offer to preserve their relationship. But by then, the De La Hoyas had decided that he was not their man.

"I don't hold anger toward Oscar," Finkel said. "I feel disappointment. It wasn't, 'I hate this guy.' I was really hurt. But we're big boys; it happens. You don't like it. You don't want it to happen. You think if you do right by people, somehow it works out. But in the end, I'm able to look myself in the mirror and know I did the right thing by him. And I couldn't get him to do the right thing as well."

The boxing world was stunned: Two upstarts from New York, landing the biggest prize—the only prize—of the Olympics, a Mexican-American from Los Angeles with movie-star looks and the potential to draw a huge cross section of the boxing marketplace.

"Bottom line is, I beat Finkel's offer, as far as total package," Mittleman says. "Bottom line is, he signed with us."

When he signed, Oscar De La Hoya turned to Mittleman and Nelson and said three words: "Let's do it."

All Oscar could think about was $1 million. Somebody was offering him $1 million. Just to sign a piece of paper. Isn't life great?

"Ooooo, I thought they were the best people for me," Oscar recalls. "Because they talked about all this million dollars. They were going to take care of me. One million, shit, that's a lot of money, you know? My father said from the start we're not going with Shelly. Because he offered like only $200,000 or something. He said, 'No, we're not going with him.' It was always Mittleman and Nelson topping every single deal. 'If anybody offers you more, we'll top it.' And when they gave me the car I wanted, I was like, 'Yeah!' That's all I thought of. I wasn't thinking about the future. They would tell me, 'Sign on the dotted line.' I'll sign, I don't care. I have what I want, that's all that matters."

But Nelson and Mittleman were not rich men, at least not rich enough to plop more than $400,000 in cash down on the spot. They needed backers. This wasn't a deal made on a shoestring, but it was close. They knew their best bet at landing instant money was hooking up with a big promoter who could seed the deal. The Duvas, obviously, were out, because they were Finkel's money backer. That left either Bob Arum or Don King, neither of whom had been involved with De La

Hoya because they had left him for Finkel and Main Events. Mittleman and Nelson needed one of the two big promoters on board, though, to fund the $1 million deal.

First up was the fidgety, short-tempered Arum, whose company, Top Rank, Inc., hadn't yet found a way to tap the vast Latino boxing market other than dabbling with light-flyweight Michael Carbajal, a bronze medalist in the 1988 Olympics. Arum wasn't wholly committed to the Latino market, mostly because he wanted a fighter that could appeal to both the Latino and general U.S. audience. Carbajal, from Phoenix, had a nice following, but he was little man, and the big fighters were the ones who made the big money.

Before the Barcelona Games, Mittleman ran into Arum in the first-class section of a TWA flight back from Los Angeles to New York and pitched the idea of teaming up to run De La Hoya's career.

"Two rows in front of me, there he was, Arum, 'the Sheik,' as they call him," Mittleman recalls. "I told him, 'Hey, I think I'm going to get Oscar De La Hoya.'"

No way, Arum told Mittleman. De La Hoya was signing with Duva. Then, as Mittleman tells it, Arum added that signing De La Hoya was no big priority. "Well, he's not the best guy on the team, anyway," Mittleman remembers Arum saying. "Raul Marquez is the better fighter."

"During the flight, I could see he was starting to think a little bit," Mittleman recalls. "By the time we got to New York, he tells me, 'You want me to take you home, I've got a limo coming, you want a ride back?' I said sure, why not? Then he's talking to me, you know, 'Top Rank could do a lot for the kid. Use my name.'"

But when Mittleman and Nelson went to Arum after they had signed De La Hoya, he balked at their price for joining the package as a promoter: $300,000 up front. And when Arum balked during negotiations, he usually ended up screaming. It wasn't quite what you'd expect from a Harvard-educated former U.S. attorney, but Arum, by then in his sixties, was as famous for his roaring, eye-bulging tirades as he was for cutting the smartest deals in the business. During the '70s, Arum promoted some of Leonard's fights, some of Marvelous Marvin Hagler's, and had a piece of just about every big fight of the era.

When the negotiations between Arum and Mittleman and Nelson bogged down, Mittleman threatened to go to Don King for backing.

King, despite some negotiations with Mittleman, never did put up the $400,000. After walking away from the De La Hoya deal, King's associate, Al Braverman, taunted Mittleman.

"He had Braverman call me a day later saying, 'What do we need Oscar De La Hoya for, we've got Pedro Sanchez!' That's one of the greatest quotes in the world," Mittleman says. "You ever heard of Pedro Sanchez? But at that time he was undefeated. We were asking for $400,000. It's hilarious."

Eventually, Arum agreed to loan Mittleman and Nelson $275,000—which funded a major portion of the De La Hoya bonus. Arum, who hadn't officially met De La Hoya yet, got the promotional rights to De La Hoya, who was about to become, unbeknownst to Arum at the time, the most profitable fighter he had ever been a part of. And Mittleman and Nelson were still stretched about as far financially as they could go.

The rest of the up-front money, about $150,000, Mittleman and Nelson laid out themselves, which drained their personal coffers. By spurning Finkel, for whatever their reasons, the De La Hoyas had turned their fates over to relatively uninfluential figures in the boxing world, who would have to scramble for cash to pay the rest of his contract. In the weird weeks and months that followed, everything that occurred stemmed from this decision, as surely as if the De La Hoyas had planned it all. Which they hadn't.

"Unless he became a world champion, any deal made with him was going to become a loss," Nelson remembers. "But if he became champion, you were going to make money. So, if he had not become champion, whatever deal we were proposing was going to become a loss. And if he did, we would come out way ahead. . . . It was structured over time. Which is something I don't think Oscar truly understood."

There were surprises for Mittleman and Nelson from the outset of the relationship with De La Hoya. In early promotional materials, they touted Oscar as a proud graduate of Garfield High, someone who wanted to study architecture in college, as soon as possible.

There was one problem, which Maria Elena Tostado, the principal at Garfield, politely informed the managers.

"She was a very nice lady and really concerned about Oscar not doing things that were wrong," Nelson remembers. "She called me up and says, 'You know, you have to do one of two things, change your line about Oscar or get him the GED [General Equivalency Diploma].' I talked to Oscar, said, 'You always told us that you graduated.' Well . . . he was pretty good at not always telling the truth."

Easy enough to resolve, Nelson said. It wasn't that Oscar was a poor student or was stupid in any way, Tostado had told him. He just always was leaving school and missing classes to train or to fight, and failed to finish all the requirements. Nelson made the arrangements for Oscar to take the GED test.

"We went like a couple of days later to take the test," Nelson says. "I remember him saying, 'This is going to be easy, I'll get the thing done in five minutes.' His words to me were, 'I'll whip this out in about twenty minutes. See ya then.' About five hours later . . . his brother and I just sat outside, he was the last one out of the class. He took the maximum time allowed. I said, 'Oscar, I guess twenty minutes wasn't a good idea. Do you think you did okay?' He said, 'Yeah, absolutely, it was just a little harder than I expected.'

"And he passed by one point. It was pretty close. But we did get it done."

There were always signs that the De La Hoyas treated money rashly, and their benefactors sloppily, Nelson remembers. Mike Hernandez, who owned a huge Chevrolet dealership in Monterey Park, gave Oscar a Corvette when he got back from the Olympics. Oscar had a few cars by then, and quickly turned around and sold the Corvette, and kept the cash.

The same questionable sense of loyalty, ironically, that had led the De La Hoyas to spurn Finkel for Mittleman and Nelson soon was bothering the new managers.

"Oscar, even before we came into the picture, he really didn't understand the value of loyalty," Nelson says. "What he did to Shelly Finkel shows he didn't understand loyalty."

Which Finkel was not about to argue. In the months that followed, Finkel sued the De La Hoyas, demanding that they pay him back the money he paid them. But what Finkel really wanted was an acknowledgment from Oscar that he knew he had done Finkel wrong.

"I called him before I sued him," Finkel remembers, "and I said, 'Look, Oscar, you didn't do the right thing. You could still be able to face me when you have to and look at me without a problem, just give me back what I laid out.'"

Finkel says that Oscar told him he would.

"And I believe he meant it," Finkel says. "His father supposedly said, 'Screw him.' Like I ever did wrong by the guy. Look at Oscar, where he is today."

Eventually, Finkel settled with De La Hoya, accepting less than $50,000—three years after the fact, and long after De La Hoya had discarded Mittleman and Nelson. But even all those years later, as De La Hoya rose to incredible heights, Finkel said he thought about his ties to the fighter, and wondered why it went wrong.

"I have this fantasy about this, and my wife says never to say it," Finkel says quietly. "But I'll say it, I don't care. . . . There's always this thing in Oscar, where he says, 'I won the medal for my mother and I did this for my mother.'

"And my fantasy is that some day, he meets his mother again. And his mother says to him, 'Why did you screw the man who took care of me medically?' And he looks, and he doesn't know what to say to her."

chapter six

The Schism

Thirteen months later, the whole De La Hoya world turned over again, and Joel De La Hoya Sr. really didn't know why.

On a smoggy day in December 1993, Joel stood in front of his new house, with the initials DLH proudly inscribed on the metal driveway gate, and wearily just put up his arms. He had no idea where his son was, where he was heading, or when he'd speak to him next.

"I don't know," Joel kept saying. "I can't say anything. I just don't know. I'm sure he'll call me soon, though. Only Oscar can talk, or his lawyer. To tell you the truth, I don't know anything. The only person who knows is Oscar, and Oscar is not here."

Joel Sr. led Oscar to sign the deal with Mittleman and Nelson. And thirteen months later, he was abandoned, left to stick his hands in his pockets in the cool Montebello breeze, and to tell the truth: Oscar was on his own, and Joel Sr. was not a part of what was happening.

Thirteen months before, the De La Hoyas were playing with their money. Now, they weren't speaking to each other. It was thirteen months of big and little steps toward this, thirteen months of Mittleman and Nelson increasingly feeling the pressure, and putting much of their own pressure upon the shy fighter. Thirteen months of success—eleven fights, eleven victories, ten by knockout—big plans, and quiet power plays.

Then it all blew up in December 1993, on the eve of De La Hoya's New York City debut, and the father was left to mumble, and wonder.

Even back in November 1992, there were rumblings.

They won the bidding, but Mittleman and Nelson quickly discovered that the bidding never really stopped. And they were not in a position financially where the endless offers could be fended off forever. Signed contract or not, the De La Hoyas were always listening to other offers, accepting other deals, and smiling and denying it to the comanagers the whole way.

Life with De La Hoya was always going to be uneasy. This million-dollar shotgun marriage was not built for the long term. If De La Hoya was willing to walk away from Finkel, who had paid to bury his mother, what made him committed to Mittleman and Nelson, who had merely paid more than anybody else?

This chapter of De La Hoya's life was a constant scramble. Mittleman and Nelson never knew who was in the house, whispering in Oscar's ear, undercutting their position with every word. Who was getting paid? Who was taking what? Who was signing what? Who was trying to take advantage of whom? It got so confusing, De La Hoya at one point had three publicists, or at least people claiming to be publicists, on the payroll, and none of the three knew about the others.

The De La Hoyas suspected the comanagers of cheating them out of money, a suspicion that was not soothed when Mittleman and Nelson started bouncing checks. Mittleman and Nelson were aggravated by the constant complaints, coming not from the De La Hoyas themselves, but from the assorted family members and friends hanging around the house.

It was going to take a lot of money, to a lot of people, to keep this relationship steady—and Mittleman and Nelson did not have a lot of money to play with after dropping the initial $425,000. They needed other sources of revenue. Nelson and Mittleman called these "income generators," side deals that would help offset their bills. And there still were at least three more hefty bonuses left to pay.

The first big score, before De La Hoya ever fought professionally, was going to be a made-for-TV movie deal, taking full advantage of his heartwarming Olympic story.

"We negotiated very very early on, prior to Oscar's first fight, a made-for-TV movie for him with a major company, Lorimar," Nelson says. "Which was headed up by Leslie Moonves at the time, who's now the head of CBS. We had a signed deal. It was a very fair deal, based on what people were paying for television movies."

It was a $250,000 deal, just to buy the rights to De La Hoya's story, from baby to gold medal, and Lorimar fronted De La Hoya $5,000 as a good-faith first payment. All the company wanted, Nelson remembers, was a few meetings with the fighter and his general cooperation. Mittleman and Nelson's commission would've been about $50,000. But every time Lorimar would set up a meeting with De La Hoya, he'd come up with an excuse, and the meeting was canceled. Three or four times, same thing. Why was De La Hoya avoiding Lorimar, even though he had already pocketed $5,000 and was risking a $250,000 deal? Nelson and Mittleman had no idea. They asked Oscar, and he said, as usual, that nothing was wrong. They asked the father. Nothing. No movement on the movie, either. Finally, Joel De La Hoya Sr. confessed: He and his son had already made their own movie deal, with another company.

"How can I let Oscar make the deal for $250,000 when I've been offered $1 million for this other deal?" Joel told Nelson. Plus, this deal included Oscar making his acting debut, portraying himself. But the $1 million was all conditional, based on sketchy promises and made by people who, according to Nelson's investigations, nobody in Hollywood had ever heard of. Lorimar wasn't interested in legal action against an Olympic hero, and walked away from the deal, letting De La Hoya keep the $5,000. The other deal, not surprisingly, fell apart when it came time to pay the money. No movie. No money. No deal.

"Our commission on deals like that was about 20 percent," Nelson says. "In our calculations for this deal we had another $50,000 toward the second part of the bonus. And of course, it never materialized. The end result of all of this is he could've had a great movie done on his life, gotten huge TV exposure . . . didn't get that. And the other deal just went by the wayside. He got nothing from that other deal. And the fact was that the iron was hot after the Olympic Games. That deal got lost, money got lost."

Mittleman and Nelson had to start watching their backs. But there was a fundamental problem: Neither spoke Spanish. And the De La Hoya household was strewn with friends and peripheral family members and friends of family members who ignored the managers and openly made business proposals to the De La Hoyas—in Spanish. Mittleman and Nelson were out of the loop, even though they were his comanagers. So they needed someone who could speak the language, someone who could make sure Oscar never turned against them—or at least could alert them if there was an attempt.

"What happened is we aligned ourselves with the father," Mittleman recalls. "We cut the father in as a partner. He wanted to be our partner. He wasn't happy just getting bonuses."

Early in Oscar's pro career, three or four months into it, Mittleman and Nelson officially cut Joel Sr. in as a partner—he would receive 5.5 percent of the gross earnings until the original partners received their initial investment back, then he would receive an equal 11 percent of the take with Mittleman and Nelson. He was their safeguard. "I always got along with the dad," Mittleman says. "He respected my boxing ability. He liked me as a boxing guy. We got along fine. Really, we still do."

Says Nelson: "We felt that we should have an ally. And even though the father received money as part of our initial bonus contract, about $50,000, and there were payments to him, we felt we really needed someone who could speak the language as a buffer for us. We felt that no matter what, if we had the father as a partner, there would be no attempt to get rid of us, if there was a problem, because the father was going to be a partner in everything that went on. And that obviously was in error."

It was a huge, momentous error.

Mittleman and Nelson misread the family dynamics, didn't recognize the unresolved, unspoken tension between moody father and quiet son. They couldn't fathom that hooking up with the father was the beginning of their end. Joel Sr., actually, was fairly loyal to them. He stopped making side deals, now that he was in on the main one. He tried to insulate Mittleman and Nelson from the outside vultures. But he was not in position to protect them forever.

"I never thought it was Joel," Mittleman says now. "It wasn't Joel who greased my skids. What happened was, as sons will do, they rebel against their fathers. It's conventional. The kid was twenty-one."

Cecilia De La Hoya, always the buffer between sons and father, was gone. It was just Joel and the children, and they were growing up. Oscar was becoming his own man and listening to his own counsel. Plus, he had all the whisperers telling him it was his money, and his career. To have a piece of him, they had to winnow him from Mittleman and Nelson. That meant the father, too.

"Actually Joel Jr. came to me and told me, he said, 'Robert, Oscar's real mad at our father,'" Mittleman says. "At that time I should've immediately jumped into gear and schmoozed Oscar to death. I should've told him, 'Listen, I'm with the father because that's what you forced me to do. But I'm on your side, I want you to call the shots.' But I didn't."

There was trouble brewing from the start, but Mittleman and Nelson had to keep plowing through.

With the momentum of the Olympics, and with the memories of De La Hoya's domination of Genaro Hernandez fresh in Mittleman and Nelson's minds—and the minds of several local boxing figures— in the heady days of August and September, there were serious thoughts of the unprecedented: De La Hoya making his professional debut in a world title challenge against Hernandez, the World Boxing Association champion.

It would be an arrogant, confident, incredible thing to do. Oscar wanted it badly.

"I tell my managers, 'Why can't we fight for a world title now?'" De La Hoya said then. "I can win now. Does that sound conceited?"

De La Hoya's family thought he could do it successfully, skipping past the usual years of slow and steady seasoning all amateurs, even the most talented, need before challenging for a title. Leonard took three years to win a title. Mittleman and Nelson were tempted, because it would mean an instant dose of money, and would stamp De La Hoya to the world as a special, special fighter. A true prodigy.

Hernandez, angered by the coverage of the workout—he was doing a favor to the kid and wasn't in top shape—said he'd gladly take on the neophyte in a real fight. Hernandez had already defended his title twice by then, for relatively tiny purses. He'd happily make a third defense for big money against an Olympic gold medalist. But there was real risk for De La Hoya. If Oscar lost to the canny, veteran Hernandez, the drop would be impossible to fathom. Start off a career 0–1? De La Hoya couldn't do that.

"I'm not convinced he would've beaten Genaro in a first fight," Nelson says. "Who knows, anything's possible . . . but to take that shot and lose would've been absolutely devastating. And we would've been called the stupidest guys in the history of boxing. I'm not saying he would've lost. But to make the first fight for a world championship, against a guy who's fairly well established. . . . You're talking about going twelve rounds before you even have a four-rounder."

There was too much to lose: De La Hoya didn't need to be profitable instantly. He needed to build up his name and adapt to professional opponents. Give him a year, then see what championships were out there. "There's no question, the first year of Oscar was definitely a learning process," Nelson remembers. "He became a real fighter in that year. But to fight for a championship, I think could've been a disastrous error."

Instead, the De La Hoya camp—Team De La Hoya, as it was emblazoned on all their sweat suits and T-shirts—decided to capitalize locally on his name recognition. They could take it easy for a while, and let his experience build.

Right after signing De La Hoya, a month or so after the Olympics, Mittleman took Oscar to a Lakers game at the Great Western Forum, where sixteen thousand roared at his entrance, giving him a standing ovation.

This was the Golden Boy, as christened, apparently, by Forum public relations director John Beyrooty in the weeks before his professional debut. The nickname, copied from the old movie, and held previously by L.A. boxing legend Art Aragon, seemed perfect for De La Hoya. And it stuck. He had a gold medal. He seemed too good to be true. And he was worth pure gold.

If De La Hoya debuted at the Forum, Mittleman figured, with that kind of reception, De La Hoya's debut was a lock to draw more than 6,000—and generate a lavish profit. Mittleman and Nelson guaranteed De La Hoya a $100,000 purse for his debut against talent-deprived Lamar Williams—with half of that scheduled to come from the Forum, assuming at least 3,500 tickets were sold. If it hit 4,000, Mittleman and Nelson would make a nice chunk.

"It was very important to us and very important to Oscar that he follow in the tradition of such people as Muhammad Ali, who in 1960 made his pro debut in his hometown of Louisville, and following the tradition of Sugar Ray Leonard, who after the 1976 Olympics made his pro debut in his hometown of Baltimore," Nelson told a Forum press conference the week of the fight. "We believe Oscar is going to be that next great boxing attraction. We wanted to make his debut before the people who have supported him throughout his amateur career."

De La Hoya very much wanted to make a splash as quickly as possible as a professional. In his heart, he knew he was better suited to the professional ranks, and he had sparred against professionals for years. He didn't want to be pegged as a light-hitting amateur, somebody content with headgear and heavy gloves, fighting three rounds and off to another tournament. As a pro, he would be fighting with eight-ounce gloves, two ounces lighter than the amateur models. And as soon as De La Hoya put the lighter gloves, he knew his hands were faster than anybody's. This was where he belonged.

"When I was an amateur," De La Hoya told his first professional press conference audience, "I guess I did pretty good by winning the gold medal. But now that I'm turning pro, my style is a lot different. I have a pro style. I can bang to the body, I can throw left hooks, I can knock people out. I had 223 wins as an amateur, with 153 knockouts. So the power is there. It's going to be very exciting. People are really going to see how Oscar De La Hoya really punches and see the art of boxing. I don't consider boxing fighting, I consider it an art. One of the boxers that I've enjoyed and I believe had the same style as me was Sugar Ray Leonard. I believe I can be the Mexican Sugar Ray Leonard. And even better, I hope."

As a publicity gimmick, the Forum finished the press conference by asking De La Hoya to officially sign the contract for the fight, for the assembled cameras to record. As De La Hoya leaned in to sign, Mittleman whispered loud enough for the microphones to capture, "Oscar, look up and smile when you sign it." De La Hoya rolled his eyes at the intrusion and grimaced.

But, dutifully, he looked up at the cameras, and he smiled.

The fight was on November 23, 1992, more than three months after his Olympic gold, and there was a party atmosphere—sombreros in the crowd, roars at every mention of his name. De La Hoya, beaming as he strode into the ring, replayed his Olympic moment by carrying Mexican and American flags in both hands. Then he made his professional debut with brute force.

Williams, who was 7–2 and said he had never been knocked down before, went down twice in the first minute against De La Hoya, and was a knockout victim before the end of the first round. De La Hoya never let him breath. "He hits like a mule," Williams said later.

But how could you really judge this performance? It *was* more of a performance than a boxing match, and this would not be the last time a De La Hoya outing was more about theatrics than piercing athleticism. Williams, for his part, gave every indication that he wanted to hit the canvas as soon as possible.

"He was in with a living dead man," said heavyweight champion Riddick Bowe, who was ringside.

That was not at all surprising. But the turnout was a shock to everybody: Though there were more than 6,000 in attendance, almost half of those were seats that did not count as paid tickets. Only 3,200 tickets were sold, about average for a Forum fight show, which meant that Mittleman and Nelson had the price of 300 tickets taken out of their check from the Forum.

"At that Laker game, he got a five-minute standing ovation," Mittleman remembers. "I was thinking, 'Jesus Christ, he's got to sell six thousand tickets.' I should've never went to that game. It fucked up my perspective."

The turnout, however, did not dissuade Arum.

Arum to this point had been a minor player in De La Hoya's career, strictly a moneyman. But with this fight, Arum saw past the slow ticket sales and into a hugely profitable future. This kid was special. Arum could feel the moment arriving. With the L.A. media asking him about the fight and the crowd, Arum did not blink.

"Oscar De La Hoya is going to be the biggest star in the history of boxing below the heavyweight division," Arum crowed. "Even bigger than Sugar Ray Leonard."

One fight into De La Hoya's career, and he was a legend?

"Arum says this when there's less than a normal audience at the Forum," Mittleman recalls. "I'm thinking, 'This motherfucker, the chutzpah.' But that's the right attitude. He's going to hype this kid no matter what reality is. What, are you going to believe me or your lying eyes? That's what Arum was telling these people. The kid couldn't draw. Ray Leonard sold out an 8,000-seat arena his pro debut, this kid couldn't do 3,300."

But that didn't mean De La Hoya wasn't marketable. His second fight was in Phoenix, on a Michael Carbajal undercard. The next one was at the venerable Hollywood Palladium, against journeyman Paris Alexander. Every month, De La Hoya had a fight, as Mittleman and Nelson worked to build his record, get him exposure on television—and build up his purses.

Though De La Hoya was gunning for a 130-pound title, he debuted weighing 133 pounds. He beat Cliff Hicks in his second fight weighing 133 again, and was up to 138 for his fourth, in San Diego on March 13, 1993, against Curtis Strong. De La Hoya developed a cyst in his right leg about a week before the Strong fight. He was in pain, and Nelson was with him. But ABC was televising the fight, and there was no way anybody wanted to pull out. So Nelson took him to a doctor, had the cyst removed, then sat up with De La Hoya all night long. De La Hoya went into the fight heavy, but knocked out Strong in the fourth round.

"When he is in there, nothing is going to get into his way of winning the battle," Nelson remembers. "He absolutely changes, his whole demeanor changes from locker room to ring. Intensity you can see in his eyes. I haven't seen it in anybody else's, maybe Duran had it in his heyday. Oscar's not playing the game, he's a changed man."

In the 130-pound division, De La Hoya had a huge size advantage over his opponents—he was five-foot-ten-and-a-half, and the 130-pound class is filled with five-five to five-seven stocky warriors. Mittleman, knowing that De La Hoya was pushing himself to make the weight, made sure to keep him away from heavy hitters in the early stages. Nobody knew how he'd stand up to a solid shot to the chin.

Starting out as a junior-lightweight was not easy on De La Hoya's body, but it gave him a better shot at his main goal: winning world titles in six different weight classes—from 130 to 135 to 140 to 147 to 154 to 160. Tommy Hearns held the record, holding titles in five different classes. The goal was to win as many titles as possible as quickly as possible, to zoom up the title chain more successfully than anybody ever had.

De La Hoya's height and his skinny, dancer's waist made him the perfect candidate. With his power and size, he was a welterweight hanging around in the junior-lightweight division, with brilliant hand speed for any division. If he could only get that 130-pound title quickly—he had to skip meals to even be close to the weight—he could break Hearns's record.

"I don't want to pat myself on the back, but any boxing expert who looks at a list of the first ten opponents I picked him will have to say whoever picked these guys was a genius," Mittleman says. "Not one guy could break an egg. I never thought that his chin was much. I didn't know. I knew he was probably straining to make the weight, actually. So we put him with no punchers."

After wiping out veteran Jeff Mayweather to go 5–0, with five knockouts, De La Hoya had some trouble with Mike Grable in an April 6 fight in Rochester, New York. Grable was knocked down several times, but De La Hoya couldn't finish him off and settled for a dominant six-round decision. De La Hoya was on TV every month, he was moving up into the rankings of the major organizations, and most important, he was getting recognition as a legitimate title contender. In the watered-down world of 1990s boxing, De La Hoya was on course to go for a title in a year.

By late summer 1993, De La Hoya was 8–0, hadn't been threatened in the ring, and was preparing to make his first appearance on HBO— on the undercard of a Roy Jones Jr. fight in Bay St. Louis, Mississippi. And once again, Team De La Hoya had a decision to make: Go get Genaro Hernandez now, or wait some more?

Under Alcazar's supervision, De La Hoya was blowing out all the little guys put in front of him, but he still hadn't made the 130-pound limit, and he looked mechanical at times, vulnerable to a fast attack.

"It was a good learning period for him," Nelson says. "We were very willing to accept being patient and not putting him into a championship fight too quickly."

A Hernandez fight, Arum figured, would get De La Hoya a $1 million purse. A fight against International Boxing Federation champion John John Molina was a similar option. Was he ready?

"We just felt it was more prudent to wait a little bit and not rush into it," Nelson recalls. "In retrospect we probably should've taken it, because [the De La Hoyas] were real anxious for the money."

And Mittleman and Nelson were struggling to come up with it.

In October, Mittleman and Nelson were a few days late on a scheduled $47,000 bonus payment to De La Hoya. And the pressure mounted, from all directions. When Mittleman and Nelson were asked about the tardiness, even warned in a letter from a lawyer who said he represented De La Hoya, they went straight to the fighter and explained the situation. Oscar just shook his head when they asked him about the letter. He seemed to accept their assurances and their smiles.

When they left, Oscar listened to the others in the house and snarled. Every time his father tried to make a pitch for the comanagers, Oscar walked away. Mittleman and Nelson were on the brink of extinction.

"They were late with payments," De La Hoya remembers. "They were ripping me off. If I had a fight, they wouldn't pay me the full amount that day. But on my next fight, they would pay me what was left of that, and I would still be owed more. . . . That happened right from the start. That's when I sensed that there was something wrong."

Said Veronica Peralta, De La Hoya's girlfriend at the time: "He was so volatile. He would just go through these mood swings. Sometimes it was just the last person he spoke to. If the last person he spoke to said one thing, then that's what he stood for. And if another person came in and sounded better, then he went with that person."

Mittleman moved to Montebello to be closer, and Nelson joined De La Hoya up at Big Bear for camp. And Big Bear became the center of the storm.

It was, more than anything, the discovery of Big Bear that turned out to be the revelation of De La Hoya's early career. Alcazar suggested De La Hoya train there for his pro debut, to get away from the chaos of Montebello and the relatives and the businessmen. Larry Goossen had a tiny gym up there, right next to the Big Bear airport, and the air was clean and perfect for high-altitude training. It was isolated, and more than a mile and a half above sea level.

De La Hoya loved the peace and quiet. Once again, he could narrow his life down to one thought: Victory.

"I think he felt it was a place where he could really relax and I think he enjoyed the training camp," Nelson recalls. "I think it's a place where he doesn't feel like he has to be the center of attention. They talk about some boxers being reluctant warriors. In some ways, Oscar's a reluctant public figure. I think he felt when we went out in public in L.A. or wherever, he had to be a bit of a showman. He had to perform and I think he wanted to relax and not always be on his best behavior."

Up at camp, Oscar brought only his most trusted associates—Joe Pajar, the clown, and Joel Jr., who took any chance to be away from their father. They had one car up there, a brown van with the license plate GOLDMINE, and for fun they went to the bowling alley or just sat in the rented cabin and made fun of each other. The lumpy, lighthearted Nelson got most the teasing—"Do you ever change clothes?" they'd yell, because Nelson almost always wore the same sweat suit and shirt everyday. "Do you like menudo?" they'd ask, about the spicy Mexican dish—and Nelson laughed it off. Wasn't that being part of the group?

"I felt it was important to keep him relaxed and not just always look at him as a guy who has to be full-time in the gym without having any amusement," Nelson recalls. "So I would take him out for some pretty amusing moments. We would go to the bowling alley. And I'm not the best bowler in the world. He was pretty good. I would take him out to the karaoke bars. He was pretty good about not getting drunk or anything like that. But I would participate with him and the other guys and try to play the role of being one of the buddies, give him some relaxation. I think he enjoyed that. He wanted to have his moments where he could just have some fun."

Nelson thought he finally got to know Oscar up in Big Bear, or at least got to know him as well as any outsider could. Mittleman, edgy, argumentative, and New York in-your-face, admits he never connected with Oscar, never knew what the kid was thinking. The much calmer Nelson thought he did.

"I don't think he enjoyed growing up that much," Nelson says. "He told me the story that when he was a young kid, he always had to go to the gym, his father would take him to the gym after school every single day. One day he desperately just wanted to get on a skateboard and skate and play in the neighborhood. And his father caught him on his skateboard and told him he couldn't do it. He was very upset about that. He didn't want to go to the gym every single day. And he basically did it from six years old on.

"His father created him. You can't take that away. He created him. From the barrio, became a multimillionaire and will never have money problems for the rest of his life. But I think there's a certain lack of emotion, a certain coldness to Oscar. The mother from what I understand was always the one who gave him emotional support. And the father was always keeping him in boxing and looking to create this superstar from the time he was six years old. I know there were several times when Oscar was very young when he tried to walk away from boxing. And the mother took the position, 'If you want to walk away, you can.' I think he needed that. I think he needed to know that he wasn't being forced into this.

"Here's a kid who should be the happiest guy on the face of the planet. And he definitely wasn't. He was like one of these child prodigies, in many ways very dysfunctional because he didn't have a childhood. He didn't have the opportunity to grow up properly. He once told me, he grew up surrounded by adults all the time. And adults looking to get things off of him."

Down the mountain, it was constant chaos. Relatives and friends and friends of relatives and relatives of friends poured into the Montebello house, proposing new deals, bringing in new potential business partners. Jerry Salas, a cousin of De La Hoya's father who worked at a nearby post office, was particularly insistent in his arguments to Joel Sr. Ray Garza, a local businessman with lots of ideas, also steered the De La Hoyas toward a more Mexican-American representation. They finally skipped over Joel Sr. altogether and went straight to Oscar, who was listening. Joel Jr., too, wanted to hear about other options.

"We believe that the father tried to keep the deal together," Nelson says. "But I think he felt he was losing control. I think what was happening is he would be bypassed because I think he was perceived as being very happy with the work we were doing and people felt they would go directly to Oscar."

Oscar was wary of his father's ties to Mittleman and Nelson, and weary of the late payment. It was easy to be suspicious: Salas and Garza and others were telling him he was being cheated. De La Hoya was furious about the missed payment, and was certain that Mittleman and Nelson were skimming off the top, then claiming poverty.

"Oscar is superficially smart but he doesn't really understand everything that goes on in terms of all these deals," Nelson says. "And if someone says he's being cheated, his inclination will be, 'I believe I'm being cheated.' Whether it's true or not true. He was pretty happy when he saw that we weren't getting any checks early on. But once he saw that we were making money, I think that's when people started saying we were making too much. The fact is that we were so in the hole at that point, between bonuses. . . ."

By late 1993, Mittleman and Nelson were looking at turning a little profit, with room to make a lot more in the next few months. But they knew there were voices in the house that were leading Oscar elsewhere.

"We knew that Garza was making a move with Salas," Nelson says. "We knew that. But you can't stop Oscar from going out and meeting with people."

The comanagers felt that once the real money started rolling in, with the help of the father, their position would solidify. Mittleman was already negotiating with HBO for a huge package that would guarantee De La Hoya entrance into the elite level of fighters—without yet having even fought for a title.

The Phoenix fight, De La Hoya's eleventh, on HBO again on a Carbajal undercard, was the calm before the conflict, a scene where all the main characters ran into each other, and several fascinating minor observers hovered in the background. De La Hoya was at the crossroads.

Renowned fashion photographer Richard Avedon was on hand, hired by *The New Yorker* to shoot photographs to accompany what was planned to be a major piece. *The New Yorker* had discovered De La Hoya in a particularly instinctual way: Editor Tina Brown, who rarely was interested in sports, told a writer that she saw a picture of the barechested De La Hoya in another magazine and immediately commissioned the story.

"We felt that it was recognition that we were ready to take Oscar to another level," Nelson remembers. "Plus, we had the HBO deal being negotiated. We negotiated the deal between HBO, Arum, and ourselves. And I think it was recognized by those trying to break us apart, that once that got signed, we were going to be in there for the long haul. And that's why the deal did not get signed."

So, as Avedon—who had apparently never even attended a boxing match previously—shot posed photos with De La Hoya and his father and his comanagers in the dressing room before the fight, Garza and Salas were in the America West Arena stands.

Alcazar, meanwhile, did his own investigating. He had been in touch with Arum, worrying that Mittleman and Nelson were wrong for the fighter. Maybe, he wondered, they'll bring in another trainer. Once again, Alcazar proved that his skills for survival were undeniable. Arum, plotting a major role in De La Hoya's career, did not exactly ignore the contacts.

"Mr. Arum is the one who will take care of us," Alcazar said up in Big Bear before the fight. "He is the smartest one out there." How about Mittleman and Nelson? "Oh, who knows?" Alcazar said, his eyes sparkling.

But all the intrigue, for a moment, was put on hold when De La Hoya walked into the ring against short, light-hitting Mexican veteran Narciso Valenzuela, a veteran of forty-nine pro fights, with a dozen defeats. The night before, Valenzuela was casually guzzling beers in the hotel bar, blissfully awaiting his bit part in the drama of De La Hoya.

De La Hoya was supposed to blow this guy out, like he had everybody else. He was so much bigger when they stood next to each other, De La Hoya looked like a heavyweight.

Then the heavyweight stumbled.

Forty-five seconds into the fight, De La Hoya got careless, dipping his right shoulder as he waded forward, and promptly found his chin at the end of a short left from Valenzuela.

Instantly, De La Hoya flopped over backward, onto the canvas, his legs flying up and his back on the floor. Wham. For his handlers, it was four seconds of halted heartbeats.

"Of course it was scary," Alcazar said later.

De La Hoya hadn't ever been on the canvas, not in over two hundred amateur fights, not in the Olympics, not in his pro fights. He was stunned, but he wasn't hurt. He hopped right up from a seated position, winked quickly at Peralta sitting ringside, then glared intently ahead at Valenzuela, who seemed more surprised than De La Hoya by the development.

It was what boxing people call a "flash" knockdown, caused by a punch that startled more than injured De La Hoya. But it was still a knockdown, and still a cause for alarm. "He was knocked down by the wrong guy," Mittleman says. "What happens when he gets in there with a real puncher?"

Once the mandatory eight-count was finished, De La Hoya shook off the embarrassment, lept at the much smaller Valenzuela, and threw a fusillade of punches that crashed Valenzuela to the canvas thirty seconds later. De La Hoya, by then wild with adrenaline, had to be restrained from attacking Valenzuela while the eight-count was still going. "I did kind of want to get him quick after that," De La Hoya said, "because I was angry."

A minute later, still in the first round, De La Hoya fired a whistling right hand that conked hard against Valenzuela's face, knocking him flat over, and out.

"That was the first time in my career that my glove touched the canvas," a smiling De La Hoya said later. "It was a new experience. I guess it's sort of history—my first knockdown. But it's never going to happen again, I guarantee it."

Then De La Hoya turned his attention to Genaro Hernandez, whom he hoped to fight in early 1994. "Hernandez probably saw me go down and thought, 'Aww, he's going to be nothing for me,'" De La Hoya said. "But after he saw me put him down twice, he probably thought twice."

Actually, it was Team De La Hoya that started to reconsider facing Hernandez anytime so soon after being knocked down by Valenzuela.

"Me and Joel watched about five of his tapes," Mittleman says. "We were talking about doing it. Then Oscar got dropped by Valenzuela, *pfft,* good-bye, Genaro."

There was another ominous sign for Mittleman and Nelson after the bout. Instead of sticking around with his comanagers of record, or even with his father, De La Hoya immediately took off after the fight with Garza, and left Nelson and Mittleman behind. They would never be at a fight with him again.

Mittleman and Nelson hadn't been ousted yet. The planning went on. If Hernandez was crossed off the list as the first title shot, who was it going to be? Would they avoid the title fight and stay with journeymen until they could make sure De La Hoya wasn't going to walk into another knockdown?

To split the difference, knowing that they needed to start selling De La Hoya as a champion—and that he was either going to win a title now at 130 pounds or else grow right out of the division before winning a title—Mittleman and Nelson booked a fight for a fringe title, with the upstart World Boxing Organization, which was only too glad to offer up unknown 130-pound champion Jimmi Bredahl of Denmark.

HBO, which was wooing De La Hoya for a long-term deal, initially balked at broadcasting a minor-league title fight. But HBO, the most powerful force in the sport, eventually relented. It wanted De La Hoya. It saw the same thing in De La Hoya that Tina Brown and Arum did.

It saw a future star in a sport whose main moneymaker had just been jailed for rape, a sport with few other star attractions on the horizon. Roy Jones was talented, but hardly a matinee idol—in mood or appearance. Carbajal was 108 pounds and without much of a personality—his draw was limited. Evander Holyfield and Riddick Bowe were both heavyweights, but flawed. George Foreman was in his forties. De La Hoya was like a teenage movie star with flying fists.

But Team De La Hoya had more prosaic concerns—most important, to keep De La Hoya from ending up on his butt after tasting hard lefts to the face. Alcazar taught De La Hoya how to march in and get impressive knockouts, but considered defensive strategy an unnecessary sidelight. But after Valenzuela, the golden chin was looking mighty suspect.

Alcazar needed help. De La Hoya was already up at camp training for his next fight, scheduled for December in New York against Jose Vidal Concepcion, and a decision had to be made.

"This was," Nelson says ruefully, "the camp where everything went to hell."

They had no idea this would start off the explosion. They didn't figure Alcazar as a vital piece of the puzzle. He didn't seem the part. He was always quiet, nodding his head, agreeable about everything. They were expecting it to come from Garza or some other big moneyman. Instead, it started from inside.

"The father was real worried when he got knocked down by Valenzuela," Mittleman recalls, "and he wanted me to bring in another trainer. I brought in the worst guy in the world."

Not that Carlos Ortiz, a former lightweight champion from New York who was driving a cab at the time, was the worst pick as trainer. It just so happened that Ortiz was one of Joel Sr.'s all-time favorite fighters. He was a worker, a slugger, a typical Latino brawler.

Once he got up to Big Bear, he also was a Puerto Rican among Mexicans, a boisterous, loud presence amid indirect, shy people, and just about the worst person to try to fit in amid the combustible elements already in the De La Hoya camp. Just when their hold was its most tenuous, Mittleman and Nelson lit a fuse.

"I picked the worst guy in the world," Mittleman says. "An abrasive personality. . . . There were a million other guys I could've picked. First of all, I shouldn't have even done it. He was fighting a stiff in New York, Jose Vidal Concepcion. I should've just told the father, 'Hey, not now, we don't need anything now.' That would've been it. 'Alcazar's doing fine, it was a lucky punch by Valenzuela, Oscar got up and finished him right off.'"

But Mittleman brought in Ortiz—after informal discussions in which both son and father De La Hoya agreed to try it out—and Alcazar immediately began to battle for survival. If Ortiz stayed, Alcazar—who had already fought off Lou Duva—was sure he would be eventually pushed completely aside. De La Hoya was Alcazar's lifeline to boxing's higher circles. Cut off from De La Hoya, from the renown and the money, Alcazar knew he'd fall back into scrambling for boxing scraps and anonymity again.

Alcazar had a contract with the fighter—he was guaranteed 10 percent of his purses, the standard trainer deal—and no one thought of giving Ortiz a percentage, yet. But still . . . the very need to make such a move had reverberations.

"I didn't make it clear to Alcazar that he was only an assistant," Mittleman recalls. "You know, I should've stood firmer with Robert. From his perspective, I can understand where he felt threatened."

Not that De La Hoya was listening to Mittleman and Nelson. When he was furious with his father, he punished his opponents in the ring . . . and he punished those who were allied with his father. Using this opening, Alcazar hammered De La Hoya: Let's get out of this. De La Hoya was particularly apt to listen to Alcazar when they were alone together, up at Big Bear, with no other voices in his ear. Alcazar insisted: The managers are forcing this man on us. They will ruin us.

Joel Jr., who liked Mittleman, tried to warn him. "Hey," he told him that fall, "Oscar's getting mad. You better do something." Mittleman didn't do anything.

This was late November 1993, and Big Bear had just been hit by a series of storms, covering the streets and trees with snow and blanketing the cabins of the Golden Bear Cottages, which housed Team De La Hoya for this camp. That meant De La Hoya, Alcazar, Nelson, and all the other spare parts of the camp were staying in separate cabins, strewn across the icy paths of the cottage layout, and secret meetings were easy to plot.

De La Hoya adapted to the new teachings relatively well, nodding at the points Ortiz was making and tossing only occasional worried glances over at Alcazar, stationed across the gym.

The New York fight was only a few weeks away. Things were tense. The second day of Ortiz's training, Joel Sr. and Mittleman drove up to watch, and Alcazar pouted even more obviously. In sparring, De La Hoya followed Ortiz's instructions—attacking more frequently and harder—and got walloped a few times as he charged in. Alcazar laughed to himself as Oscar moaned, and watched his face swell.

The third day of sparring under Ortiz's watch was the last day. In the middle of the sparring, De La Hoya jumped out of the ring, threw off his headgear, and signaled that he was done. De La Hoya hated confrontation, but he was no longer interested in watching his face become laced with welts. And he was a powerless little boy again, running and crying.

"I felt like I was stuck with this trainer," De La Hoya recalls. "And I had the worst beatings in the gym three days in a row. I was getting hit by guys I would just knock out any time. One time I was getting hit so bad . . . not bad, but just getting hit. And I got out of the ring, I took off the gloves, and headgear, and I just started crying. I was crying. I couldn't take it. My father comes up to me, 'What's wrong? Be strong.' And I said, 'I can't take it anymore. I don't want him to be my trainer.'"

Ortiz and Nelson just thought he was tired. They were wrong.

"That was our first experience with that," Alcazar recalls. "It was a real hard experience for me. But at the end, he decided. He could tell the difference between us. It was only a few days, but it was real hard for me. In those few days, he was bleeding all over himself, he was another Oscar."

After De La Hoya cut short the session, Alcazar grabbed him and took him to one side of the gym. The trainer knew his pupil too well. A furious Alcazar thrust De La Hoya in front of a mirror. Then he told De La Hoya to look over at Ortiz, standing thirty yards away, his rough-hewn face a sea of old bruises and welts from his brawling days.

"This is the face of your trainer!" Alcazar told De La Hoya. "You won't fight a year, and you'll have the same face."

De La Hoya touched the wounds on his own face and sagged visibly. The tension of the camp, and the hopelessness of the sparring sessions, wore him down.

Alcazar chuckled years later at the memory. "You know what he did?" Alcazar recalls. "He took the gloves, he threw them against the wall, and he walked away from the gym. He came back to his room, he picked up the phone, and he fired everybody."

Not everybody. Alcazar was beside him, supporting him, and demanding that he follow through on the emotion.

"He was kind of confused," Alcazar says. "He didn't know what was the right thing or wrong thing to do. He was unhappy about the moves the managers were making. He didn't know how to express his feelings. But then he decided. . . . Things never stopped from there."

That night, De La Hoya surprised Nelson, telling him that things had to change.

"I want him gone," De La Hoya said.

"Are you sure you want it done this quick? You've only worked with him two days," Nelson replied. But De La Hoya, so slow to speak his mind, was set on it. Ortiz had to go.

"Turns out, I went the next day," Nelson says. "So I didn't last much longer myself."

The Ortiz move changed everything. It convinced De La Hoya of all the things that Garza and Salas and so many others were telling him: The managers were screwing around with his career, and with his money. They were manipulating him. They were harming Alcazar. They were plotting with his father.

"Oscar heard so much from so many different people," Nelson says. "I don't think he could trust anybody. But I think if we had not brought Carlos in, even though Oscar was in on it. . . . If we kept Alcazar and the father happy, it would've been tougher to break."

Mittleman says John Ellis, the brother of former heavyweight contender Jimmy Ellis, was involved in offering De La Hoya a lucrative deal. And that Ellis hired attorney Michael Norris, who did a lot of the early legal work for the breakup.

"They offered Oscar another million, so that's when all that shit hit the fan," Mittleman says. "Next thing I knew, we were out."

De La Hoya, apparently, never got the $1 million or whatever he was offered. He has always denied that he ever accepted any other offers, saying only that he had to leave Mittleman and Nelson. In the confusion, things needed cleaning up. And that brought the arrival of Mike Hernandez, the Chevrolet dealer in Monterey Park, who had experience dealing with high-strung athletes after developing friendships with former Los Angeles Dodgers Fernando Valenzuela, Manny Mota, and Steve Howe, among many others.

There was chaos, and then, finally, Oscar made a call to Mike Hernandez, and things started to calm down.

"They might've come up with $25,000 or something," Mittleman says of the outside bidders. "And I think Mike Hernandez returned it to them."

On Friday, December 3—only days before De La Hoya was scheduled to fly to New York and meet the East Coast media—Nelson found a stuffed envelope lying at the door of his cabin. In it was a request to refrain from any further contact with the fighter—although it was nonbinding because a Los Angeles Superior Court judge had refused to sign it.

For all intents and purposes, the envelope was the notification that De La Hoya had fired the managers.

"We made mistakes, but the mistakes we made were impossible to fully comprehend," Nelson says. "We just didn't think that he would dump the father. And I know they've reconciled. But I don't think his relationship has ever been the same. He dumped him once. He can dump him again."

Would De La Hoya be dumping anyone else? The logical extension of the firing was the promoter, Arum, who only recently had gotten close to De La Hoya and the camp. But Arum had real money. Arum had the company. For a few days at least, even Arum didn't know if he was in or if he was out. He couldn't get ahold of De La Hoya and fumed as the fight had to be canceled. The promoter, the man who paid for the fight, was powerless.

But by establishing himself as the calm center of things, and blaming everything on Mittleman and Nelson, Arum did not get extinguished.

"They're all crooks and thieves," De La Hoya said at the time. "Bob Arum is just the straightest, nicest crook."

Of course, since Arum's loan to Mittleman and Nelson had enabled them to pay De La Hoya, Arum could help make them go away, too. He could broker this thing. Which is what he did, making sure both sides got enough to stay out of court. And in the process, he signed up De La Hoya for another five years.

Mittleman and Nelson sued Garza and Salas for $10 million, alleging "tortuous interference" in their contract with De La Hoya. De La Hoya stayed isolated, making a single call to Arum, who insisted he fight in New York. Randy Gordon, the chairman of the New York Athletic Commission, had already warned that he probably would try to suspend De La Hoya if he was pulling out of a fight for noninjury reasons.

"I'm not going to fight," De La Hoya told him. "My hand is injured."

Arum roared that nobody can cancel like that, not so close to the fight, that money would be lost and reputations splattered. In New

York, the center of the boxing media, the headlines screamed their disapproval. De La Hoya was spoiled. He was a baby. He didn't care. But Arum finally agreed, because he had to. The fight was canceled.

"Then I called my father," De La Hoya recalls. "I told him what was going on. I told him that I was tired of this trainer and how I can't fight because my hand was injured."

He had to gulp a few times, because his father was arguing. For once, for maybe the first time in his life, Oscar had to override his father. His father was brainwashed, Oscar decided, had spent too much time with Mittleman and Nelson.

"Mittleman and Steve would tell him every day," Oscar recalls, "telling him that without them we're going to lose everything: the house, the money, everything. My boxing career would just go down the drain. And my father would believe it, you know? He was convinced I needed them. I knew what was going on. They would give my father 11 percent, something like that. They knew that my father could control me, so they wanted to control my father by giving him 11 percent. There were times when my father and I couldn't talk to each other. I hated my father for being on their side, you know?"

But they were gone, Oscar decided. And it was time for his father to realize that. Then he made his final point. "'I'm going to ask for one favor, just one favor,'" De La Hoya said, and his father was quiet. "'Support me in what I do. *Support me*.'"

His father listened, then he spoke. It was an important moment.

"Son, I'm going to support you in this," Joel Sr. said in Spanish, severely. "And if you're wrong, then we all go down."

For a moment, Oscar blanched. What if it all did blow up? What if he was wrong? What if he had overreacted, just because Alcazar was making things tense up in Big Bear with Ortiz, just because Mittleman and Nelson missed a few payments? His new favorite term was that he was "swimming with the sharks," something Alcazar kept telling him. What if he had fired the wrong guys?

But Oscar had had a whole career of hirings and firings. He was used to change-ups and sudden dismissals. He *never* was with the same people for very long. The one thing that always stayed constant was him: Everybody wanted to be a part of him. A few months away from his twenty-first birthday, Oscar De La Hoya drove down from Big Bear and came out of hiding. He knew his father wasn't with him. And, proudly and publicly, he just didn't care that much.

He looked quite young and nervous wandering through a Montebello shopping mall, a baseball cap on backward, strolling from store to store with Pajar and a girl, buying a new Italian suit for his dramatic appearance at a press conference the next day, called to try to explain the breakup. He wanted to look mature for the press conference, and in charge. But at the mall he was just a gangly kid who giggled when he recognized a reporter and said, "You got me." Nobody at the mall seemed to recognize him, and he sat down and ate french fries in the food court.

De La Hoya was wearing a long soft cast on his left hand, painted in the green, white, and red of the Mexican flag. Laughing, De La Hoya said that he went to the doctor to try to verify that he canceled the New York fight because he was hurt, and to his surprise, the doctor found actual serious damage in his left hand—probably from working with the heavy bag for the first time in his career under Ortiz. "He put his hand in his car door right before the doctor's appointment," Pajar joked.

"My mind was a little kind of confused," Oscar said, "but that's not enough to pull out of a fight. Now I've found out that I tore a tendon, really."

Why did it all have to happen now? he was asked. What was so bad about Mittleman and Nelson that he had to fire them, instead of just serving out his contract? And the kid who had sparked a coast-to-coast controversy just shook his head mischievously and told his interviewer that he had finally stood up for himself and was feeling tremendous that he had. He sounded like he felt released.

"I'm young, I'm kind of like a seed, I'm just beginning," De La Hoya said that day. "And I wanted to have it all straightened out before it all starts. This is perfect timing. When they breached the contract once, I wasn't happy. But they're such smooth talkers, they pressure you so much. Me, I'm a kid of twenty years of age, I was nineteen back then [when he signed]. What can I say? I could never say no. I'm a nice guy. . . . But this is a move we had to make.

"First of all, they did not do what they promised in the contract. Breach of contract. They've breached the contract so many times. . . . We found out they had no money to support what they had to do. It was a very scary, very tough decision. But I put my foot down and that was it. It was a case of two people coming from New York and giving me $1 million. It was good for me, I was nineteen, I had just come back from the Olympic Games. I said, 'Wow.' I knew what I could do in the future and I know what I can accomplish. They didn't come through and messed me over. I'm not worried that people think I've done wrong. Because I'm doing what's best for my family and myself. This is business. You have to swim with the sharks.

"They weren't being with me, they were with my father. They talked to him so much, they were confusing him, he changed his mind so much. . . . It's like Mittleman was always at the house. And it was like, 'Mittleman's going to take you to court, he's going to sue you.' My dad was scared. I mean, he was scared. They tried to get to my father because they figured, 'Oh, he has respect for his father.'

"Steve would be there pressuring me every day, and it's hard to train and do things. My personal life, I didn't have one because he would always be there. I've never heard of any manager being so close. A block away from home like Mittleman; Steve being in camp every day. A manager just stays away, does his job, phone calls, makes fights. But he's not in camp every day. . . . I don't see how I could've handled it differently. I kept thinking about it a lot. For me to be happy, everything had to be running smoothly, everything had to be running the way it was supposed to be. And I wasn't happy, so I did what I had to do. We have to see what is the best thing for me. We can't see what the best thing is for Mittleman or Steve or Bob Arum. We have to see what's best for me and my family—that's all I can care about. It was a very, very tough decision. But I put my foot down and that's it."

("We lived up to every obligation we had," Mittleman said in response. "What's he going to say? 'I took $1 million from Nelson and Mittleman, used them up until I got the HBO deal, and then left them when somebody else gave me more money'? Yeah, how did we mismanage him? By getting him to 11–0 and getting him a multimillion-dollar HBO contract? He's making things up now.")

The future, suddenly, was his own, Oscar explained. The hardest part of the whole experience, he said, was feeling tied down by other people's limited vision.

"My career is going to go into entertainment, into commercials, into the movie business, into everything," De La Hoya said. "It's going to blast off like a rocket, go up into the stars. That's the way I see it and that's the way it's going to be. They were making decisions without us, they were doing things behind our back. Hiring Ortiz could be one of the reasons that triggered it, one of the many, one of the ten, twenty reasons that we're doing this. My father will be behind me. Team De La Hoya will be back together. Robert, my brother . . . Arturo [Islas, the cook], that's Team De La Hoya there.

"The whole world will know what's going on, they will know I am a good guy. We have so many things planned. I mean, this is not all about money, this is about taking care of my family. I've got a sister who's eleven years of age, she has a future, I have a future, my father has a future. If I have these problems now, what could happen in the future when I don't have anything? So might as well take care of it now and really, really focus on my boxing, make my money, and be happy."

That night, back at the house, Joel De La Hoya didn't know about the future, because he didn't know what was going on in the present.

"I don't know anything about new managers," Joel said. "These are a surprise for me."

And a few minutes later, Mittleman could only shake his head in sad acknowledgment of the moment. "Joel, if your son doesn't show honor to you," Mittleman told him, "then I sure as hell guess I can't expect him to show honor to me."

Many months later, Oscar tried to explain the conflict in the context of his life and family.

"If my mother was still alive, I would probably just have a happier life," Oscar said. "And she would've fired those guys long ago. The first problem that I saw and explained to her, she would've told me to fire them, get rid of them. I wouldn't have had the problem of my father being against me and she would've talked to him. And everything would've worked out fine."

chapter seven

Star Power

Now, all he had to do was win.

As he sat up in his Big Bear cottage a few months later, under layers of snow and scrutiny, De La Hoya was alone, and brooding. He had taken a stand. For once, he risked butting up against his father. Every other time, he ran away from confrontation, crying. As a boy from a piñata, as a teenager from his father time and again. He let others make the choices, and he was happy to do it.

Now, he had made a decision. Risked a choice. It made him want to hide.

"Nobody could get ahold of me—nobody," he recalls. "I was scared. Man, I was very scared. It was all on me. I finally felt in charge of what I wanted to do. With Mittleman and Nelson, I never felt that way. I always felt they were pulling me everywhere. I finally felt in charge, 'Yeah, shit, I'm calling the shots.' But yeah, I was feeling scared. 'Shit, somebody help me. Somebody hold my hand.'"

He couldn't turn to his father, of course. His friends and his brother were not a part of the equation—they went whichever way he pulled them. Though Alcazar had been the trigger to the explosion, ultimately he was too narrowly focused to depend on. All Alcazar really cared about was training De La Hoya and getting the credit for it. If De La Hoya was going to vault to the elite level, as everybody had been predicting for years, he needed some support. And he found it—in Arum, and, to a greater extent, in businessman Mike Hernandez.

Hernandez had been around De La Hoya for a while, most notably when he gave Oscar a new Corvette for winning the gold medal. He also provided cars for Joel Sr. and Jr. And, unlike all the other grabbers and moochers, Mike Hernandez was rich enough and proud enough to stay away from the cash trough. Hernandez was trustworthy—and, most important, independent. When everybody else was yammering and uncertain, Hernandez moved quickly and decisively. With his shock of thick, white hair and rough, grumbling voice, he projected the aura of Anthony Quinn: cunning, bawdy, and impossible to fool. His eyes were flashes of impatience. And, De La Hoya noted with great satisfaction, "He scares the hell out of my father."

When Mike Hernandez said something, there was not a lot of chaos bubbling in the background. Things quieted.

"What I noticed is they needed a lot of help and I didn't see anybody willing to give him a hand after they got rid of Mittleman," Hernandez said. "They were hiding. Roberto [Alcazar] called me one time and I didn't really think they knew what the heck was going on. They didn't know if Oscar was going to fight anymore. So I talked to them. Later, he talked to me. You got to do everything legally, if you're going to do it. Can't be lying or trying to screw Mittleman. This kid needed some help, and I somehow solved it."

When Hernandez got a close-up look at De La Hoya's business dealings, the $5,000 handshakes, the contracts, the agents, he decided he had to step in and shake things up. De La Hoya was spending up to $10,000 a week. Money was flying out the door of the Montebello house with every new pitchman who spoke to Joel Sr. or Oscar. In addition to his NSX and his latest Corvette, he leased not one, but two Lamborghinis. One red, one white.

The cars would be Hernandez's toughest argument with De La Hoya, who found release on the highways of L.A., flying through traffic with his foot on the pedal and a complete confidence that his was not a life destined to end in a crash. Anybody who saw him drive was not so sure.

"I hate that Lamborghini so bad," Veronica once said. "I hated the red one before he got rid of it, I hate the white one. I fear for him, when you have so much power and just want to see how much power you can get. When you're driving on that freeway and people see that car, they look at you. What if somebody loses control and hits you or you cause an accident? I tell him, 'You know what sweetie? I don't need you to be king of the ring so you can die on the road.'"

Other than the cars, though, De La Hoya's life became a little more measured under Hernandez's guidance.

"He started bringing in CPAs and more lawyers and he made me aware of what I had in my bank, my assets," De La Hoya said. "I was like, 'Wow, I fought for this and this is what I have in the bank?'"

He had signed a million-dollar deal after the Olympics, and thirteen months later was left with only $3,000 in the bank. Hernandez immediately decided to get Oscar out of the house and into one of his own apartments in Los Angeles. Oscar needed some room. Then Hernandez cut off the financial bleeding by, in his typical venomous rumble, "getting rid of the leeches."

A few months after the firing of Mittleman and Nelson, Hernandez called the first Team De La Hoya meeting, held inside his dealership in Monterey Park. Twenty people showed up, some who had real roles, some who did not. Hernandez turned to Oscar, who shrugged sheepishly.

"Before this meeting is over," Hernandez told De La Hoya in front of the others, "two of these people have to be fired. There are too many."

The supplicants blanched and argued. De La Hoya was silent. Then he just nodded. By the end of that meeting, more than two people were cut off of the De La Hoya payroll. And there would be more to come.

"It was tough, you know, but I managed to tell them," De La Hoya said soon after the firings. "If they were really true friends or true family that really stuck by me, they'd understand. I would pay them good and then I would come out really bad. My financial situation was really bad. So they had to understand, and they did. I confronted them, and they did. Which was something good, but it was tough, tough to deal with. . . . I went from spending $10,000 a week to spending $1 a week. No more cards, gotta get rid of these people. It was just like that."

Hernandez mediated the Mittleman-Nelson negotiation—the two were given a 50 percent share of his next several fights, paying them vastly more over the short term than they would have earned as his managers.

"Mittleman's not a bad guy," Hernandez said then. "We're not out to screw anybody."

Calmed down, Mittleman and Nelson dropped the lawsuit against Salas and Garza, and any claims to De La Hoya's management. Salas and Garza, meanwhile, were pushed away, too, by Hernandez, who wanted to streamline the operation as much as possible. They were only agitators, he decided. They weren't people who would be worth much to De La Hoya's career over any kind of long haul. Hernandez also directed most of the decisions through Arum, winnowing the chain of command and letting Oscar in on all the major choices, if he wanted.

"I think without him I wouldn't be here," De La Hoya said of Hernandez in 1995. "He's the one that made me more aware. He wants to take care of my financial problems and he wants to see me as a very successful Hispanic boxer. And he's been doing his job very well. He told me in the beginning, 'When you get richer and richer, you're going to have more problems, more problems.' I'm believing that. Hopefully, I'll have him for the rest of my career, because without him, I can't do anything."

Now, to justify his decision to fire his first professional managers—and continue his career basically without any official replacements—all he had to do was win.

"I wouldn't say I'm my own manager now," he said right after his twenty-first birthday, celebrated in Big Bear with an untouched birthday cake sitting on top of his small refrigerator, in the same cabin that was the headquarters of his breakup. "But I'm *on* my own. I have my legal advice, my senior adviser, and I have all these people who, when we have something to discuss, we all get together, kind of talk it over. It's like a jury in some ways. It's much better. Now, we don't have people doing things behind our backs, doing things under the table. And I make the final decision."

By De La Hoya's twenty-first birthday, Mike Hernandez had become his most essential adviser—and the central figure in all his business dealings.

As Hernandez sat in an East L.A. restaurant in 1994, with De La Hoya's career still a few years short of his huge earning days, he fidgeted his way through an outline of the young fighter's future.

"He can make $50 million, and there's not many out there who can do that," Hernandez said. "He can be real, real special, this kid. Look at his face. Just look at him."

For years, Hernandez was known in East L.A. as a businessman who liked to be associated with local athletes, help them through financial and personal difficulties. He was a good friend of longtime Dodger Manny Mota, and advised Fernando Valenzuela and Ramon Martinez, among others.

De La Hoya, though, was the greatest possibility yet for Hernandez. Oscar needed help, Hernandez saw, but essentially he was a good kid. He had a troubled family. But just a little help could nudge him into greatness, Hernandez thought. This kid could be greater than any other Latino athlete in America, ever. And Hernandez liked the idea of being the mentor for such a giant. Celebrities, especially sports celebrities, Hernandez had long ago learned, didn't need less help. They needed more. Hernandez was glad to provide it.

"He can be a role model for the kids," Hernandez said. "I want to keep him clean. That's important for this community. I'm tired of seeing them ruin themselves. Oscar can be a great role model for this community. He can be the biggest."

Alcazar, for one, recognized swiftly that Hernandez was a man who could take De La Hoya places.

"What can I say for him, if it wasn't for him, we wouldn't have made it this far," Alcazar said. "Things were kind of up in the air, and then he came in, and we went in the right direction."

With Hernandez's guidance, De La Hoya's career marched on. The key to it all was HBO, which merrily waved away the manager disputes as something all fighters have to deal with at some point.

There was a loud message for De La Hoya in all this. As long as he stayed on top of his game and created high ratings, all that mattered was him.

"It was perfect," De La Hoya said with relish at the time. "[Mittleman and Nelson] were very anxious to sign the HBO deal, and that's when we fired them. Then we signed it, and they didn't have anything."

Though the manager firings and the hand injury postponed the official signing of the HBO deal, the offer never was taken off the table. De La Hoya signed the five-fight, $7.5 million deal, with HBO's option to renew for five more fights, sending the package into the $20 million range, in early 1994.

By then, he already had a $250,000 deal with B.U.M., the sports apparel manufacturer, and smaller deals with several other firms. HBO, the home of the young Mike Tyson and the middle-aged Julio Cesar Chavez before Don King took them both to rival Showtime, badly needed a new young star, and the executives were pretty sure De La Hoya was the answer. The ratings already said so. And he hadn't even fought anybody famous. He had controversy, he had a great story, he had looks. Now, for HBO to start making back its money, he needed a title.

Enter Jimmi Bredahl.

The first title fight, planned by Mittleman and Nelson in the weeks before they were dumped, was still on: Bredahl from Denmark, the cocky southpaw WBO champion. Even though the HBO long-term deal hadn't yet kicked in, De La Hoya's purse for the fight was an incredible $1 million. As per the settlement, Mittleman and Nelson got half of it.

After the catharsis of the management crisis, and the criticism from New York, Arum needed a setting for this fight that pitched De La Hoya against a larger canvas—that took advantage of his star qualities. There was an obvious candidate: the remodeled Olympic Auditorium in downtown Los Angeles, the fabled fight palace of the '50s, '60s, and '70s that was home to just about every major Latin fighter of the era, from Carlos Palomino to Mando Ramos to Bobby Chacon. No less a figure than Jack Dempsey had dug the ceremonial first shovel of dirt at its ground breaking seventy years earlier. For Arum, there was an irresistible capper: Both Joel Sr. and Vincente De La Hoya had fought at the Olympic, before it was closed in the early '80s.

The Olympic, with its low-slung second level and perfectly centered floor, had been shut down for several years, a victim of a worsening neighborhood, careless ownership, and the domination of Las Vegas for major fights. But Olympic owner Jack Needleman wanted to revitalize the area, and Arum wanted to forge himself an L.A. headquarters. De La Hoya himself was excited about the prospect—he was going to be the man who reopened the Olympic. What other L.A. fighter could do that? The answer was as obvious as the hundred-foot banner Arum hung from the building's rooftop: OSCAR'S NIGHT, it read, next to a gigantic picture of De La Hoya. The juxtaposition was remarkable: This old arena, famous for bloody battles and not a few riots, was being reopened strictly on the star power and famous face of someone who had never been in a real boxing war in his life.

As the cleaned-out and remodeled building opened, De La Hoya acknowledged that he had undergone some refurbishment, too. It was March, and because of the management problems, he hadn't fought since October—easily the longest layoff of his professional career. Up at Big Bear in the weeks before this fight, De La Hoya trained ferociously. Even amid the worst of the controversy, De La Hoya never let himself get badly out of shape—the quiet discipline of his childhood was just too powerful.

For this fight, though, there was something more. De La Hoya's training sessions were always intense and unflagging: the pace of his movements, the power of his punches. But in this training camp, he seemed to throw himself into each jab and hook, hungry for impact, searching for the perfect destructive moment. With Alcazar wearing hand pads, De La Hoya shouted, almost involuntarily, with every shot to the pads, "Ha! Ha-ha-ha! Ha!" and with each shout came a corresponding, clean, violent *smack*, right in the heart of the pad. Alcazar at times could only move his hands back and shake them in pain after De La Hoya's piercing attacks.

"The time off came at a perfect time for me," De La Hoya said then. "I had a few problems with my managers, and the pressure was getting to me. I kind of had to refocus. Now I feel great. I don't feel rusty at all. I want to show that [the firings] did not affect me whatsoever. I'm still the same person, I'm still the same guy that came out from the Olympic Games with a gold medal. Nice person and everything. Just because I split up from my managers, there's been a few bad publicity things. But I'm sure that after a few fights, people will just forget about all that and remember again what Oscar was."

He knew there were critics. There were critics of him from the beginning, and there were plenty more now. If he wanted to seem even more of a dilettante than he did in the beginning of his career, if he wanted to seem more of a preener and a complainer, he had followed the perfectly petulant path.

The boxing world didn't ignore it. Great fighters, argued Dan Duva, the respected head of the Main Events operation, don't display the cut-and-run tendencies De La Hoya so eagerly and recently displayed. Great fighters stick it out and endure the consequences of their own decisions—in the ring and out.

"The change in management doesn't by itself lead to problems, but it's indicative of what I believe is a flaw in someone's character," Duva said. "The fighters that have really been the most successful, like Marvin Hagler, Michael Spinks, Sugar Ray Leonard, Evander Holyfield, Muhammad Ali, they kept the same core group of advisers with them throughout their careers. Loyalty shows strong character— because there are always people waving money in your face. It takes a very strong person to not give in to that temptation. It takes the same kind of strong will to win tough, grueling fights when you're hurt, out of gas, and need to dig down deep."

Bredahl was the first step, then, of De La Hoya's answering the critics, or proving them correct.

De La Hoya was slightly annoyed when Bredahl's camp discovered a little-known WBO rule that mandated the weigh-in occur the day of the bout, instead of a day earlier. That meant that the much bigger De La Hoya had less time to rebuild his strength and natural weight after making the 130-pound limit, which De La Hoya hadn't officially made since he was eighteen years old.

More irksome for De La Hoya was Bredahl's playful cockiness. Because of De La Hoya, Bredahl took home $300,000 for the bout, by far his highest purse, and a sign of rich things to come for all future De La Hoya opponents. But the skinny left-hander, who was 16–0 but hadn't fought any name fighters, talked amiably about knocking De La Hoya down in the first round, and cheekily passed out invitations in the days before the bout inviting one and all to his post-fight victory party.

"I will be your worst nightmare," Bredahl warned De La Hoya at the final press conference as he handed him a party invitation.

Said De La Hoya, in a cool glower: "I know he's a good boxer, a good technician. but he has no power, I know that. His record shows that and the fights that I've seen, he doesn't show power. I'm not going in there thinking I'm going to walk right through him, but he will not beat me."

Arum, however, misjudged the audience for this show. He took the fight to L.A. for the energy of the local crowd, and the atmosphere of the golden age of boxing, but charged Las Vegas casino prices for tickets: $500 for ringside, and $50 for the cheapest seat. De La Hoya's presence alone could not justify the pricey ticket. The L.A. market simply wouldn't dish out high-roller cash. Though there were more than 5,000 in attendance (with 7,100 seats available), only 3,100 paid for tickets. In an echo of De La Hoya's Forum debut, he failed once again to prove that he could draw the local audience to one of his glitzy matches.

Still, it was a good TV show.

De La Hoya surprised even himself at the eight A.M. weigh-in by coming in at only 128¾ pounds, and rested up the rest of the day in a downtown hotel. By fight time, he bounded in the ring wearing canary yellow and looking very strong—buoyed by the warm reception and electric feeling inside the old building.

The earlier fight on the card charged up the audience when super-middleweight champion James Toney—who would have been the main event on any other show—floored Tim Littles in the fourth, one round before doctors were prepared to stop the fight, forcing a draw, because of a deep gash in Toney's forehead.

Then it was De La Hoya's turn. Chants of "East L.A.! East L.A.!" rumbled down from the balcony, and the HBO microphones and cameras ate it up.

In the first minute, Bredahl, who had never been knocked down before, took a short right to the chin and plopped to the canvas, as De La Hoya calmly nodded his head and smiled to the crowd. In the second, Bredahl tried an awkward attack, but De La Hoya slammed the champion with a short left and Bredahl slumped to the canvas again.

But there was no quick finish to this one for De La Hoya. Instead of finishing him off, De La Hoya stayed back a little, patiently picking pieces of Bredahl's face to punish, one at a time, round by round, welt by welt, as Bredahl weakened and the left side of his face puffed red.

By the ninth round, De La Hoya snapped a left that clearly bent back Bredahl's nose and sent a jolt of pain through the Dane's body. After the round, he yelped to his corner, "My nose!" Bredahl went down again in the tenth. After that round was over, the ring physician peered down at the champion, a map of red bruises stretched across his contorted face, and just shook his head.

It was over. De La Hoya was a champion. Bredahl immediately leaped up from his stool and dashed over to hug De La Hoya, who hadn't sat down yet. And as a startled ring-card girl walked by, the two fighters hugged.

"My strategy was to kill his stomach," Bredahl said, "but he killed my face first."

De La Hoya inflicted more damage in this bout than he had in the rest of his pro fights combined. But, not so impressively, it took him ten rounds, and he never seemed to have a coherent course of attack against Bredahl's quick circling tactics. De La Hoya claimed he was only trying to prolong Bredahl's agony.

"What I really wanted to do was make him suffer," De La Hoya said. "Because he was saying things, like dropping me in the first round. So I wanted to hurt him and end the fight on my terms. Which is what I did."

So he was a champion. . . . But it was the minor WBO title, against a minor figure even by WBO standards, in a weight classification that De La Hoya dominated physically. When would he be fighting for a major title against a major champion who actually had a chance of defeating him? When would he get into a real fight?

"My timetable is to develop a little more experience," De La Hoya said that night. "And eventually I'll be fighting the best in the world. Only I know when I've developed the strength and power to beat anybody out there."

The performance against Bredahl, though, gave further ammunition to those who wondered how so much could be given to a fighter who had proven so little in the pro ranks. He still looked like an amateur at times, letting the smaller, light-hitting Bredahl dictate the pace of the bout, even if he could do little to harm De La Hoya.

The former managers were blamed and fired for daring to bring another trainer to help Alcazar. But the Bredahl fight did nothing to disprove the need. Ever vigilant about his own position in the sport, Alcazar was visibly agitated by the criticisms. A few months later in Big Bear, training for De La Hoya's next fight, against Italian Giorgio Campanella, Alcazar spoke fast and fervently.

"I don't have the kind of experience like [other trainers] claim to have, but how many of them have won a gold medal together and then won a world title together? We just need time."

How much longer Alcazar would get, however, was anybody's guess. As the criticism built, De La Hoya knew Alcazar was feeling the pressure, and did only a little bit to ease it. De La Hoya didn't completely appreciate Alcazar reaching to take control of the entire boxing operation, and he felt that Alcazar was getting increasingly paranoid about his position.

Hadn't De La Hoya fired Mittleman and Nelson to get rid of Ortiz? De La Hoya, meanwhile, harbored hopes of bringing in his personal idol, Alexis Arguello—who, like him, was tall, dark, and lankily powerful—to take over the training. Alcazar was too tense and reminded De La Hoya too much of his amateur days.

"He's a good trainer," De La Hoya said of Alcazar at the time. "He suits my style. And he adds on to my style. He doesn't take away anything. When people say I have to bring in somebody else, it's no problem. I probably will in the future. But it has to be somebody suitable for my style. Robert has no problem bringing somebody in and helping us out, somebody more experienced, maybe like an Alexis Arguello, somebody who has my style."

But Arguello was not a trainer, had no interest in training anybody, and even launched a comeback at about the same time, at forty-six years of age. Without a clear alternative, De La Hoya and Alcazar stayed together. They had survived Ortiz, survived Mittleman and Nelson, and survived even Joel Sr.'s worries. If De La Hoya could just win a few fights impressively, the second-guessing of Alcazar would surely cool down.

When the May fight at Las Vegas's MGM Grand hotel and casino arrived, Italian journeyman Giorgio Campanella seemed to pose little real threat. Campanella was 20–0, but had only thirteen knockouts, and stood five-foot-four, almost seven inches shorter than De La Hoya.

De La Hoya already was eagerly anticipating a move up to the 135-pound division, straight to a title fight in a few months against veteran Jorge Paez for a crown that the WBO conveniently was vacating just for that fight. The former title holder, Giovanni Parisi, did not appreciate it, but that's the way boxing handled these things: The star name gets the star treatment. The WBO wanted De La Hoya as a champion, and did what it had to to make sure of it.

Campanella, De La Hoya's first-ever title defense, was just the appetizer.

"What I'm looking forward to is eating," De La Hoya said coyly days before the Campanella fight.

A few weeks earlier, De La Hoya was summoned to a rare meeting with reclusive MGM Grand chairman Kirk Kerkorian. How rare? Kerkorian did not even meet personally with Mike Tyson two years later when the company cut a $20 million deal with the heavyweight. Kerkorian told De La Hoya that the MGM very much wanted to be in business with him. De La Hoya and his handlers said they'd see what they could do.

The MGM Grand was not bashful in its pursuit. In promotional materials, it highlighted De La Hoya's fight—to the virtual exclusion of the title defense by Roy Jones Jr., a far more seasoned fighter, on the same card. Jones, who was chafing under a promotional agreement with Arum at the time, was on the undercard of De La Hoya–Campanella, and wore a dog collar to the main press conference to announce his frustration with the lower billing.

"I came here with an attitude," Jones said, staring at De La Hoya. "The reason I have an attitude is I'm 25–0, an Olympic champion. What else do I need? And still I have not seen my face on the cover of a major boxing magazine or headline a card in Las Vegas? Why? I want to know."

De La Hoya just smiled and stayed silent. Why argue about the obvious? He was the draw. He always would be. He was a magnet. Other fighters wanted what he had.

For the Campanella fight, De La Hoya was paid $500,000—$250,000 of which went to Mittleman and Nelson, as the final installment of the settlement. The rich Paez fight was up next. All De La Hoya wanted and needed was to get rid of Campanella.

"I think of Campanella as a plate of fettuccine," De La Hoya said. "And I love fettuccine."

On May 27, 1994, the night of the fight, De La Hoya walked out of his dressing room last, with some fashionable delay, and let Campanella stew in the ring for a few minutes. On his way out, De La Hoya smiled at the girls in the crowd, blew a few kisses, and kept on grinning even after he hopped into the ring. Focused? Not exactly. It was more like he was the happy headliner in a Vegas revue. Meanwhile, Campanella was preparing a buffalo charge.

De La Hoya meandered out of his corner at the opening bell, but Campanella fired out, charging into De La Hoya fearlessly. As De La Hoya dropped his right to throw a hook, Campanella powered a hard left straight into De La Hoya's jaw.

Suddenly, it was happening again. De La Hoya collapsed backward, shockingly, onto the canvas fifteen seconds into the bout—his second first-round knockdown in three fights. But, unlike the Valenzuela fall, this was not a flash knockdown. De La Hoya was hurt, and woozy. This time he toppled, his legs kicked out from under him.

Then he staggered to his feet slowly and in a daze. In the corner, Alcazar threw his hands up.

"I told him, told him, told him," Alcazar said later in exasperation. "This guy is a little Mike Tyson. He's going to be coming right at you."

As De La Hoya teetered, referee Joe Cortez reached the eight-count, restarted the fight, and still De La Hoya looked vulnerable. His face tightened. He did not pounce on Campanella as he had on Valenzuela in October. He was wary, cautious, hanging on for the rest of the first. Then, after the round break, he seemed to get the ground back under his feet.

He moved his feet, avoided Campanella's left hand, and gave himself a chance to breath again.

"I started out trying to be that big, macho fighter, bang with this great banger," De La Hoya said. "By the second round, I realized that I could easily outbox him, get him from the outside using my reach advantage, and stay away from that left hook."

Campanella couldn't catch him, and then De La Hoya started

turning on his own firepower. Campanella went down in the second round—and De La Hoya showed his antsiness by firing four punches at Campanella when he was on his knees, which easily could have led to a disqualification. De La Hoya ended it in the third, following up a second knockdown with a swarm of shots at Campanella's head that caused the Campanella corner to throw in the towel and end the fight.

Once again, it was good theatrics, but it was not the enlightening performance of a sure-thing superstar. Campanella wasn't a terrible fighter, but he was hardly a knockout warrior; he was much smaller than De La Hoya, and yet he had taken De La Hoya to the brink with a quick left over a lazy De La Hoya defense.

De La Hoya knew one thing for sure: He was never going to fight at 130 pounds again. He felt weak this time trying to make the weight—he probably grew out of it months ago, but stayed unnaturally light at 130 to grab the title and defend it. Once.

"If Oscar De La Hoya had never fought at 130, and gone straight to 135 as a pro," said boxing observer John Beyrooty, "maybe we'd think he was the greatest fighter ever. Those knockdowns were all about having to make that ridiculous weight."

A few weeks later, De La Hoya wandered into the Forum for one of the building's regular Monday night fight cards. This time, though, he was not bathed in applause. He was booed, hard and loud, by the mostly Mexican and Mexican-American fight crowd. This was a crowd there to watch Paez, the jokester, the pranky "Clown Prince of Boxing," win a setup match, and Paez delivered.

Arum and Alcazar wanted De La Hoya to fight Paez because Paez was a famous name with almost no knockout power. Paez was charming, and he was theatrical—his ring arrivals were always an event: Would he come in dressed as a clown, a bullfighter, or a bride in a wedding dress? Paez had done all of those things, but he had never knocked out a strong young champion. It would be a nice, easy, crowd-pleasing victory, the De La Hoya camp figured. Paez might be cagey, but once he got hit, there shouldn't be any problems for the younger fighter.

By the time De La Hoya showed up at the Forum to watch Paez, the fight was already signed. But if De La Hoya's handlers thought they were setting up a fight in which their fighter would be cheered as a hero, they were wrong. There were other, stronger forces at work. At the Forum that night, De La Hoya arrived, and the boos rained. De La Hoya looked nervous, but then simply waved to the crowd and sat down. The men shouted catcalls, but the women lined up for autographs. Love and hate. De La Hoya, not even fighting, was the center of the attention, for good and bad. Forever.

"This kid doesn't deserve that," Alcazar, with him at the Forum, said of the boos. "What he did for this country and for those people's country, Mexico.... He put that country way up on the top. I don't think Oscar deserved to hear that."

De La Hoya's response? "That's boxing," he said at the time, with a weary shrug. "And all those guys, their girlfriends all wanted my autograph, didn't they?"

Later, in a less flippant mood, he added: "Since the Olympic Games, I've been 'the Golden Boy' and this and that. And now it's, 'He's this rich kid.' People want to see me go down.... You have to put on a good show because they pay the money. I'm going to do that, but I'm going to get my money and run. Of course, I want to win world titles and have a big name. But I want to have as few fights as possible and make the most money. My image is like a star image."

That's what the Forum crowd was booing, an image ... his carefully cultivated image. Why, the loud fans wanted to know, was De La Hoya so famous and so rich when he hadn't beaten anybody? Gradually, but inevitably, as De La Hoya's career bloomed, the hardy boxing fans of his hometown grew ever more disaffected by his rise. De La Hoya was treasured by corporate America because he had crossover appeal, because he had that mysterious smile. De La Hoya looked like a super-model and fought like a demon. People across America cared about him, and cared for him.

But the Mexican nationals and Mexican-Americans in Los Angeles watched him closely, and noticed that he stuck to himself and avoided the old neighborhood. When it counted, De La Hoya acted like a privileged, protected white fighter, not a rambling, rumbling Latino. Roberto Duran was Panamanian, not a Mexican, but to many Latino fight fans, he was the feral epitome of the species. Julio Cesar Chavez, the king of Mexican fighters, was a man of the people, symbolic of their inner strength and need for macho heroes.

De La Hoya, with his squeaky voice and distant manners and no-name opponent list, was not anything close to the perfect Latino superstar.

"I guess there's a lot of jealous people out there," De La Hoya said. "People want me to fight against good fighters already, at the early stage of my career. All I have to do is get a few more fights under my belt and people will know who the real champion is. A lot of people are going for Paez. That makes me want to train harder because I want to knock him out in the first or second round to show people how much better I am."

Everybody in camp knew that De La Hoya was so much stronger and faster—and hungrier—than Paez that this fight was more of a statement than a real athletic contest. Maybe the doubters thought Paez had the guts and guile to pull off a surprise victory, but not Team De La Hoya.

This was an easy camp for the fighter, because it was for the vacant 135-pound WBO title, and De La Hoya relished the five extra pounds. Finally, he could eat ribs or steak or whatever he wanted up at Big Bear. He ate at the one decent Mexican restaurant in the area, and he got an account at the Sizzler, for the nights when he was in the mood for all the fried shrimp he could eat.

"The so-called critics say that Paez is going to be my toughest opponent," De La Hoya said then. "But they've been saying that since I fought maybe Troy Dorsey [in June 1993, his eighth fight]. Paez fought

Troy Dorsey [in July 1990], took him twelve rounds to win a decision. And I stopped him in one round."

Things were so loose leading up to the Paez fight that De La Hoya and his handlers shrugged off the temporary loss of legendary cut man Chuck Bodak, who had been in De La Hoya's corner for his whole pro career. Bodak, renowned for his colorful language and his habit of sticking pictures and signs on his huge bald head during fights, had served Paez's corner for years, and decided that he didn't want to choose between the fighters.

Either way, Bodak was turning down a $10,000 payday out of principle. "I'm a great believer in loyalty," Bodak said. "I've worked with both, think the world of both, and to me, loyalty is a lot more important than money. Even if I was destitute, I'd do the same thing."

De La Hoya and Alcazar were so certain that Paez would hardly touch him, and were so fearful of bringing in any new voice to the corner, that they enlisted none other than Joel Jr.—who had zero experience handling cuts—to be the cut man for the fight. Todd duBoef, Arum's stepson and right-hand man, first heard about the possibility of Joel's new job a few days before the fight and immediately panicked. "They can't be doing that," duBoef said. "That's crazy. It must just be a joke."

It wasn't. Joel was the cut man. What if De La Hoya got cut? Alcazar said that was impossible.

"I think Oscar's going to destroy Paez with the jab," Alcazar said. "He's going to cut his face all over."

Alcazar's words were not lost on the Paez camp, which, over the weeks leading up to the fight, had moved from cheeriness at getting such a big payday ($175,000, versus De La Hoya's $800,000), to simmering anger at the perceived insults. Alcazar said from the outset that "this is going to be Oscar's easiest fight yet." Though Paez had sixty-three fight's worth of experience (53–6–4), Alcazar was brimming with confidence.

"No question in my mind, Oscar's going to knock him out," Alcazar said. "How many rounds, who knows? It all depends on how many rounds it's going to take Oscar to catch him with a clean punch. That's as long as the fight's going to be."

Privately, De La Hoya called Paez "basically a clown, and that's it."

How could he say that about such a veteran? Paez was twenty-eight, a former featherweight champion, and probably not powerful enough to do significant damage to De La Hoya. But Valenzuela and Campanella weren't exactly devastating punchers, and both had knocked De La Hoya down. Both of those fighters seemed surprised by the knockdowns, then overwhelmed when De La Hoya rose to fight again. What if a veteran, someone who had been in against Pernell Whitaker and Freddie Pendleton, hurt De La Hoya, then kept up the attack?

"De La Hoya has never been taken into the deep water where we can see if he'll sink or swim when it gets tough," said one of Paez's trainers, Alex Sherer. "He's never been in a fight, even the knockdown fights, where he's had to go head-to-head, fist-to-fist, fighting for survival late in the fight. He hasn't fought anybody who could do that to him. That's what Paez has to do, and I think will do."

Actually, De La Hoya's most heated and debated moment of the fight came a few days before the matchup, when Alcazar represented De La Hoya in a coin flip to see who would be given the honor of entering the ring last. Because they were fighting for a vacant title, both fighters had equal claim on the traditional champion's prerogative. Both wanted it, too. Alcazar called the toss, and lost, which meant that Paez came out last. De La Hoya was not pleased.

"He's mad at me more for that than anything else ever," Alcazar said with a laugh before the fight.

De La Hoya looked mad when he came out of his locker room that July night. This time, De La Hoya did not grin as he walked out into the ring. He glared straight ahead and ignored the crowd in the MGM Grand Garden. No Vegas revue this time.

"The objective is to come into the fight focused, kind of have some blinders when I walk in," De La Hoya said before the fight, "so I will not pay attention to the crowd. And afterward I can have the Golden Boy image and meet the people." And when the two fighters met in the middle of the ring for instructions, De La Hoya stared straight up, into the darkness, as a way to gather his focus and pay tribute to his mother.

It was a serious time in Las Vegas. Just a week earlier, welterweight Robert Wangila had died from the head injuries he suffered in a local fight, casting a temporary pall over the sport. But, as always, there were fights to put on. De La Hoya–Paez just happened to be the next one.

Paez skipped his usual frantic ring entrance, but it was hard to ignore "Zedillo," the name of the recently slain Mexican presidential candidate, carved into his hair. Otherwise, Paez looked like a man attempting to ration his power and courage for a long battle.

Once the fight started, Paez tried to take the fight to the taller, younger boxer, and De La Hoya stumbled a little under the fire. No major punches landed, but De La Hoya once again appeared stiff and predictable.

"I was trying to get his game plan, see what he has to offer," De La Hoya said of the first round. "I knew he was going to start off fast and try to throw lunging punches like that. So the first round was kind of a feeling-out process. The first round of my last fight, and with Valenzuela also, we were coming out too strong in the first round. Kind of being overconfident. I was more focused. I just felt I was here with Paez and nobody else was in the room."

For the first time, if he was listening, De La Hoya heard another man's name being chanted during a fight—"Jor-ge! Jor-ge!" And, with the noise building, De La Hoya gave the Paez partisans hope by throwing tight, insignificant punches, one at a time. Paez easily fended them off. After the first round was over, Sherer yelled to Paez, "He's scared! The man's scared!"

Alcazar to De La Hoya: "Beautiful. Nice."

Then, twenty seconds into the second round, Paez bobbed in front of De La Hoya, and, as the veteran moved in for a right uppercut, De La Hoya landed a short left to Paez's chin that jerked Paez's entire body

The proud child, with trophy and Joe Minjarez.
PHOTO COURTESY OF JOE MINJAREZ.

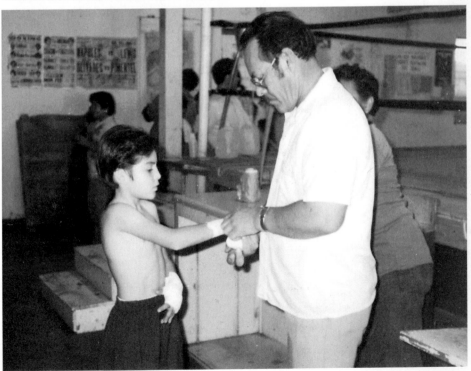

Even before he was a teenager, De La Hoya was deeply focused on fighting. Here the young fighter gets his hands wrapped by Joe Minjarez at the Eastside Boxing Club. PHOTO COURTESY OF JOE MINJAREZ.

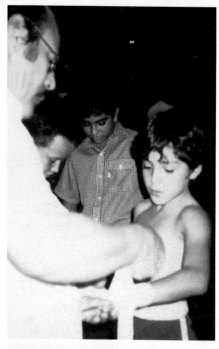

De La Hoya liked to wear the same red shorts as often as possible. PHOTO COURTESY OF JOE MINJAREZ.

Even before he got to the Olympics, De La Hoya's cover-boy looks and obvious talent pegged him as a future star. PHOTO BY MIKE POWELL/ALLSPORT.

De La Hoya at home with some of his family, including cousin Adrian Pasten (far left) and father Joel (back right). PHOTO BY MIKE POWELL/ALLSPORT.

As an amateur, De La Hoya spent the early mornings running through the streets of East L.A. to train. PHOTO BY MIKE POWELL/ALLSPORT.

A relieved and tired De La Hoya hearing the announcement that he has been given the narrow decision victory over Korean Hong Sung Sik to move onto the gold medal match in the 1992 Barcelona Olympics. PHOTO BY DAVID CANNON/ALLSPORT.

In each one of his Olympic bouts, De La Hoya took a moment after victory to drop to a knee and look up in tribute to his mother, who passed away in 1990. PHOTO BY MIKE POWELL/ALLSPORT.

De La Hoya, in the flush of his Olympic fame and minor fortune, driving the streets of L.A. in his new Corvette. **PHOTO BY MIKE POWELL/ALLSPORT.**

Oscar De La Hoya, proudly showing off his 1992 Olympic gold medal. **PHOTO BY M. MORRISON/ALLSPORT.**

Nineteen years old
and gleaming bright.
PHOTO COURTESY OF JOE
MINJAREZ.

Robert Mittleman (left) and Steve Nelson (middle) outbid everybody to be
his first professional comanagers, but there was always a sense of distance
between them and De La Hoya, including at this press conference at the
Great Western Forum to announce his professional debut in November
1992. PHOTO BY HOLLY STEIN/ALLSPORT.

Keeping up his crossover appeal, De La Hoya entered the Great Western Forum ring for his pro debut wearing a sombrero and carrying the flags of his two national identities. PHOTO BY HOLLY STEIN/ALLSPORT.

Two of his favorite things: enjoying the sun and posing for pictures, in 1993. PHOTO BY SIMON BRUTY/ALLSPORT.

In perhaps the most stunning moment of his career, De La Hoya hit the canvas in the first moments against journeyman Narciso Valenzuela in October 1993 in Phoenix. De La Hoya got up quickly and knocked Valenzuela out later in the first round.

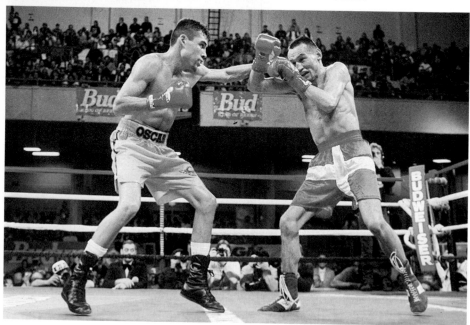

In front of a festive crowd at the newly reopened Grand Olympic Auditorium on March 5, 1994, De La Hoya measured up then out-muscled Jimmi Bredahl to win the World Boxing Organization lightweight title—De La Hoya's first world title. PHOTO BY HOLLY STEIN/ALLSPORT.

Two rounds after suffering a shocking knockdown at the hands of little-known Giorgio Campanella, De La Hoya let loose against the smaller Italian, recording a third-round knockout on May 27, 1994, in Las Vegas. PHOTO BY HOLLY STEIN/ALLSPORT.

De La Hoya, out and about with unidentified woman, watching the fights at the Forum as his professional career was about to hit the stratosphere; June 11, 1994. PHOTO BY HOLLY STEIN/ALLSPORT.

De La Hoya star-
ing down at a
defeated Jorge
Paez, seconds
before Paez was
counted out in the
second round of
their July 29, 1994,
fight in Las Vegas.
PHOTO BY AL
BELLO/ALLSPORT.

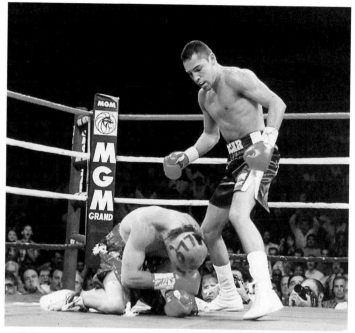

With perhaps the cleanest, best punch of his career, De La Hoya leveled
Rafael Ruelas in the second round en route to a breathtakingly easy knockout victory on May 6, 1995, in Las Vegas. PHOTO BY HOLLY STEIN/ALLSPORT.

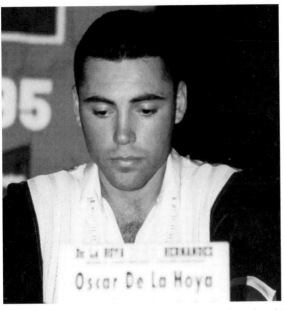

A quiet moment during a press conference before his 1995 fight against Genaro Hernandez.

De La Hoya fought Genaro Hernandez, his bitter L.A. rival, cautiously in their September 9, 1995, fight but eventually broke his nose and forced Hernandez to quit at the end of six punishing rounds in Las Vegas. PHOTO BY JED JACOBSOHN/ALLSPORT.

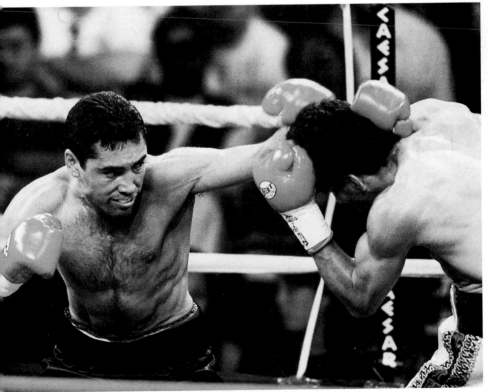

Though De La Hoya, as always, took the public events seriously, Julio Cesar Chavez (foreground) showed little interest in anything De La Hoya had to say during their press tour before their June 7, 1996, fight in Las Vegas. PHOTO BY AL BELLO/ALLSPORT.

During the long press tour before the 1996 fight with Julio Cesar Chavez, De La Hoya spent what little free time he had with friend Joe Pajar (foreground right), trainer Robert Alcazar (standing), an unidentified reporter, and brother Joel Jr. (far left).

Oscar, in his element, during the Chavez press tour.

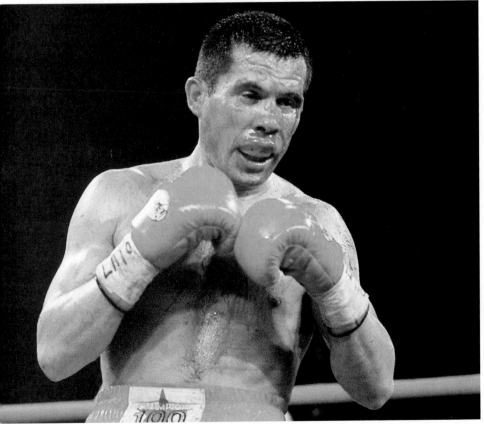

Chavez, drenched from pore to pore in his own blood, wobbling toward his technical knockout defeat to De La Hoya in June 1996. PHOTO BY AL BELLO/ALLSPORT.

Frustrated and often flailing at the defensive-minded Pernell Whitaker, De La Hoya, out of character, mocked Whitaker near the end of De La Hoya's disputed victory on April 12, 1997, in Las Vegas. PHOTO BY JED JACOBSOHN/ALLSPORT.

A velvet-wrapped De La Hoya strolls into the ring before his blistering second-round knockout of an overmatched David Kamau on June 14, 1997, in San Antonio. PHOTO BY JED JACOBSOHN/ALLSPORT.

Wilfredo Rivera, oversized and overmatched, couldn't do much against De La Hoya in their December 6, 1997, meeting, except duck and hope De La Hoya missed. De La Hoya won by technical knockout in the eighth round in Atlantic City. PHOTO BY AL BELLO/ALLSPORT.

De La hoya flashing a thumbs-up at a charity event at his alma mater, Garfield High School, flanked by actor Esai Morales (far left), publicist Debbie Caplan (center), and Anthony Kiedis, lead singer of The Red Hot Chili Peppers.

Looking comfortable on some of the poshest golf courses in the world—including this one, Riviera Country Club in the Pacific Palisades—hasn't endeared De La Hoya to the core of Latino fight fans in East L.A. PHOTO BY J. D. CUBAN/ALLSPORT.

Two enormously successful white-collar fighters: De La Hoya, who has patterned his career after Sugar Ray Leonard, and Leonard, who has admired De La Hoya's rise, pictured in April 1994. PHOTO BY AL BELLO/ALLSPORT.

As both a tribute to his deceased mother and a way to avoid his opponents' eyes before the start of action, De La Hoya always stares to the sky during the pre-fight instructions. Here, De La Hoya ignores Genaro Hernandez before their September 1995 fight. PHOTO BY JED JACOBSOHN/ALLSPORT.

to the left. Paez's eyes blinked in pain. That was followed up with a short right to Paez's nose, and, as Paez's head dipped down, De La Hoya ripped a glancing left hook to the side of Paez's head, jolting the older fighter backward. Paez was teetering and tried to avoid any more shots, but De La Hoya fired another left to the side of his head, as Paez's knees buckled. He wasn't down yet, but he was barely hanging on.

A few seconds later, with Paez still trying to regain his senses, De La Hoya sent a left to Paez's chin, and Paez crumpled like a balloon out of air, slowly and exhaustedly, to the canvas. His feet weren't knocked off the ground, but the rest of his body just fell flat to the mat, and his head toppled forward, straight to the canvas.

As Paez rolled in agony onto his side, then his back, his hands over his face, De La Hoya threw his left hand into the air.

By the time referee Richard Steele reached the count of two, it was obvious. At nine, Paez moved his hands off of his forehead, but made no attempt to rise. It was over, thirty-nine seconds into round two. And De La Hoya had his second WBO title, and a victory over an until-now respected opponent. Twenty-five seconds later, Paez was still down, his eyes still closed.

The crowd murmured in frustration, and there were loud boos after the fight was waved off. Was Paez just going through the motions? "Fix!" several people shouted. But those quieted a bit when the large-screen replays showed that some of the punches—which looked so quick and so glancing live—did land solidly, and probably did cause some pain.

"I call the punches forty-fives," De La Hoya said afterward of his quick, half-hook lefts, "because they come at forty-five-degree angles when I throw them right." And they did the damage of bullets fired from a gun.

Still, it was unclear exactly what De La Hoya had proven on this night: That he was a terrible destroyer, capable of wiping out a cagey veteran with what appeared to be glancing blows? Or that Paez was in it for the payday, and once he found a safe place to fall, there he went?

Probably it was a combination of the two. De La Hoya did wound Paez, and though the shots were not the kind that usually sent a fighter like him out (earlier Paez had been knocked down five times and gotten back up five times against Rafael Ruelas), they were the kind of punches that made a man not *want* to get back up for more.

"Coming into this fight I knew the whole world was going to be watching," De La Hoya said. "Afro-Americans, Anglos, Mexican-Americans. . . . I knew I had to prove to them that I can do a good job and I am a good, game fighter for them. You're always going to have critics, and it seems like in boxing there are those that still don't believe in me. But I feel very good about winning my second world title in just my fourteenth pro fight. There were a bunch of people who were saying to me that Paez is too experienced for me, that I wasn't ready. I think the Mexican fans were kind of confused about me, they didn't know who to cheer. But you see when I knocked him out, they were cheering me."

Ringside, George Foreman was impressed, too, by the shock knockout: "Only a Sugar Ray Leonard could do this."

Said a dazed Paez, through a translator: "I don't remember anything after getting knocked out. I don't remember the second round at all. De La Hoya was too strong and hit too hard. I've never been hit that hard by a punch before."

In the moments after the knockout, Joel Sr. couldn't contain himself. Things were going too well to stop him from traipsing through the media room headquarters at the MGM, singling out writers he knew and chortling.

"After this fight," Joel Sr. said, beaming, "all we've got to say is, *Who's next?*"

Hours later, De La Hoya and his friends marched down from a victory party in their suites and through the MGM. Where were they going? "To McDonald's," Alcazar said sheepishly. "Oscar wants Big Macs."

It was getting big. Now, the whole boxing world wanted to know the answer to the same question: Who *was* De La Hoya fighting next?

The De La Hoya camp knew who it wanted: Rafael Ruelas, the newly crowned International Boxing Federation lightweight champion from the San Fernando Valley, a tall, gangly fighter who had received a great deal of publicity as a young pro. Ruelas was born in Mexico, came to America when he was a child, and never thought about the Olympics, turning pro at seventeen to support himself.

The Ruelas fight moved from possibility to sure thing in the summer of 1994, when Arum bought out the company that promoted Ruelas and his brother, Gabriel, also a champion. Arum now controlled the two most bankable young Latino fighters in America—and he could make a huge star out of the winner of their matchup. The De La Hoya–Ruelas rivalry, though not quite as peppery as De La Hoya's with Genaro Hernandez, was brewing, because both knew that they were headed toward a collision.

Both trained in Big Bear, both at Larry Goossen's gym (run by the brother of Ruelas's trainer) right by the tiny airport. Sometimes Gabriel and Rafael would see De La Hoya during morning runs and wave. One afternoon in 1994, while both were preparing for fights, De La Hoya showed up at the Goossen gym a few minutes early, with Rafael still training. Joe Goossen, Rafael's trainer, jumped up when he saw the De La Hoya camp wander through the door, finished up with Rafael, then grabbed Alcazar.

"You fucking ever come early again," Goossen screamed at Alcazar outside the gym, "and I will personally kick your fucking ass! You got that?"

They got it. And they realized something, finally: If De La Hoya was going to keep using Big Bear as his training base, as the stakes rose, he couldn't keep wandering into other people's tiny gyms and living in rented houses. If he was a champion, he needed to copy Ali's compound in Deer Lake, Michigan. He needed his own house, his own training facility . . . or else always risk walking on other fighters' toes. By early 1995, De La Hoya already had plans for his Big Bear facility, and by late in the year, the compound would be completed. His own Deer Lake.

Meanwhile, waiting for the Ruelas deal to be completed, De La Hoya paced himself with two lesser-profile fights—knockouts against Carl Griffith and John Avila in November and December, respectively. The Griffith fight, on an MGM Grand Las Vegas card that also featured Ruelas, elicited one memorable example of De La Hoya's growing public confidence. In previous press conferences, he had always been demure about his opponent, speaking quietly and without rancor. But against Griffith, in the promotion's last press conference, he announced that he would "walk back to L.A. if I get hit with even one punch" by Griffith.

After the third-round knockout, De La Hoya grinned and pointed to a light scrape on his face.

"Okay, I'll walk one mile," he said. "I must say he hit me with one punch. I'll walk to the Excalibur."

De La Hoya was on a knockout spree—he had knocked out his last ten opponents. Team De La Hoya wanted Ruelas next, and in November 1994 the deal was cut, guaranteeing De La Hoya more than $2 million and Ruelas $1 million. It was a big investment, bigger than any two young nonheavyweights had ever commanded for a pay-per-view fight. The cable companies weren't sure about this one: Neither fighter had ever led a pay-per-view card before, and neither could be certain of drawing an East Coast audience. To pay for the purses, this fight would have to draw more than 200,000 pay-per-view buys, something that was anything but certain.

Arum wanted that fight to fall alongside the lucrative Cinco de Mayo celebration in Las Vegas, and he wanted more buildup. So Arum had to give De La Hoya another opponent in February of that year, one who could help his credibility but not endanger the Ruelas bout.

The choice was John John Molina, whom De La Hoya hadn't fought when Molina was the IBF 130-pound champion. But Molina, who hadn't lost a fight in almost five years, had recently moved up to lightweight, and badly wanted a shot at De La Hoya. Molina, a tough, tested, 36–4, also was cotrained by Lou Duva, which gave the promotion, named by Arum "Ready or Not," a neat little edge.

For fun and for tactical advantage, Duva jumped all over De La Hoya in the press conferences, questioning his intestinal fortitude and blasting him for walking away from Finkel after taking $100,000 from Finkel and Main Events.

"I don't give a shit what he thinks of me," Duva said. "What I have against him and his father is the way it was done. The way they abused Shelly, didn't give him the courtesy of sitting down and working it out."

Said De La Hoya, who earned $1.25 million for the fight (about $700,000 more than Molina): "I want to put the Lou Duva camp out."

For Alcazar, too, this fight had personal overtones. Alcazar had feared Duva's involvement in the Finkel offer back in 1992, and had steered De La Hoya away from Finkel because he fretted about Duva's meddling. Two titles and sixteen victories into De La Hoya's pro career, he was up against a Duva-trained fighter. Alcazar wanted to show the world he was ready for the moment. He not only wanted to beat Duva, he wanted to prove to the TV viewers that his advice was as legitimate and wise as any more experienced hand. To do that, Alcazar needed to speak English in between rounds, when the cameras peered in and the microphones picked up every syllable.

It was not a good choice. Born in Mexico, Alcazar usually spoke to De La Hoya in Spanish, he thought in Spanish, and though he could understand English perfectly, sometimes Alcazar struggled with the correct English words even in the most relaxed situations.

Meanwhile Molina—who used this fight to debut a new, startling hairpiece after losing his hair over the previous few years—was going through some of his own corner palpitations. Duva was the main voice in his corner, but Molina's older brother was becoming more involved in training, and both had been ignoring Duva for most of the past several weeks.

With Ruelas looking on calmly from ringside, De La Hoya came out firing at Molina, who immediately lowered his head and started a pattern of butting. De La Hoya howled in protest to referee Mills Lane, who for the most part let the roughhousing go unchecked. If the shorter Molina could stay inside and tangle up De La Hoya's arms, he could take advantage of De La Hoya's hesitant infighting and stay away from De La Hoya's dangerous hooks.

De La Hoya managed to throw off Molina for a few seconds in the middle of the round, and, furious from a particularly serious head clash, slammed Molina with a hard right to the chin that wobbled the challenger. Fifteen seconds later, still unsteady, Molina marched in close again. But this time he was a little slow, and De La Hoya landed a hard left hook with a following right that flung Molina off his feet and onto the canvas for only the third time in his long career.

But Molina hopped back up quickly and shrugged off the dizziness. He was not Jorge Paez, and he was not looking to avoid pain. He survived the round and never let De La Hoya get such a clean shot at him again for the rest of the fight. Instead, Molina frustrated and at times hurt De La Hoya, grappling with the taller fighter, getting under his chin, and hurtling his head up as he chopped at De La Hoya with obviously illegal shots to the back of De La Hoya's head. Lane either didn't see or didn't care about Molina's rabbit punches, as De La Hoya complained louder and louder.

De La Hoya ruled the second round, too, but it was clear Molina wasn't going anywhere soon. After the second, Alcazar glanced at the HBO camera behind him, then stumbled over his English: "Breath-breath-relax and breath, son," he said quickly. "You're working beautiful."

As the fight went on, it got even sloppier. Both fighters swung and missed, tied up in clinches, and started hitting each other in the clinches, before Lane could separate them. By the fifth round, De La Hoya looked a little tired from the wrestling, and his composure was escaping him. As a long chain of Molina elbows, head butts, and even some punches rocketed off all parts of his body, De La Hoya glared at Lane, giving up opportunities to score as he moaned for protection. After the round ended, Molina raised his arms in celebration and as a goad to further frustrate the younger fighter.

"Don't throw this fucking fight away!" Alcazar yelled to De La Hoya after the round.

Something was going wrong. Though De La Hoya still was landing the harder shots, suddenly, in the sixth, he started having problems breathing through his nose. Early in the round, after another Molina charge and butt, De La Hoya glanced over to his corner in exasperation.

After the sixth, De La Hoya no longer even looked at Alcazar.

"You're letting him in too much, son, don't let him in," Alcazar said. Then there was mostly tense silence. Finally, in a desperate half-whisper: "You've got to box, *mijo,* you've got to box!"

In the Duva corner: "Don't run in, John John! Go side to side. He can't take it in the belly."

De La Hoya gritted his teeth to start the seventh, and would later admit that about then he abandoned any coherent game plan other than brawling for survival. This was time to leap into battle. De La Hoya finally landed another meaningful combination in the seventh, nearly sending Molina to the canvas again. But Molina came right back at him and dug several shots to De La Hoya's body.

Before the eighth started, Alcazar was too nervous to speak, so the corner was silent as the fight seemed to slip away. De La Hoya stared straight ahead, furious.

"I was just going on instinct," De La Hoya said later. "Robert wasn't telling me anything. So I just had to win the fight on instinct."

In the last four rounds, the fight was up for grabs. De La Hoya's face was swelling, and his body ached. Molina wasn't in great shape, either, but he had been to the late rounds in title fights before, and he looked stronger, hardier.

As the fight went on before him, Ruelas smiled knowingly. Don't let Oscar lose now, Ruelas thought to himself, not before I get to him. This is somebody I can beat.

"It confirms what I've been saying about De La Hoya," Ruelas said later. "He lacks the experience and he doesn't take the initiative. He lets guys fight their fight. You saw what happened. Molina is not a big puncher, but he did hurt him a couple of times. If I hit him with a big shot, he's not just going to get hurt, he's going to go down."

Could De La Hoya lose this fight? By anybody's reckoning, after the dizzy De La Hoya middle rounds, it was a close fight, maybe Molina's fight by now. De La Hoya had to grab it back. De La Hoya had never been beyond ten rounds—and only into the tenth once, against Bredahl, who barely touched him and had nowhere near Molina's toughness and savvy.

De La Hoya flew into survival mode in the ninth, eagerly chopping away with illegal rabbit punches to answer Molina's own, and meeting head butt with head butt. He even snarled at Molina in a clinch, before De La Hoya flew into another attack. Lane was struggling to control this fight, and then he lost it. A few rounds later, Lane couldn't tug Molina loose from a clinch, screamed at him, and actually rapped him hard with his hand.

"Come on!" he urged in the tenth as both piled up the rabbit punches and inside wrestling moves.

Alcazar woke back up after the round. "Listen to me, Oscar . . . you've won the fight already, don't go tight with the motherfucker," he pleaded. "Don't risk the fight. Use the experience! Don't do that macho shit no more! You've won the fight already! Okay, son?"

But De La Hoya cast his eyes away and instead seemed to be listening to his friend Joe Pajar, who told him to keep attacking. Running on fumes, De La Hoya flew at Molina in the eleventh and slammed the tiring Molina with several punishing shots. Late in the round, De La Hoya, out of character and out of spite, taunted Molina.

"Be smart, son!" Alcazar said after the round. Then, in a panic, he looked at the microphone, then lowered his head and started whispering feverishly in Spanish.

This was De La Hoya's first journey into the twelfth round, and he discovered that it wasn't that bad. He felt energized by the challenge.

If the fight was in doubt, he rescued himself here, pounding the now stationary Molina to the body and to the head in the first minute, then throwing a raking left to the body that all but ended the Molina forward momentum.

"He didn't look pretty," respected trainer Teddy Atlas said of De La Hoya. "But he showed a fighter's temperament, I'll tell you. It got tough, it got ugly, it got testy. Molina was trying to frustrate him, rough him up. But in the long run, De La Hoya showed more than flash. He showed he had something of substance. Even though he didn't look pretty, he stuck his toes in the canvas and he did not submit. If he had it in him to submit, he would have done it in the Molina fight."

With 1:30 left in the fight, Molina was about to topple over, and instead he stumbled into De La Hoya and held on tight. De La Hoya screamed to Lane, "Get him off of me!" Molina stayed on his feet, but when the final bell rang, De La Hoya knew he had won the fight. And knew he had finally had his first real struggle as a pro. With an aching face and body to prove it.

The judges—Jerry Roth (who scored it 116–111), Chuck Giampa (117–110), and John Rupert (116–111)—all gave De La Hoya a decisive victory, though it felt like it should have been closer. As the scores were read, Alcazar leaped into Arum's arms, and De La Hoya moved away, climbed on the corner ropes, and gestured happily to the crowd.

According to CompuBox statistics, De La Hoya landed 115 more punches than Molina, and landed them at a higher percentage. It wasn't a thing of beauty, but it was a clear victory.

"I had to become a warrior," De La Hoya said after the fight. "John John's more experienced, but I should've boxed more.... I fought a very unintelligent fight. But, with only seventeen fights, nobody in their right mind would've gone up against a great fighter like John John Molina. So you have to give me a lot of credit because I went up against a great champion."

Could he survive this sort of performance against Ruelas? "Rafael Ruelas is going to be a tough fight," De La Hoya said. "But he has no balance whatsoever. If I catch him with a good left hand or a good right hand like we were exchanging back and forth, he's going to go and stay down."

There was work to do, however, and wounds to heal.

After the fight, De La Hoya skipped the press conference and grumpily ended up back in his hotel suite, as his left eye began to swell from the repeated Molina head butts. He couldn't sleep, his head hurt, and he moaned in pain. During that bleak night, Veronica sent out for raw steaks and put them on De La Hoya's eyes to keep the swelling down. De La Hoya had never been through something like this before, and he was scared.

De La Hoya froze when he saw himself in the mirror the next morning: "Will you still love me?" he said plaintively to Peralta. "Nobody will love me! Look, I'm ugly."

He didn't want to go downstairs, lest his fans see him. He was nearly in shock—not from the punches, or from the hurt, but from the bumps on his face, from the temporary scarring, marring his ultimate treasure. Never again, De La Hoya swore. I will never allow myself to get hit like that—to get marked like that—ever again. His face was too precious to be a punching bag.

There was more fallout from the Molina fight: As observers wondered if De La Hoya was just a blown-up gold medal winner without true boxing intelligence, Alcazar took the brunt of the blame.

"I would wait for instructions, and he wouldn't say anything," De La Hoya said of Alcazar. "I would hear the assistant, Joe, say things, but I would look at him, and Robert wouldn't say anything."

Later, Alcazar admitted to De La Hoya, "I know I didn't explain to you up in the ring. I felt nervous. I felt like I was in the Olympics again, very nervous for you, scared."

"He couldn't talk much," De La Hoya said of Alcazar. "I understand. He's learning."

Predictably, Alcazar reacted to the criticism by firing back. By chance and talent, Alcazar had been given the responsibility—and the joy—of training a prodigy. He understood he'd be scrutinized, but he was hurt by it. But he wasn't going to walk away, not even close.

"This is what I say: If all these people say that Oscar is green and that he makes a lot of mistakes, I say fine. I accept your opinions," Alcazar said after the Molina fight. "But there are over twenty gyms in the Los Angeles area, full of young fighters. If Oscar De La Hoya is not enough fighter for you, go ahead and make another one. Why aren't they making their own Oscar De La Hoyas? How come I am the only one?"

Alcazar was particularly pained by rumors in the Mexican press that the De La Hoya camp would soon be turning to Ignacio (Nacho) Beristain, widely considered to be the savviest trainer in Mexico. (Alcazar was widely considered to be the luckiest in America.)

"If we continue getting these results, I see myself up there with any other trainer," Alcazar said. "I beat Lou Duva, and look at the position he's got in boxing. I'm going to beat Joe Goossen. And I hope I'm going to have the opportunity with the one who calls himself the best trainer from Mexico, Nacho Beristain. What I say is I'd rather have what's in my bank account than have something on my wall. And I'll take my bank account compared to Nacho's any time."

From the Molina fight, De La Hoya went straight into preparations for the Ruelas showdown, set for May 6 at Caesars Las Vegas, which outbid the MGM Grand, as Kerkorian's casino saved its money to pay to become the fighting home of Mike Tyson, once he got out of jail.

This was a pivotal point in De La Hoya's career—he was past his management shakeup, and about to try to assume the mantle of one of the sport's top money magnets. If he could beat Ruelas, and draw major pay-per-view dollars in the process, at twenty-two, his place in the sport would be guaranteed. This was his moment, if he grabbed it.

"I really feel that I have, in Oscar, an emerging star," Arum said at the time. "I mean, Oscar was the victim of high expectations people had for him coming out of the Olympics.... If you lived through it and you remember all the stuff about 'Oscar's fighting bums.' But he wasn't fighting bums. He was an inexperienced fighter trying to find his way. He was matched very, very well, and he was in the spotlight all the time. And then of course, when he fought a real top-of-the-line professional in John Molina and handled him, I thought, relatively easily, I think that's when he made his bones.

"Oscar really relishes this moment. This is a guy whose not intimidated by the moment. This is what he's been living for. He's a superstar, and a superstar wants as many bright lights on him as he can. It's about more than the money, it's the idolization. I look at the parallels between his career and Ray Leonard's career. Ray had three crowning fights: Ray had the [Wilfredo] Benitez fight, which was like Oscar's Molina fight; then he had the Duran fight; and the Hearns fight. The Hearns fight, I think, was certainly his crowning moment. He was down, Hearns was beating him, and he showed guts and he came back and won the fight."

In other words, Leonard finally earned his Hall of Fame credentials by testing himself against the best of his era—losing a few fights along the way—but valiantly rallying back in the face of the most savage odds against Hearns. Which is why, Arum plotted, Ruelas was a perfect rival for this point in De La Hoya's career. Exactly because so many people questioned De La Hoya's heart, and admired Ruelas's grit, this was the fight for this time.

"In Rafael, I had a fighter whose biggest asset was his heart," Arum said. "I mean, Rafael's a very, very good fighter. But he's also very vulnerable, and what gets him through and makes him as good as he is, is his incredible heart, the fact that he can recover from punishment and come on. But I realized with a fighter, maybe he's not going to be around forever. And this was his opportunity for a big payday, it was a match that was just a natural, there was a gentlemanlike animosity between them. It was my feeling that I couldn't conceive down the line that there would be a better opportunity of making this fight. It wasn't that I could say a year from now that the fight would be bigger. I thought the time was propitious, everybody would recognize it as a big fight, and it's really taken off.

"I think Oscar's ready. And I think that he's in a position now where he's going from really good to great. . . . He really shows a new kind of maturity. He's not as suspicious, he's not as money-driven. He's more relaxed with himself. . . . I mean, you've got to realize for a twenty-, twenty-one-year-old kid, this all must've been terrible, everybody pulling at him, pushing at him. That was a disaster waiting to happen. But once Hernandez was in the picture, I felt that would straighten itself out because Hernandez spoke so much sense and he commanded so much respect in that community."

There was a difference in De La Hoya during these days. With some of the biggest crises gone by, his twenty-first birthday long since past, and the Olympic glory now a fading memory, it was time for reassessment—and for finding a new passion in life.

If you're going to make big deals, and deal with big businessmen, Hernandez told him, maybe you ought to try golf. On the golf course you can socialize with corporate executives and stay away from the East L.A. catcalls, Hernandez said. And you might find you like the game.

A few times out on the course after the Molina fight, and De La Hoya was in love. He loved the culture—the wide open spaces, the male bonding, the pressure putts—and he loved the challenge of the game. Immediately, he talked about playing enough to qualify for the Senior Tour by the time he turned fifty, or maybe even the regular tour once he retired from boxing. He joined Hernandez's club, the Friendly Hills Country Club, and hit the links every moment he could. Golf was all about focus and isolation—and De La Hoya couldn't have found a more perfect fit.

"I'm into it now, I'm really into it," De La Hoya said. "Because you can retire at fifty and go into the Senior PGA and still make a ton of money. It's just that the sport is very challenging. It's a mental game, you don't get hit, you can make money, get exposure, all that stuff. The golf course is where you don't get mobbed by people, you don't sign autographs . . . that's where you can go out there and focus and pay attention.

Golf is very frustrating, that's what I've learned. You have to keep on with it, never give up, because if you give up in the first week, then you'll never know how good you can get....

"I think boxers should get into golf more. First, it could create a cleaner image for boxing, and boxers have this eye coordination with everything. It's there, the timing ... everything's there. I think I'm the only boxer right now that's playing golf. The only one that's playing is Sugar Ray Leonard, but he's retired."

If it kept De La Hoya off the freeway and out of the nightclubs, Arum, for one, was all for De La Hoya's golf exploits.

"Tommy Hearns used to give me a heart attack driving around in these racing cars," Arum said. "Or Toney and these other guys used to play these serious games of basketball.... I'd rather him play golf than do the other things. They've got to do something, or else they get in trouble."

Golf was just part of the new De La Hoya look on life. With Hernandez prodding him, De La Hoya started glancing into his own future beyond boxing. His life had always been all about boxing, and only about boxing. But eventually he would have to get out. With the Molina fight fresh in his mind, he *wanted* out before his face was ruined and his bones beat down. De La Hoya looked around at some of the heroes of his youth—the sad Arguello, the tired Chavez, the embarrassing comebacks of Leonard, the disturbing Ali—and swore to himself that he would avoid those paths. De La Hoya was rich enough to do what few boxers ever could: walk away on his own terms.

"I would say I'll retire at maybe twenty-six, twenty-seven, about that age, depends, maybe I'll get tired of boxing earlier, or maybe it'll be after, you never know," De La Hoya said. "Maybe one fighter hurts me really bad or something. But around that age, twenty-six, twenty-seven, that's when I'm really focusing on. Make enough money, play it smart, and not work at all for the rest of my life. Go into golf, and win money there.

"I'd say most of the fighters think about living the fast life, having a few dollars in their pocket and spending them on whatever, new clothes, a car, and that's it, it ends there. I think about the future. I think about when I retire. I want to retire good. I don't think about having a fast life for one year and that's it, it's over. Then I have to go work at McDonald's or something. . . . I look at the mistakes of other fighters, and I learn. I just don't see myself like that. Because I have the right people behind me."

If talking about retiring before he got hurt made him seem soft in boxing's harsh light, De La Hoya suggested that he could take it. It did not mean that he was short on the desire to win, to absorb punishment if that's what it took in the ring, or to be a warrior. Sometimes, it was convenient to see him as a windup soldier—bigger and stronger than everybody else, but missing something burning inside. Asked once if he burned to win, De La Hoya dropped his fork at breakfast, and, for once, stared straight at his interviewer.

"I don't lack the hunger," De La Hoya said. "My record is clean, my record is undefeated, so I'm doing something right. If I wasn't going in with any hunger, then what am I doing in the ring? I go in with hunger, but people just don't see it. I show it with my fists. I knock these guys out. I beat these guys and that's it. I want to be like Sugar Ray Leonard. I would like to be the way he made his money and was very smart— exactly like that. Stay clean. I think he got cut one time. That's it."

But, his interviewer reminded him, Leonard ignored logic and came out of retirement three or four times, looking sadder and sorrier each time. De La Hoya heard that and sighed.

"Yeah, he did, and that wasn't very smart," De La Hoya said. "But I don't think it was because of money. I think it was because of the love of the sport, the attention. I hope I don't have that problem."

Joel Jr., as usual, knew what his little brother was really saying. Oscar said he wanted to retire quickly, but also said he wanted world titles in six different weight divisions. There was no way even Oscar De La Hoya could pull that off in less than four or five more years of fighting.

"He wants to get out clean, that's what he wants," Joel said. "He's already building the status. I wouldn't want to get all messed up, either.

He wants those six titles in a couple more years, because he doesn't want to be like those other fighters. And a lot of people criticize him because he's not in there with all those blood-and-gore fights like everybody wants to see, because he just doesn't want to get hit like that. He just refuses."

Would Oscar ever get himself into a war to prove that he was great? Joel shook his head.

"That's a tough one," he said. "He just doesn't like to get hit."

Oscar was reshuffling his life in other ways, too. In a very symbolic move, before the Ruelas bout, De La Hoya bought his own luxury condominium in Whittier—about twenty minutes away from Montebello. For the first time in his life, De La Hoya was truly on his own and out from his father's watch. It had grown increasingly uncomfortable in the Montebello house because Joel Sr. had remarried, ironically, to a woman named Cecilia.

"Anybody but that name, you know?" Oscar said, shaking his head. "Of all the names . . ."

With Ruelas, finally, De La Hoya was facing a peer. Only a few years older, a little taller, and with a nice record of defeated opponents, Rafael Ruelas was somebody even De La Hoya recognized as a near equal. Ruelas wasn't washed up or tiny or timid—De La Hoya had to be at his best to win this one. De La Hoya knew Ruelas; Ruelas knew De La Hoya. De La Hoya and Alcazar got the idea of training in Big Bear from Ruelas and Joe Goossen. And De La Hoya knew that Ruelas, while a bit awkward, feared nobody, and had a far larger following among the Latino fight crowd than De La Hoya.

Maybe because of these pent-up worries, the weeks in Big Bear leading up to Ruelas were strange and tension filled in the De La Hoya camp.

There were a few threats made in phone calls to Hernandez's office—the new home of the Oscar De La Hoya Fan Club—and a few times, confronted by taunting fight fans or chased by overaggressive females, when De La Hoya felt uncomfortable out with only Pajar and a few other friends. It was time, Hernandez felt, for De La Hoya to hire some bodyguards. Their first, best option was a big, burly twenty-four-year-old man from Montebello named Eric Purvis, who apparently got to know De La Hoya from a mutual friend—an actor from the NBC teenage sitcom *Saved by the Bell.* Purvis said he was a police officer and had the badges and guns to prove it. He swaggered like a cop, talked like a cop, and De La Hoya felt safer around him, mostly because Purvis surely was a man who wasn't afraid to use some effective violence.

Oscar, Joel Jr., and Pajar were stunned and excited when Purvis showed them his arsenal of weapons, and laughed when Purvis said he could protect them from anybody. Hired before the Ruelas fight, Purvis quickly became De La Hoya's shadow—wherever De La Hoya appeared, at a publicity shoot, at a restaurant, on his runs, on the walk to a fight—Purvis was there behind him, smiling for the photographers and casing the crowd like a Secret Service agent. Purvis's smile ended up on the cover of *Boxing Illustrated,* standing right behind De La Hoya, when the magazine named him its Fighter of the Year.

There was always something sly and mysterious about Purvis, though. On the streets of Montebello, he was known as "John Wayne," a vigilante who liked to pull over suspected gang members and rough them up. Purvis was arrested twice. On the first occasion in March 1996, according to Burbank police, he dressed in an LAPD uniform, complete with a loaded pistol, went to actor Richard Lee Jackson's house, and tried to interrogate him. At the time, Purvis said he was there to "play a joke" on Jackson. Purvis was released on bail, and resigned from any position with the LAPD.

Purvis had worked at a local fire department, and he was an LAPD "technical reserve officer," which meant that he had gone through training but was not authorized to conduct investigations, carry a gun, or use a squad car.

All the while, he was working for De La Hoya. But the Jackson arrest gave police a thought: Was Purvis the man who masqueraded as a cop between August 1995 and May 1996, stopped gang members on the streets, searched them, drove them around in his car, then dropped them off far away from where they were picked up? According to one probation report, the bogus cop, "John Wayne," pointed a gun at two brothers and threatened to kill them before letting them go.

Purvis was arrested again on June 4, 1996, and bail was set at $2 million. He entered a no-contest plea a few months later. The judge, a former LAPD officer, gave him a two-year prison sentence and orders for Purvis to undergo psychological testing.

Publicly, it was never disclosed that Purvis was so closely associated with De La Hoya for most of the time in question. And De La Hoya later insisted he had no idea that Purvis was engaging in any illegal activities. In fact, De La Hoya worried for his own safety—would Purvis stalk him, too? De La Hoya fired Purvis, then hired several more bodyguards, to protect him from his fans and from his old bodyguard.

But in spring 1995, with the Ruelas fight coming up, Purvis was a huge part of De La Hoya's camp, serving as part-bodyguard and part-gatekeeper, eagerly keeping almost everybody away from the camp and the fighter. Up at camp, De La Hoya was more and more isolated, dreaming of the day he didn't have to rent a cabin or go to a public gym, when he could just train by himself, alone.

With their father pushed to the background by the management flap, Joel Jr. was Oscar's main family bond—Oscar still idolized his big brother, and still wanted him around as much as possible. But Joel was eternally restless and looking for the next good time.

Around this time, Joel crashed and totaled the team van, the one with the GOLDMINE license plates, and Hernandez angrily demanded that Joel seek alcohol counseling. Oscar, not for the last time, made a passionate appeal to the judge in the drunk-driving case, and Joel was not punished harshly.

Sometimes Joel brought his friends up to camp, and they drank and screamed all night long, as Oscar tried to get his rest. Sometimes Joel just disappeared for days, before reemerging, desperately needing sleep.

"Joel is an addict," Mike Hernandez said, disgustedly comparing him to Dodger Steve Howe's travails. "Oscar needs him, Oscar loves him, and Joel is never there. The family is a mess."

Said a former close friend of Joel Jr.: "He's drinking to escape reality. He's living in Oscar's shadow his whole life, wasn't he? I mean, his whole thing is he wanted to play baseball and his dad couldn't give a shit if he went to baseball practice or not because he was so concerned with Oscar. So it was like he was the black sheep living in the shadow of his brother. Bitter because he didn't get to do it.

"He'd always say, 'You know, I was boxing first. Oscar couldn't even punch when he was little. And he would cry. He was a sissy.' I think Joel was just living in his shadow, just couldn't hold up to the image. He could've left. He could've taken the money and done his own identity. But he couldn't. He was too weak of a person. He didn't have anything without that name and backing."

Oscar, though, always made sure to take care of his older brother. Joel Jr., who was often missing from camp and who provided little in Oscar's corner during fights, was cut in for a 4.5 percent cut of all of Oscar's purses. And that only kept up his self-destructive moments and his wild quests for attention.

Said the former friend: "There was one time when they went out drinking and he was coming out and getting off the freeway right at the off-ramp to his house and the cops pulled him over. He was speeding, over a hundred, they ran his plates, saw the name, let him go. He was like, 'I just drank a little bit.' And they would let him go because of the name. He'd say he was invincible, nobody could touch him."

But it wasn't his name that was getting him out of trouble. Not *his* name.

"I am always getting him out of trouble," Oscar said quietly of his brother. "Always. I think it made us closer. Because I'd do anything for my brother. I've gotten him out of some trouble. Big time. I'd do anything for my brother and he'd do anything for me."

Said Veronica Peralta of the brothers' relationship: "I think they love each other. But I think they're very resentful of each other. When Joel would get drunk, and Oscar wasn't around, he'd say, 'Hah, Golden Boy?' I think he was angry that maybe his brother fulfilled the dream that his dad wanted him to fulfill."

Joel Jr., though, made a point to be around the camp for the Ruelas fight as much as he could. Oscar still felt angry with their father for the management crisis, and Alcazar was becoming an increasing irritant. Behind his back and to his face, Joel and Pajar made fun of Alcazar, giggling about the way he talked and the eagerness with which he grasped onto the De La Hoya dream. Oscar himself signaled his cooling feelings toward Alcazar by deciding that Alcazar, for the first time since they started going up to Big Bear, would not live in the same cabin as he, Pajar, and Joel.

After the mute performance against Molina, Joel Sr. himself fretted all over again that his son was getting amateurish training from Alcazar. So, for the second time in a little over a year, the De La Hoya inner circle reached a consensus: Alcazar was not the right man to lead De La Hoya's training. Alcazar, of course, resisted this tug fiercely. He had fought off Ortiz before, and he buckled down to fight another challenge.

Arum didn't initiate the move, but, listening to Hernandez, who was listening to Joel Sr., Arum played facilitator. He called his friend, Rafael Mendoza, a boxing agent with vast connections in Mexican boxing. This time, there was no way they would bring in a personality like Ortiz. This time, Arum wanted to make sure they brought in a low-key personality, someone who could work with Alcazar and let Alcazar take as much credit as he wanted. Upsetting Alcazar could upset the camp, they knew, because it had happened before.

"Robert's an excellent trainer, but you know, he's not Eddie Futch," Arum said, referring to the Hall of Fame trainer. "Oscar was not a fully polished fighter. There were a lot of things he was doing that were wrong."

And things needed to be fixed before De La Hoya faced Ruelas, a fighter with the power and tenaciousness to make De La Hoya pay dearly for obvious mistakes. If De La Hoya fought Ruelas as he had fought his last few fights—straight up, predictable—he could get beat.

Arum asked both his own matchmaker, Bruce Trampler, and Mendoza to draw up lists of potential training candidates for De La Hoya. "More or less," Mendoza recalled, "they were the same names. George Benton, Emanuel Steward . . ."

But the De La Hoyas wanted a Mexican if possible, and Mendoza had a candidate: Jesus Rivero, who trained the famous flyweight Miguel Canto—one of the best defensive fighters of his era—then disappeared from boxing to Mérida, his hometown on the Yucatán peninsula, when Canto retired in 1980. Arum, Mike Hernandez, and Joel Sr. all were immediately intrigued by the idea of this defensive specialist, whom they figured would not draw attention and could help keep Alcazar satisfied. De La Hoya had the power. Now he needed what Arum called "fine-tuning," and a trainer who could teach him some of the evasive tactics he lacked.

"Rivero was right because he knew how to teach," Mendoza recalled.

But, despite the interest, Mendoza wasn't sure Rivero would take the job. A few months earlier, acting at the behest of none other than Alexis Arguello, making his comeback, Mendoza had contacted Rivero, and the old trainer had refused.

"Please try," Arum told Mendoza. They wanted Rivero.

Loaded with tapes of De La Hoya's last few fights, Mendoza flew down to Mérida to meet with his old friend. When he showed Rivero the Molina fight, the little man stirred.

"I can see that the kid has potential," Rivero told Mendoza. "But he doesn't know nothing. He's out of balance. He doesn't use his reach."

So he'd train De La Hoya? "No, no, I am retired," Rivero said. "I am just telling you, he cannot do this, he cannot do that."

But Mendoza kept pushing. "I started working in his mind. I started challenging him," Mendoza recalled. Finally, Rivero gave a little ground. "Is he a nice kid? Is he a bragging guy?" Rivero asked Mendoza, who quickly shook his head. "Okay, I'll tell you what I'm going to do," Rivero continued. "I will see him and I will talk to him and I may stay with him, I may not stay."

After that meeting in Mérida, Rivero, on his own, flew to L.A. and met with Joel Sr. and Mike Hernandez at Hernandez's dealership. The next day, he was on his way up to Big Bear, to join the early stages of the camp and decide how long he wanted to stay.

"And the guy who was driving him was Mr. Alcazar," Mendoza said. Alcazar pounced on Rivero. "We don't need nobody to teach nothing here," Rivero remembers Alcazar telling him on the drive. "He's winning."

Rivero looked at Alcazar, puzzled. "Why is he telling me this?" Rivero thought to himself, and later recalled to Mendoza. "Why did he call me? Doesn't need a teacher? This guy was out of his mind. He's stupid. He thinks I'm going to take his job. Alcazar didn't want me here, he wanted to push me aside. I asked him, 'Where do I start? What should I do?' He said, 'I don't need you. There's nothing to teach. Oscar is the champion of the world, there's nothing to teach him. You're not supposed to change his style now.' I saw that he was wrong. There were a lot of things to teach him."

In his fit of fury, Alcazar accomplished exactly the opposite of what he wished. Rivero was uncertain before this conversation, but Alcazar's harangue provoked his stubborn spirit and challenged him in a way nobody else could.

Said Mendoza: "That made Rivero's decision to stay there. To prove that Alcazar was wrong. Not only for Oscar, it also was for Alcazar."

Up at Big Bear, because they of course couldn't share the Goossen gym with Ruelas, De La Hoya worked out in a converted karate gym about two miles away from Ruelas. In the first few days, Rivero showed up and watched De La Hoya work out, staring silently as Alcazar maneuvered to keep De La Hoya as far away from him as possible.

When a reporter showed up unannounced early in the training, Alcazar flushed in surprise, rushed over to Rivero, and pleaded with him to leave the building. Rivero, confused, did as he asked. Later that night, Alcazar told the reporter that Rivero was "just somebody I've hired to clean the floors." Meanwhile, De La Hoya, Joel Jr., and Pajar just rolled their eyes and laughed at Alcazar's uneasiness.

"Rivero realized that Oscar didn't respect Alcazar," Mendoza remembered. "He knew that Alcazar didn't know what to do in the corner. They used to make jokes about Alcazar giving instructions . . . you know, 'blah-blah-blah . . .' something nobody understands. They used to make jokes, Joel, Oscar, and the other kid, Pajar."

Rivero showed up, and Alcazar apparently even tried to make De La Hoya think that he was just a cleaning man. He was supposed to introduce Rivero to the fighter, but he didn't. He was supposed to explain that Rivero would be assisting training, but he tried to ignore him.

"Alcazar should've introduced me, but he never did," Rivero said later. "Two days after I was in Big Bear, Pajar and Oscar came and shook my hand. Robert never did that."

For two weeks, Rivero just watched, letting Alcazar run the training. Oscar would occasionally cast an interested glance over to Rivero, wink a hello, but Rivero stayed to himself, then went back to his own cabin. Alcazar would be too bothered if he made a move too swiftly. He knew about the Ortiz fiasco.

Then, at last, he asked Oscar and Pajar to come to his cabin after training, just to talk. He could tell they were intrigued.

"You probably don't even know my name," Rivero told them. "Do you know my name?" They didn't. They just called him "sir," or, in Spanish, *"don."*

"I was very careful," Rivero recalled.

"My name is Jesus Rivero," he told them. "I was the trainer and manager of Miguel Canto, Mendoza recommended me. . . . I want to tell you something. If you want me here, I can stay. If not, I don't need this. First, before I go, I want to tell you this: Your balance is wrong. You don't do that. This is wrong."

Faced with the blunt language, De La Hoya was momentarily startled.

"I want to prove to you why," Rivero said quickly. "It's very easy to say this or that. But it's very difficult to tell you the reason. I'm going to tell you how. And after that, I will leave." Rivero recalled later, "Then, Oscar started liking it. He started having the confidence in it."

Said Mendoza: "That's when the connection started. He was very clear since the beginning. Nobody talked to Oscar like that. Rivero liked to argue with him, like a teacher to a student."

As the camp wound down, De La Hoya was visibly changing his style—fighting more fluidly, moving back and forth with his hips, easily avoiding hard shots and flicking inside and out for his own counterattacks—and it was fairly evident that he had altered his training situation. The sparring partners started telling outsiders that there was a strange little man doing most of the training, while Alcazar fumed.

The rest of the De La Hoya camp was ordered never to disclose Rivero's name or hint that Alcazar wasn't totally in control. The only public title for Rivero was "the Professor," and beyond that, publicly, nobody would say a thing, in a not-very-subtle attempt to keep Alcazar from going crazy. Rivero wasn't even going to be in the corner for the Ruelas fight, or introduced at press conferences, or even recognized in public. But in the gossipy world of boxing, where nothing at such a high level stays secret for long, Rivero's name became public knowledge.

"We know he's insecure," Mike Hernandez explained of Alcazar. "We know he has a problem with that. He should be friends with Rivero. He shouldn't think they're going to take Oscar away from him. Oscar can't replace Roberto. Nobody can do what he can do for Oscar. No one will work harder to protect Oscar. They belong together."

Arum could only hope for peace in the camp, as Rivero helped De La Hoya along. Maybe, Arum wished, Alcazar could stay under control and actually learn from Rivero, who lived in Mexico, and at sixty-three was hardly in this for the long haul.

"There's plenty of room for Robert to learn," Arum said. "And one of the things 'the Professor' is doing is teach both Oscar and Robert. Listen, the best lawyers go to courses after practicing law. There's nothing wrong with that. Oscar was not a fully polished fighter. There were a lot of things he was doing that were wrong. And this polishes him up and enables him. . . . It's like opening a book and saying, 'Oh, my God, *right*!' And you keep learning as you go along. A lot of stuff, he got away from, stuff he had as an amateur and got away from. This guy was able to help teach that, so it came back."

Arum said that Rivero was not a publicity seeker, or a rambunctious personality like Ortiz. Rivero wanted to refine, not redo, De La Hoya.

"Ortiz had a completely different style of boxing and tried to make Oscar into that style," Arum said. "You can't do that. This guy doesn't do that. This guy improves what Oscar has."

Right there in Big Bear, Joe Goossen, Ruelas's trainer, couldn't help but see what was happening—and wonder if a change of trainers in De La Hoya's camp, announced or not, would throw De La Hoya off stride for Ruelas.

"I feel sorry for Robert. He's a nice guy," Goossen said then. "It looks like the inmates are running the asylum. A lot of people have been telling me it's a panic move. I think it's kind of a rotten thing."

In the big picture, Ruelas was just a single step. The final goal, as it had been from almost the beginning of De La Hoya's career, was Julio Cesar Chavez, the most famous Latino fighter of the era and a Mexican hero. The De La Hoya camp looked at Ruelas as a necessary precursor for Chavez. Ruelas wasn't as strong as Chavez, and was much more awkward. But he had a version of Chavez's hardheaded stubbornness, and a willingness to take shots in order to deliver them. And he could hammer.

Ruelas had passion. And Ruelas knew that De La Hoya's heart was his biggest question mark.

"He's doing it more for the money," Ruelas said, "than for the sport."

The Ruelas story was long familiar to L.A. fight fans: He was born impoverished in Mexico to a large family, then spirited across the border with his older brother, Gabriel, when both were under eight years old. The brothers ended up living in Sylmar, over the hills from Los

Angeles in the San Fernando Valley, where they learned to read. To earn money, the boys sold candy door to door. As the tale goes, thirteen-year-old Gabriel showed up at the Goossen Gym in Van Nuys selling candy, saw the fighting, and soon was a regular member of the gym. Rafael followed him, and soon the "Candy Kids," as they were relentlessly hyped by the Goossens, were born.

Gabriel was always the flashier, more athletically talented fighter; from their early days, Rafael was more of a plugger, a straight-ahead, give-and-take brawler. He was a gentle, humble person, naturally introspective. But he hit hard. Coming up to the De La Hoya confrontation, Rafael only had one loss—a freak knockout to journeyman Mauro Gutierrez, when Ruelas suffered a flash knockdown, then lost track of the referee's count while he looked over to his trainer and was counted out while he was still on one knee. In early 1994, Rafael beat his brother to a title, winning the International Boxing Federation lightweight title at the Forum in a crunching war with champion Freddie Pendleton. Ruelas crawled up from the canvas twice in the first round, wobbled several more times the rest of the way, but stormed back to take an incredible unanimous-decision victory.

Rafael Ruelas was not anybody's pick as the next Sugar Ray Leonard. But he was tough. He was taller than De La Hoya. And he was in his prime.

Once again, Alcazar brushed off the competition.

"I see Molina as better than Ruelas by at least 50 percent," Alcazar said. "Ruelas, he has a big heart. And, of course, he has a big punch. But basically, he's got no talent in this sport. He doesn't even know how to walk into the ring. What, is he going to dance like Muhammad Ali? No way."

Ruelas and De La Hoya fought several times in the amateurs—both won fights against the other. But that was when De La Hoya was twelve and Ruelas fourteen. When De La Hoya was readying for the Olympics, Ruelas was already a pro, and Alcazar was looking for some tough sparring. So a sparring session in the Goossen Gym was set up.

They went at it for a few rounds, to mixed reviews. But, as Ruelas sat in his rented Big Bear house a few weeks before the big fight, he said he had learned something important from that quick session.

"I learned he's not very strong up here," Ruelas said, pointing to his heart. "I learned that he doesn't like pressure, which is what he's going to get. He's always gotten it from me, and he'll get it again. And bringing in a new trainer shows me a little bit of weakness. He doesn't want to get hit. I don't like to get hit, either. But I'm going to be there. I'm going to take my shots and take chances of getting hit in order to hit him as soon as I can, try to get him out, the sooner the better. I don't see a way this won't be an action fight. His style is like Hearns's style, a counterpuncher, a hard puncher. And my style is go after it. . . . Things came a lot easier for him. Maybe they came too quick, too sudden."

De La Hoya was already rich, and he was barely twenty-two. Ruelas, who had been fighting professionally since January 1989, three-and-a-half years before De La Hoya won in Barcelona, was just starting to make decent money. In forty-four fights, Ruelas's previous high purse was $375,000. De La Hoya already had five fights that paid him more than that.

"That happens to most of the people who win gold medals," Ruelas said. "I don't feel it should, but that's the way things go. That's okay. This is the confrontation. After May 6, Oscar won't be there anymore."

De La Hoya was equally cold in his evaluation of the fight. "I don't see it going the distance at all. I'm too smart for him. Too smart. Even though he wants to go get into a brawl, I'm just too fast. I'm too strong. I'm going to keep on throwing until he just lays there. He's gotten up before, but a human can only take so much, you know?"

The bigger debate in the days leading up to the fight was about the potential impact of the fight itself. Was it a "regional fight" between two L.A. fighters who did not intrigue the East Coast, as ESPN's Charlie Steiner said (enraging Arum), or a fight that should stir memories of the Leonard-Hearns-Duran-Hagler glory days of the nonheavyweight classes?

HBO, which would broadcast the fight on its pay-per-view arm, watched and waited. Caesars Palace, for its part, kicked in $2 million to host the bout, as a big chunk investment in the power of De La Hoya's personality.

"You look at the pay-per-view figures, you ask the people in that end, they'll tell you the Hispanic buying audience is a very strong audience," said Caesars executive Rich Rose. "That is a fight audience that supports its stars. I don't think it's just beginning, I think it's begun. This is helping to take it to the next level. If you look at the dominant personalities who are Latino fighters—Duran, Chavez—neither one spoke English. These guys, they're well-spoken, good representatives of the sport, can speak the languages, and can make the transition. It has never happened before."

And after that night, there would be only one of them.

On the night of the fight, May 6, 1995, the omens were not good for Ruelas, not from the start. Though the threatened rain held back, the skies were gloomy, and the air was thick.

In the next-to-last fight, immediately preceding the main event, Gabriel Ruelas defended his World Boxing Council super-featherweight title against veteran Jimmy Garcia, from Columbia, who had trouble making weight in the days before the fight. But Garcia, beaten by Genaro Hernandez a few months earlier, had made it, and said that he was going to give Gabriel a rough fight. He was knocked out by Hernandez, and Garcia had sworn to his sister than he would never be knocked off of his feet again.

It was a disastrous fight. Garcia looked slow and listless, and Ruelas pounded him for ten long rounds, blasting shots off of Garcia's head throughout the bout. But Garcia would not go down. His brother shouted at him to stay up, to keep fighting, and Garcia, on wobbly legs, with blood oozing out of his nose in the 95-degree heat, did just that. Dangerously, but bravely, Garcia absorbed shot after shot, and Ruelas blasted away.

Finally, the fight was stopped. And a few seconds later, Garcia slumped down in his corner, sinking deep into unconsciousness. He cocked his head involuntarily back and to the left, against the corner post, and he would not recover. Miguel Diaz, working as a cornerman, screamed: "He can't hear me, he cannot hear me!"

Garcia lapsed into a coma, never emerged, and died thirteen days later.

But on this night, as the emergency medical personnel carried Garcia out of the ring on a stretcher, Oscar De La Hoya and Rafael Ruelas got ready to fight.

De La Hoya again lost the coin flip, and he had to go out first, even though they both were champions—De La Hoya held the WBO belt, and Rafael the IBF. In an act of typical boxing gamesmanship, Joe Goossen locked his door for an extra four minutes when it was Rafael's turn to come out, hoping to ice De La Hoya in the ring.

The odds were 2–1 against Ruelas. Gabriel hurriedly showered and changed so he could watch the fight. As part of his own gamesmanship, once both fighters arrived in the ring and referee Richard Steele called them to the middle for a brief conference, De La Hoya was careful to make Ruelas wait a few extra moments.

Rivero, as scheduled, was in the crowd, not in the corner, and Alcazar very showily clapped his hands on De La Hoya's back, or flicked away imaginary specks of dirt on De La Hoya's back, just to be touching him, to seem in charge. But the night before, Alcazar betrayed his true nervousness. In a Caesars bar with two reporters, Alcazar angrily railed at Rivero, and predicted forthcoming disaster.

"He's screwing up Oscar, I'm telling you," Alcazar snarled. "This guy is going to lose us the fight. He's going to get him knocked out with that shit."

Then the bell rang, and Ruelas tried to take De La Hoya's head off. Ruelas fired out of his corner and swung a hard left at De La Hoya, who bent away from it easily. Ruelas kept on charging, but, like in the Pendleton fight, he left himself open every time he threw one of his looping shots. And De La Hoya did not miss. He wasn't blasting away, but the punches De La Hoya was throwing were dead on the money.

The first big De La Hoya flurry came a minute into the fight, when a left caught Ruelas flush on the chin, sending him rocking. He stayed up, but he kept eating jabs, and could never put the effective pressure on De La Hoya that he needed. De La Hoya was too strong.

Joe Goossen tried to encourage his fighter at the break: "Beautiful. Rafael, you keep working. All right, you took a little shot, you got a little dinged, you came right back good. I don't want you to stop moving . . . give him a target either. Keep on doing it, you'll track him down."

As a measure of how accurate even his hardest shots were becoming, how much this was like target practice, De La Hoya landed forty-four of his eighty-nine punches in the round—Ruelas connected only on sixteen out of seventy-one thrown.

Ruelas stepped up the pace in the second, knowing that he had to hurt De La Hoya soon, or else he would be in deep trouble. And he snuck in a hard left hook about fifteen seconds into the round, but De La Hoya wasn't bothered by it and instead just kept up his body movement.

De La Hoya was in rhythm, bouncing back and forth, and ready for the swooping kill. He found it a minute into the round. Wading ever forward, Ruelas moved into De La Hoya, who shoved Ruelas off with his right shoulder, fired a glancing right to Ruelas's chin, then a picture-perfect left flush onto Ruelas's chin. The sound of impact was audible throughout the 16,000-seat arena, a *thud* that was clean and violent.

Later, De La Hoya would call it "the best punch of my career." It had to be the loudest.

There was no alternative, no way Ruelas could avoid what happened next: He rocketed backward, stumbling before collapsing to the canvas. Looking stunned, Ruelas rose from his back and was up at the count of seven. Steele checked his eyes, then continued the fight as Ruelas bounced once to regain his balance. But the end was near, and De La Hoya could feel it.

"I caught him flush on the chin," De La Hoya said, "so I was a little shocked he got back up. But I knew his legs were going to be wobbly. I knew if I feinted him to the body, I'd catch him to the head. And I knew it would just be a matter of time."

De La Hoya missed with a left as he flew at Ruelas, but landed a right to the chin, and Ruelas, who no longer had his feet under his own control, hit the floor again. He tried to get up, but was spinning on his knees in confusion. He put his arm on the rope to pull himself up, wobbling badly. But he made it to his feet at five, hanging on to the ropes, and Steele sent him back out. Ruelas had 1:23 to survive the round, and De La Hoya's eyes were wide in anticipation. De La Hoya crashed into Ruelas without fear and bashed three straight shots to Ruelas's face, as the skinnier fighter angled by instinct away and toward the ropes again, his hands covering his face.

Finally, De La Hoya threw four blistering shots at the helpless Ruelas, one of them pointing Ruelas's chin to the sky, his mouth clenched, just trying to stay on his feet by force of will. But Steele aptly stepped in at that moment, 1:43 into the round, and stopped the fight as Ruelas spread his arms in protest and Joe Goossen leaped into the ring to argue.

De La Hoya jumped for joy—his biggest show of emotion since winning the gold medal—and happily flexed his muscles to the crowd.

In Steele's arms, Ruelas just shook his head: "No, no, no.

"I tried maybe to get things going faster than I normally do," Ruelas said later. "And he caught me with a good one. We knew he was fast and we knew he was strong, and we knew I would be coming at him. Which I was doing. I knew I had to get inside. He just caught me with a clean shot before I caught him."

It was a breakout fight in every facet for De La Hoya. He got his rousing triumph. He got his first non-WBO title. He crushed his first real rival. And, possibly most important, the pay-per-view numbers were astounding: 330,000 purchases, at $30 apiece, which meant that the fight grossed $10 million, topping several of the recent major heavyweight attractions. These were numbers that lifted De La Hoya's earning power in quantum fashion and made him the obvious rising heir to Chavez for the Latino boxing throne.

A week after the bout, De La Hoya flew to Cabo San Lucas with Mike Hernandez (and without Peralta) for a golf trip, his first visit to the resort that would become his favorite place in the world. There, he heard scraps of news about Garcia's condition.

"I think he's going to be all right," De La Hoya guessed. "I really hope so."

And there he was feted like a conquering king, toasted and saluted by the tourists and the locals. In quieter moments, he and Hernandez argued about Veronica. Hernandez worried that he would be tying himself down just when he was at his peak—when he could have any actress he wanted, and when a wife would only complicate the business and the marketing.

"Are you going to marry this girl?" Hernandez asked angrily.

"I know," De La Hoya argued sternly, "Veronica's the one I love. She's the only one. I've made up my mind."

But as Hernandez continued to critique her, De La Hoya fell silent, and his eyes turned down. Then he went back to the revelry.

"I think it was the Ruelas fight that changed him," Peralta said later. "I guess boxing is a sport where you have to get psyched up to where you believe you're the man. But he got more and more into that hype out of the ring. He went through all these power trips after that fight. He kept telling me that I was the luckiest girl in the world to be with him. 'I'm the man, I'm the shit, everybody wants to be with me.' I loved him, but you don't want to hear that. As time went by, he was so egocentric and so full of himself. The more full he was, the emptier I felt."

chapter eight

Rivalry

Distinctly out of character, but with cold sincerity, Oscar De La Hoya peered into a camera and said he hated Genaro (Chicanito) Hernandez. "I hate his guts," De La Hoya said a few weeks before he was to face his bitter rival at Caesars Palace. "I've never hated an opponent more."

Which seemed funny to Hernandez. Why should De La Hoya, the kid who had been handed titles and delivered millions, hate *him?* Hernandez stood up in the ring on September 9, 1996, thinking about that. He hates me? "What did I ever do to him, anyway?" Hernandez said the day before. "Steal his girlfriend?"

What did I ever do?

"They said, 'Oscar doesn't like you,'" Hernandez retorted. "I said, 'Yeah, I'm glad he don't like me. Because I like women.'"

Hernandez danced and jogged as he waited in the ring, waving to the crowd. Okay, he thought, maybe it's not my crowd, but it's definitely not Oscar's crowd. They were there to boo De La Hoya. Fine.

"They're going to be cheering for me only because I'm fighting Oscar," Hernandez said earlier. "A lot of the people, they don't like me that much. But I think he's gotten bigheaded, and the people just want to see him go down. I'm their vehicle."

And this fight was his vehicle.

Hernandez wanted what De La Hoya had. For years, Hernandez wanted it. And finally, after the offers and taunts and promises, Hernandez had the chance to take some of it for his own, some of the fame and the money. Most especially, with the big house and the big house mortgage and the wife and the little daughter, Genaro Hernandez wanted and needed the money.

"This is like my lottery ticket," he told himself. "Oscar is my lottery ticket."

This is why, though those who did not follow the ways and moods of the L.A. boxing community could have never guessed it, the Hernandez fight was the most impassioned of De La Hoya's career. De La Hoya trained for it the hardest, worried about it the most, and ached to win it more than any of them since the Olympics. He burned to beat Genaro (Chicanito) Hernandez, burned to hurt him, to humiliate him. He knew him best. He hated him most.

Why? Because, in the hearts and eyes of the community of fighters they both came from, Hernandez was the anti-Oscar: the fighter who received the raw end of the financial deal, who persevered the longest, and who was changed the least by his ultimate success. Hernandez was the kid from the streets, with a smile. He had a huge, rambunctious, and loving family. He had a brother who was his closest friend and most trusted adviser. He had a wife and a daughter he cherished. He had a fighting style that made up for physical attributes that did not include overwhelming speed or power. He could never be an Oscar De La Hoya.

For all these things, good and bad, Hernandez was the fighter, and the man, Oscar De La Hoya could never quite figure out how to be. Every moment he spent in L.A. was a reminder of that. The gyms were full of Hernandez's friends. The streets were full of his fans. The world at large followed De La Hoya. The boxing community of L.A. was Hernandez territory. It was as if Hernandez was stalking him, chasing him, and always highlighting what he wasn't.

It did nothing to harm the contentiousness that De La Hoya had attended Garfield High in East L.A., and Hernandez had gone to Roosevelt, which was on the South Central side of town. The two schools—with two of the largest enrollments in the nation—were bitter rivals, the twin Latino teenage tribunals of the Southland, and Arum played it up, holding press conferences at both Garfield and Roosevelt before leaving for Las Vegas.

But this wasn't really about high schools. This was about symbolism and character and aggravation. Just the way Hernandez talked about De La Hoya . . . it was so deeply detailed, so studied. So irritating to De La Hoya, who listened intently.

"Everybody talks about him being so strong," Hernandez said, "but if he really is a knockout puncher, how come he hasn't laid out anybody flat? I see they stop the fights, but I haven't seen anybody stay down. I'm not sure about his strength. He hit John Molina flush on the jaw, and Molina gets up—and he's a 130-pounder. He hits Ruelas flush on the jaw, Ruelas gets up. So I mean, I saw him against John Avila, he was beating his brains out, but he didn't knock him out. Narciso Valenzuela, he could've gotten up, but he told me his ear was kind of numb and that was why he didn't get up. That guy from Denmark, he got up. That tells you Oscar's not as hard a hitter as everybody thinks. I give him that he has good conditioning. But other than that, I haven't seen that really powerful punch everybody should be afraid of. He's quick, he's strong because he's young, but is he smart enough for me?"

So this was a brawl between two familiar opposites, intimately knowledgeable about each other, and intrinsically opposed. So De La Hoya burned to win this fight. Genaro Hernandez was an obstacle— not to becoming nationally famous or being recognized as one of the best fighters in the world. Hernandez was a mental obstacle. A natural rival. Beating him would equal beating all the neighborhood kids who booed him—who even tossed an egg at him at his own Garfield appearance; beating him would explode De La Hoya beyond the reach of anybody in L.A.

Burned . . .

At twenty-nine years old, middle aged for a fighter, Chicanito Hernandez had his chance September 9, 1996, at Caesars Palace in Las Vegas, to reroute the course of boxing.

He was better prepared for this, by far, than the slow and gangly Ruelas. Why not Chicanito? If someone was going to knock off the

Golden Boy, it should be someone from the neighborhood, someone who stuck to the neighborhood, who trained in the neighborhood. Who had to scramble for everything, scramble harder than anybody else. He had scrambled all the way here, to Caesars Palace, at dusk, with Oscar De La Hoya standing in the opposite corner.

"This is the biggest fight of my career," Hernandez said during his training. "This is the fight that's going to tell me if I'm going to be making bigger money or if I'm going to stay where I'm at. And I don't want to stay where I'm at. People think I'm a millionaire, and I tell them, 'If I was a millionaire, I wouldn't be fighting.' My brother asked me, 'If you won the lottery, would you still be fighting?' Because he's into all this. I say, 'Are you dumb or what?' *Of course not.* I'm here to make money, not to get beat up. I play the real lottery, and I hope I win it."

It was about a man trying to make a living for his family. So Hernandez burned to win this fight. De La Hoya was the obstacle to Hernandez making real money, big money, retirement money. De La Hoya was the strong kid who was already a millionaire, before he was twenty-three. De La Hoya was the cocky kid who left the neighborhood as fast as he could. The natural rival.

"I think the money got to him," Hernandez said. "Everybody that knows him and they talk to me, they go, 'You know what? He's changed a lot. He thinks he's it.' I'm not surprised that happened to him. I'm glad he's making the money, but it shouldn't be getting to his head. Because people hate him. I went to the DMV today, people said, 'When are you going to drop him?' I think that's what people are waiting to see. Been waiting for the longest time. They didn't think Rafael was the fight he needed because Rafael didn't last longer than four or five rounds. With all due respect to Rafael, I think I would give him a harder time. I can fight him inside and I can fight him outside.

"I've got a little more pressure in this one, because a lot of people want to see Oscar go down, and they think that I'm the person to do it. Hopefully, God willing, I am the person to do it."

Chicanito was the father with a mortgage to pay, who drove a Camry —with a baby seat—not a Corvette. He was the one who actually went to the DMV. He was the one who moved to an airy house in a Mission Viejo cul de sac because he wanted to make sure his daughter grew up safe.

Said his wife, Lilliana: "He's not in there because he likes it—he's in there because he saw that as a way to make good money. Hopefully, he can wrap it up soon."

De La Hoya had character, but nothing made De La Hoya seem like more of a soulless creation of media and muscle than comparisons to Hernandez. Hernandez had fame and some degree of wealth, but no one made Hernandez seem like more of a luckless scrambler than De La Hoya. They were the perfect pair.

Hernandez had to move up from his natural 130-pound weight (and give up his long-held WBA junior-lightweight title) to get this fight; he had to wait two years and bargain Arum up to an acceptable payday. All along, he had to listen to De La Hoya deride him like De La Hoya had derided no other fighter.

"The way he's been talking, he's not showing any respect," Hernandez said. "He's disrespecting other people and he's disrespecting me. And hopefully we'll show him he has to have respect for people. I just found out in one of the interviews that he said he was going to punish me for six or seven rounds and he'll knock me out after that. Who does the guy think I am, a punching bag? I'm not going to stay there and get punished. Nobody punishes me. I'm a little more smart than that. If I see I don't have a chance, I'm going to do the right thing and just call it quits. I'm not going to go in there and get hurt."

Who does the guy think I am?

That, Hernandez figured, was what this fight was all about. It was the chance for L.A. to see who was real, and who was the brittle creation. To see what happened when De La Hoya was handed a difficult situation, when Genaro Hernandez threw punches that the Golden Boy had never seen before. To see somebody who knew he could drop Oscar De La Hoya. Who went into the fight sure of it.

For this fight, there was a chip on Genaro Hernandez's shoulder, and anybody who knew L.A. boxing knew why.

De La Hoya, too, seemed to sense some of this. For years, he had praised his next opponent, but found a way to jab at Hernandez. He called him "Generic" Hernandez, because his technical, tactical style rarely resulted in spectacular shows. He called him "Chickenita" because he charged that Hernandez was afraid to fight him.

Afraid? Hernandez had campaigned endlessly to get into this ring.

"He's just an ordinary fighter," De La Hoya said. "This guy's saying he never got respect and he got jealous because I came back from the Olympic Games and received all the attention and this and that. . . . It doesn't really matter. I beat this guy, and I move on. That's it."

Acidly and accurately, he pointed out that Hernandez didn't make big money because he wasn't a particularly interesting fighter to watch, all arms and defense, little star power.

"You have a boring fighter like 'Generic' Hernandez," De La Hoya said, "then people won't want to see you fight for the next one. You have to put on a good show, keep on thinking about the future. I fought Avila on CBS [last December] and my next fight was on HBO [in February against John John Molina]. We still have the best ratings on HBO. So, now that's going to get better buys for pay-per-view and my next fight after that is going to get even better buys. You have to keep on thinking that."

Now, as Hernandez stood in the ring and waited for De La Hoya, he had a chance to hit the Golden Boy.

One hundred three degrees of desert heat blazed off of the Caesars Palace outdoor arena floor—a tennis court, usually—creating not so much a furnace, as something like a giant blow-dryer . . . hard, heavy heat, bouncing upward, back up into the night. De La Hoya had been at the mall earlier in the day, drove there from his Desert Inn bungalow that sat right next to the famous golf course. Then he went to Caesars Palace and barely spoke a word for hours that led up to the fight.

"He wants to knock this guy out more than anybody he's ever faced," one friend of his said that day. "He wants to destroy Chicanito."

If De La Hoya's was the face the marketers saw when they thought of L.A. boxing, Hernandez's was the real face of the community sweat and struggle. Hernandez had literally stayed in place during his career, and the community loved him for it. A man who had battled through five surgeries to his fragile hands (fragile *hands* for a fighter!), he was the L.A. fighters' fighter, trained by his combustible older brother, in L.A., tossed into a sweaty gym with all the other fighters struggling and working and staring up at De La Hoya.

Where Chicanito trained became almost instantly the center of the L.A. boxing scene, because everyone else gravitated toward him. The best boxing was where he went. The L.A. boxing culture is tightly knit and full of talent. The gyms can change, but the champions find time for sparring with up-and-comers, just like Hernandez did with De La Hoya when De La Hoya was preparing for the Olympics, and just like Hernandez did with the cavalcade of local contenders, from the fighters coming in from Mexico for fights at the Forum to soon-to-be champion Shane Mosley of Pomona.

One hundred and fifty miles away, in Big Bear, De La Hoya trained in his newly built private gym, in the mountains, away from everybody else. The cabin was still under construction, on the same two-acre lot as the gym, which was already up and running. Around the site was a high black gate, and wherever De La Hoya moved, his bodyguards followed. De La Hoya only saw people by appointment, and imported his sparring partners from L.A.

"No way. I couldn't do that, I'd get bored," Hernandez said, talking about De La Hoya's mountain isolation. "The way I see it, it's the people who can't control themselves who are the ones that deserve to be put away like that. I don't do those things. My life is just going to the gym and back home, that's it. I don't go and party. I don't go drinking or anything else. I live a clean life. It may be kind of boring to everybody else, but it's the job."

Hernandez trained where he always trained—among the sweat and swearing of the L.A. gym scene. It was a fifty-mile commute from

Mission Viejo to L.A., but he couldn't be among his brethren any other way. And he was urged on by those same fighters: "Kick his ass, Chicanito!" "Beat up that pretty boy!" Hernandez heard that every day, every workout. He heard a lot. His wife, Lilliana, put a picture of De La Hoya on their bedroom mirror. "For inspiration in the morning," she said, chuckling.

"It's just like *Rocky IV*," she said. "You remember? The one where Rocky has to fight the big Russian fighter because he killed Rocky's friend, and the Russian is training with all this fancy equipment and expensive methods, and Rocky is in a barn with nothing. That's like Oscar, who has his own private gym and everything up in Big Bear. And Genaro, who's at the Brooklyn Gym."

The Brooklyn Gym—later closed down to make room for a restaurant's expansion—was as famous as it was tiny. It was two rings in a large garage on the property of a restaurant and a gas station. The main ring was about five feet from the parking lot, and the garage door was always open. Hot or hotter. And at just about two P.M. on just about every day, there was a war in there. It didn't matter exactly who was fighting whom, but it was always two skilled men, speaking Spanish, smiling, and pounding away.

The Brooklyn Gym is also where De La Hoya and Hernandez held their famous May 1992 sparring sessions, when Oscar was seventeen and Genaro was already the WBA junior-lightweight champion. Hernandez (23–0 at the time) was just warming up for his second title defense in Japan. (He won the title in France on November 22, 1991, by knocking out Daniel Londas.) De La Hoya was getting ready for the Olympic Trials.

"Robert Alcazar came to me one day and asked me if we could spar with Oscar," recalled Genaro's trainer and older brother, Rudy. "I told him, 'Hey, man, if we can help you in any way that can make him successful to get that gold medal, yeah, we'll put our share in.' Genaro had just come back from a fractured hand and had taken six months off.

"So Oscar gets in the ring and gets the better of Genaro. That was Tuesday. On Wednesday, he was getting the better of Genaro, then in the third round, Genaro hit him with a solid left hook and a right hand that kind of left him standing there, knocked out on his feet. Oscar left that day with a swollen cheekbone. And then the next day, Thursday, Oscar didn't show up. And then he didn't show up on Friday either. Then on Saturday, we read an article in the *Los Angeles Times* that he would knock Genaro out. We're like, what?"

In that article, which actually came out more than a week after the sparring, Alcazar was quoted in a happy, happy mood. "Oscar sparred a couple of days with Genaro Hernandez, but Oscar handled him easily," Alcazar said. "In fact, Hernandez told his people he didn't want to work with Oscar anymore."

Genaro Hernandez was not entirely pleased when he read that remark. At the time, he was L.A.'s only major world champion. And he was being disrespected. "I ain't going to help that motherfucker! Why didn't he come back on Thursday?" he screamed to his brother.

Rudy recalls of that period: "Genaro would've knocked him out of the gym if Oscar had come back." Genaro remembers: "He was always quick. But people, they come and they take advantage of me because I'm not ready, I'm not in shape. And when I'm in shape, they don't come back."

From that moment on, there was bad blood between the camps. And both sides knew there would be a time when they would face each other in the ring, for money. It couldn't happen any other way. De La Hoya and his family wanted it so badly that they considered making the pro debut against Hernandez, just to show clearly how little they thought of his experience.

"I've got to think he could've beat Genaro, but it was too risky," Alcazar said later. "It was too risky because of Genaro's experience. Even when we had the offer, we turned it down. Give us some time."

Hernandez and his family wanted it so badly, that each time the negotiations broke down, they egged on De La Hoya a little harder, and got a little testier. In 1994, Arum offered Hernandez $300,000 for the fight. Hernandez refused, knowing that this fight was worth more, that *he* was worth more. De La Hoya already had earned a $1 million purse by then, and Hernandez had never earned more than $130,000.

"Robert Alcazar started calling us 'Chickenita,' because we refused $300,000," says Rudy Hernandez. "And I'm like, that motherfucker!"

The combustible, garrulous older brother felt angry enough that he made a point of showing up at a De La Hoya press conference at the Biltmore Hotel in downtown L.A. and making his views known loudly and with a physical exclamation.

At the press conference, with a gaggle of reporters and cameras in the ballroom, Rudy charged at Alcazar. "Hey, you piece of shit, why are you talking all this shit? Why? Why? You think $300,000 is a lot of money?" Rudy screamed. "I'll tell what you can do for your $300,000. You can shove it up your ass."

Then Rudy put his hand on Alcazar's face and shoved him backward, and chaos broke out at the Biltmore. Before further festivities, Arum cut in and separated them.

The rivalry burned, white-hot.

"Those people are crazy," Alcazar said then. "I know we can beat them, but I am afraid of what will happen if they fight. They are crazy people."

On at least two occasions, Arum presented Hernandez and his handlers with offers to fight De La Hoya, but both were much lower than Hernandez thought he deserved. The first was for $250,000, the other for $300,000. So De La Hoya went off to fight Bredahl and Paez instead. Had Hernandez lost his chance?

"I was so mad at Genaro when he turned $300,000 down," Lilliana said. "How could he do that? But I guess he knew what he was doing. I'm glad he did it now, but back then, I was very upset."

Finally, Arum approached Hernandez in the summer of 1995 at, of all places, the wake for Jimmy Garcia, the fighter who had died after his beating at the hands of Gabriel Ruelas. Hernandez was there because he knew Garcia, had sparred with him, and had actually defeated him a few months before. But Hernandez had just fought Paez, and took eight rounds to dispatch him, on cuts.

"I thought it was over," Hernandez said of his De La Hoya chances. "But I think they saw my Paez fight and they figured, 'Well, if we can knock Paez out in two rounds, maybe we can take Genaro out, too.'"

At the Pond of Anaheim, the Orange County indoor arena, Rudy decided to advertise his distaste for De La Hoya as loudly as possible. When he walked into the ring with his brother, Rudy was wearing a T-shirt that read brightly and boldly: DE LA HOYA SUCKS. And there was a picture of a middle finger raised in defiance. The crowd loved it, burning with the same frustration: They wanted to see Genaro fight Oscar, too.

"A friend of mine made it and he let me have it," Rudy recalls. "I thought it could get more publicity. I put it on and I was walking at the Pond, making sure everybody saw it. And that's what got us the fight."

Genaro wasn't completely proud of his brother. In fact, he was embarrassed by the provocation.

"It was crazy," Genaro says. "I almost thought he was disrespecting them. Obviously, it was never my intention to have anybody who worked with me to go out there and act like that. I don't, so why should somebody else do it? But obviously, he did what he had to do to get the fight for me."

The T-shirt punctuated the emotion: If De La Hoya was to be L.A.'s signature fighter, he had to fight Hernandez. He could go and be famous and rich and incredibly celebrated, but in L.A. he had to fight Chicanito, or everything else didn't matter. By then, Alcazar and De La Hoya knew it.

"We were human," Alcazar remembers. "We were both proud of our jobs. And what happened to me . . . I kind of lost my control. I got into the fight like a fan. Because of the promotion before the fight. It was a big promotion, it was South Central versus East Los Angeles, and it was something personal. It was pride. It was personal."

But Arum was also reconsidering Hernandez's worth as an opponent after the financial performance of De La Hoya–Ruelas. That pay-per-view jackpot had put De La Hoya in a whole new strata, and Arum could afford to dole out a little more to fight a personal rival.

"For Oscar to accomplish what he wants to accomplish," Arum said, "he's going to have to beat all of these guys. I don't want anybody left saying, 'Hey!' So Hernandez is part of that business."

Rudy Hernandez said at the time, "If Oscar's so confident, how come he waited so long to fight Genaro? How come he made us wait until he got the fight at lightweight? Because he didn't want to fight him at junior-lightweight. That's our division. I think ego got this fight made. His ego couldn't stand it. And ego will be his downfall."

At the Garcia wake in Las Vegas, Arum guaranteed Hernandez a chance to challenge for De La Hoya's new 135-pound title, and guaranteed him what he had been asking for all along—$500,000. Hernandez didn't really care that De La Hoya would be making double that. At last, Hernandez was dipping his toe in the big money pool.

Once again, though, boxing luck went against him almost immediately. Though Hernandez thought he could get a waiver from the WBA to fight for De La Hoya's title at a higher weight, a few days after he signed for the fight he learned differently. The WBA told him that if he fought De La Hoya, he would be stripped of his 130-pound title—which he had held for more than four years, one of the longest terms in boxing at the time.

De La Hoya gets titles tossed to him, and Hernandez loses his because he is fighting De La Hoya?

"I worked so hard for the title," Hernandez said. "I mean, it's been a dream for me to own a title. And there are a lot of fighters out there who don't win one. It just doesn't seem fair. They asked me to write a letter asking for permission. I wrote a letter. They give me permission, I sign the contract to fight Oscar, a week later they turn around and deny the permission. So they can take the title, because the title's not going to pay my bills. This fight is."

Another piece of timing and luck: If Hernandez had taken the fight earlier for less money, he could have gotten De La Hoya at 130 pounds—when De La Hoya was punishing his body to make the weight and susceptible to early knockdowns. And before he hooked up with the Professor.

When fight time arrived, De La Hoya stayed in his dressing room trailer a little long, then finally ambled out, a phalanx of bodyguards circling him, and drew a rambunctious, very mixed greeting. Shrieks of joy from the girls, boos from some of their boyfriends, and loud applause from the Vegas high rollers, who knew whom they had come to see.

As De La Hoya climbed into the ring, with Alcazar making a show of himself to prove to everybody that he was still the man in the corner, Hernandez nodded. Here it goes, he thought.

Then, after the national anthem was played, he bent down to have his brother, Rudy, take off his cross necklace. As he did, it caught on his nose, and he winced in pain.

If you wince when a necklace comes off, it is not a good sign for when the punching starts.

Genaro had debuted professionally as an eighteen-year-old in September 1984, with no fanfare. Rudy by then was in semiretirement, and their father, Rudolfo, who had been Rudy's trainer, was training Genaro. But the best sparring competition for Genaro, even though he only weighed 130 pounds, was Rudy, who was tipping in at about 200.

Though Genaro quickly proved to be a skilled and adept fighter against Rudy or anybody else, his rise was further slowed by fragile hands. Altogether, in the years leading up to the De La Hoya bout, Hernandez had five hand surgeries—three on his right, two on his left, including an intricate fusing of several of his bones in 1994. Eventually, Hernandez just learned that he was going to have to adapt to pain in his hands.

"I didn't worry about it. The time came, either it's going to happen or not going to happen, you can't worry about that," Hernandez said.

And he had his brother with him, every step and moment of the way. Which somehow made the obstacles seem more bearable.

The oddsmakers did not give Hernandez's experience very much weight against De La Hoya—the younger fighter was a clear 4–1 favorite. De La Hoya was definitely stronger and faster, and he liked fighting people as tall or taller than he was. That meant he didn't have to worry about head butts or bull charges. He could just stand and fight, and, he figured, he'd nail Hernandez eventually.

But Hernandez had a plan.

"I was going to knock him out," Hernandez says now.

He sure wasn't going to copy Ruelas and walk straight into De La Hoya's left hook. The truth was, Ruelas had no other option—he knew only one way to fight, and that was not going to be the way to beat De La Hoya. Fight that fight one hundred times, Ruelas would fight it the same way, and lose one hundred times. Hernandez, though, was far different—harder to categorize, impossible to plan for. No way was he Ruelas.

Years of fighting shorter fighters had forced Hernandez to learn how to fight both inside and out—he almost seemed to like it when he had to bundle up his long arms and whack the little guys with short, stinging uppercuts. His trademark was to let the little guys charge him into the ropes, then lean back on the ropes expertly and use his long arms to pick apart the opponent. He also figured he knew how to fight tall, fast fighters.

"I have a lot more body movement than Ruelas does," Hernandez said before the fight. "I respect Rafael. But they just had a wrong plan. They went toward Oscar, and Oscar just caught him."

The bell rang, and the two men met in the ring.

Hernandez was taller than De La Hoya, as he already knew from their appearances together. He had longer arms, he was looking down on De La Hoya, something De La Hoya hadn't experienced often. Hernandez looked down on De La Hoya, and came at him.

Don't get tagged early, he thought. Don't dare do that.

"He's going to try to hurt me, and one thing's for sure, he's going to lose his head coming after me," Hernandez said before the fight. "And I hope he does. I have the advantage of being able to fight both inside and outside. Oscar's saying he has four different styles of fighting, and I only have one. Well, he's going to have to choose one of those and he's going to have to try to hit me."

But Hernandez still started out as the instigator, because De La Hoya was being cautious. De La Hoya was staying away, staying outside, bending and moving, watching, moving his head. He barely threw a punch in the first few moments.

Hernandez watched and measured.

"Our fight was to start from the sixth round and go to the twelfth, that would be our fight," said Rudy. "Get him frustrated and then go after him. Eventually he was going to have to get out of his plan and fight Genaro. Because he just stuck and moved. He didn't want to fight him."

It was a little startling. De La Hoya wasn't engaging. He was being fancy. He was impossible to hit.

This was the mark of Rivero, who wasn't even in the corner because Alcazar still felt too threatened to allow that. Rivero didn't have much of a part in the Ruelas fight, because he had just been brought on and because it wasn't a tactical fight. But for the Hernandez fight, something clicked between Rivero and De La Hoya.

You could tell it in the way he moved this night. He was listening. There wouldn't be any more first-round knockdowns.

"When I came to him, I saw he was a champion in trouble," Rivero said. "He was too fragile and he could easily be knocked out. The first thing I tried to do was give him a good defense."

By then, it was hard for Alcazar to cut Rivero off—De La Hoya was flourishing, so much so that he told Mike Hernandez and his father that "I've learned more in ten months than in the past twelve years."

Still, Alcazar seethed. Rivero wasn't in the corner, and Alcazar made a big show of jumping into the camera's view whenever it came by—chewing the scenery, grabbing attention, fiddling with De La Hoya's hood incessantly on the way to the ring, so much so that Joel Sr. had to wave at him to stop.

"I felt like I built this wall, then I saw someone else come and knock that wall down," Alcazar said. "But I wanted the best for him, and if that's what he needed at that point in his career, I had to give him the opportunity."

Before the fight, Genaro Hernandez got the best shot in of all. At the final press conference, after Alcazar had said this would be an easy fight for De La Hoya, Hernandez leaned into the microphone and said: "Who cares what he says? He isn't even training him anymore. I know Robert Alcazar is not training him. Right now, somebody else is training him."

Alcazar emphasized that Rivero was only helping out at camp—and that he would probably only be around for a little while. That, at least, is what Alcazar hoped. But that is not what was developing.

"Oscar saw that I was teaching him," Rivero says. "I was teaching him everything that Oscar had never seen in boxing. He discovered there were so many things he didn't know and so much still to learn. That was my task. Oscar had a lot of confidence in me as his teacher in boxing."

And he started talking to Rivero, whose plump, tiny frame, craggily voice, and wild eyes gave him the air of a cartoon character. Unlike Alcazar, who, perhaps wisely, swore never to delve into De La Hoya's private life, Rivero did so freely, especially during the early stages of the camp, when De La Hoya was clearly moping through training, his mind at least a hundred miles away.

"Do you have a personal problem?" Rivero asked De La Hoya after one particularly dismal workout. "You're young, you have women.... What's the problem?"

De La Hoya said nothing. But about a week later, he went alone to Rivero's cabin.

"I do have a problem," he told Rivero. "I'm in love with my girl-friend, and we had a fight."

De La Hoya was moping, and it showed in his training. Veronica had caught him with another girl and had stormed out of his condominium.

"Don't deceive her," Rivero told him. "Send her flowers, be up front. Recognize what you did. She cares for you, but how can she if she sees other girls around?"

Who had De La Hoya ever spoken to about these things? He told Rivero he couldn't talk to anybody else. Later, Rivero smiled at the thought. "I feel like I'm a Celestina—a mediator for love. Like a Shakespearean character or like a character in Cervantes."

There were definite Shakespearean moments in De La Hoya's life at times, since Veronica and Joel Sr. clashed almost every time they met. And Oscar was powerless, watching between them.

"His dad yelled at me in public once after a fight," Peralta recalls, thinking back to the night of De La Hoya's victory over Angelo Nuñez in Beverly Hills. "It was a table of ten, two tables of ten, Oscar's family was there. And Oscar didn't do well. He won, but not according to his dad. He didn't do good enough. When the fight ended, he goes to me, 'You, it was your fault! Because of you, my son didn't do well. You're going to be the cause of his failure and his destruction!'

"I was just stunned, and everybody at the table was just looking at me. I was not about to get into a discussion with this man. I was just overwhelmed that he would do that in public. So I turned my back.... I couldn't cry because I was in public. And later on, I talked to Oscar and I was just in tears. And he just told me to ignore him, told me he was crazy....

"And another time, we were barbecuing in Oscar's backyard at the house in Montebello. I remember I was sitting in the pool, I had my feet in the water, and Oscar and I were being silly. He had the thing that you clean the pool with, that big long pole ... and the dad once again just came barging in and started yelling and saying I was a good-for-nothing girlfriend, that I was the cause of his son's destruction, that I was just after him for his money. He was on one side of the pool and thank God Oscar was on the other side. And then Oscar started yelling back at his dad and his dad started yelling back at him. It was horrible. They got into this horrible yelling match. And then Oscar came to his dad's side. . . . At that point I got up and I asked Oscar to please stop yelling at his father because no matter, it was his father and he shouldn't be yelling like that. His dad was yelling at me and Oscar was defending me.

"I guess after that his dad felt stupid, so his dad stormed out of the backyard. At that point, I ran into the bathroom, locked myself in, and I just started crying. And I left. We didn't have the barbecue after all."

Oscar caused a bit of turmoil himself, of course. At events she attended with him, he'd tell girls who asked that Veronica was his cousin. And he'd take their phone numbers, right in front of Veronica.

"In high school, he was always gone training," Peralta said. "He didn't get to go to his prom. He always kept to himself. Now he gets the girls, they're following him all around. . . . And some of them have no shame. I look at them, 'God, give me a break, have some self-respect. Or at least respect the fact that he's with his girlfriend.' And I guess some of that is alluring to him. These girls don't realize what he really is, don't know him when he's lonely, when he's sad, when he's depressed. . . .'"

The last thing Rivero said on the day De La Hoya went to him was: "Soon you will learn that changing women is not like changing clothes."

With that advice, De La Hoya sat down to write his love letter to Veronica. It was an awakening for him—he had never said he needed anybody else, not since his mother died.

"It's a peace of mind," De La Hoya said then. "My mind now is just focused on the fight. I mean I don't have to worry about my girlfriend, I know she's there, and I love her a lot. We have no problems whatsoever. Everything now is just so perfect. I think it's very important because you can be in the best shape physically, but if your mind is not there, you can lose a fight, easy as that."

The letter arrived by Federal Express one afternoon, while Veronica was getting ready for a date, and she was back together with De La Hoya by the end of the week. It was only temporary, but it settled De

La Hoya for the Hernandez fight. He locked back into training and cut loose for Hernandez.

Rivero would have more to tell him, but that would come later.

"At first, he would talk about the past champions, like Joe Louis and Willie Pep and all that," De La Hoya said then, "about his fighters, Miguel Canto, the old days, and how I would have to use those styles today to be a very successful fighter. And I really didn't really pay attention to that. I thought, 'Hey, we're in the '90s, and you have to use different styles to win fights.' But now that he's been teaching me, I know the old style really works. Using the combinations the old champions used to use really works.

"Back when I was just starting, I wanted to go in and just knock somebody out. I would worry about, if I didn't knock somebody out in two or three rounds, it was like, you know, 'What's going to happen? I'm going to run out of condition and run out of air and just get tired.' Now, I want to go the distance. I want to fight ten-twelve rounds, because I have the skills and the moves to do so. When I got knocked down, I was a young fighter who didn't know what was going on."

In the fight's early minutes, De La Hoya kept feinting, not punching. And Hernandez picked up the rhythm, jabbing off of the feints as De La Hoya bent his body down, peered up, and threw a few light shots.

Hernandez came at De La Hoya in sections—shoulder first, then a right; one leg forward, then two lefts to the body. But nobody was landing anything serious.

"He wasn't going to do that the whole fight," Hernandez recalled. "Because the shots I was giving to the body...that was going to add up."

Finally, in the last minute of the round, De La Hoya cut loose, firing back-to-back uppercuts that landed hard.

"You're boxing very well," Alcazar told De La Hoya in between rounds.

De La Hoya felt strange. In the middle of the round he felt his back twinge, and it was sore now. Then, when he hopped up from his stool to start round two, he felt a pull on his right side. His tried to loosen his right arm, but it was not responding. And round two had already started. De La Hoya says he hurt his shoulder from twisting strangely. But Rudy Hernandez says it definitely came from his brother's digging to the body—digging De La Hoya had never felt before.

In the second, De La Hoya was tighter—more constricted, less athletic. "I couldn't lift my right arm," he said.

Hernandez came out jabbing, throwing the left hand to keep De La Hoya from finding his own punching rhythm. If he could control De La Hoya's jab with his own, he could find a spot to launch a power punch to the body. And see how long De La Hoya liked that.

"My intention was just to hit him. I didn't care where they landed. Just hit him," Hernandez said. "And hopefully later on . . . later in the fight, he would wear down. He wasn't doing that much. The way I saw it, I take away his jab and his game plan is going to be thrown off. His game plan always starts with his jab. And if you can take away that jab, you can make it a hard night. Because he can't follow it up. I guess he loses his mind a little bit if he can't land that jab. It always starts with a jab."

This was Hernandez's style—take away the best thing of his opponent, and make him adjust to it. Hernandez didn't have overwhelming power or dangerously fast hands. . . . What he had was a hard chin, long arms, a five-eleven frame, and the smarts to beat you from either the inside with his wiry strength and knowledge of angles, or from outside, with his long arms and elusiveness.

In thirty-three fights—which could have been many more if not for his persistent hand problems—Hernandez had only one blemish, a draw against Raul (Jilberto) Perez in 1993—and he quickly turned around and destroyed Perez with a savage single body punch three months later. The last time he was knocked down was in 1984, when he was just starting out.

"As far as I'm concerned, Genaro could've won the featherweight title first, the junior-lightweight, lightweight, and the junior-welterweight," Rudy says. "Because he has the talent. If you look at all the top ten pound-for-pound fighters in the world, Oscar's the only one that I think does any kind of adjusting in the ring, as compared to all the others. The others will never leave their game plan. They know one style and one style only. And if that doesn't work for them, fuck, they're kind of lost, you know? . . . I think one thing makes a fighter great. It's the accomplishment inside of the ring and who he's fought and how long he's been up there. And the ability to adjust in the ring. I thought he'd be a better fighter than Oscar. I thought that's why Genaro would beat him. And if Genaro could rock him in the gym like he did when they sparred, who says he can't knock him out in a fight? That's what I was thinking."

Recalled Genaro: "I thought it was just a matter of time."

Hernandez, though, was altering his own style. He was chasing De La Hoya, lunging at times, and not being particularly judicious about it. He tried to lure De La Hoya to the ropes in the second, but De La Hoya backed away.

"My thing is this . . . what would've happened if Genaro had landed one good solid shot, that's all," Rudy says.

Genaro: "I landed one, but it was right on the cheek. It was on the cheek, it wasn't on the jaw."

Rudy: "That's all I wanted. Just one punch, that's the only thing I wanted."

A minute into the second round, De La Hoya landed a quick left hook to the chin, and Hernandez smiled back at him, the universal sign that the punch got his attention. De La Hoya sensed that he had figured Hernandez out. He had known he would do it, known it all along.

"This guy's no dummy," De La Hoya said before the fight. "He's going to try to box me and use his left jab. But the training that I've been doing is going to be too much for him to handle. I know that for a fact. At this point, I don't think anything can be tricky anymore. I've been working on a lot of things, a lot of body movement, a lot of counterpunching. I'm going to be doing a lot of counterpunching, that's going to be the key."

Then, with only fifty-five seconds left before the bell, De La Hoya sent a wicked left hook that struck Hernandez directly on the nose. He followed that up with a hard right, on top of the nose again. And Hernandez was smiling again. Wobbly, but smiling.

Though it wasn't clear until later, this was the punch that ended the fight. Because Genaro Hernandez had been hiding something for several weeks—trying to hide it from De La Hoya, from Arum, and just a little bit, from himself.

Genaro Hernandez went into the biggest fight of his life, against the hardest, most precise hitter he'd ever faced, with a fractured nose.

In mid-August, three weeks before the De La Hoya fight, on a sweltering day at the Brooklyn Gym, Genaro Hernandez's nose was cracked by Shane Mosley—the same blur-handed future world champion who gave De La Hoya his first loss in the amateurs.

Mosley was not as tall as De La Hoya, but his hands were just as fast, possibly faster, and Hernandez wanted to test himself against it. (A year later, after several hard sessions with Mosley, former junior-welterweight champion Zack Padilla suffered from a blood clot in his head, and was forced to retire.)

Shane Mosley did not mess around. They whacked each around plenty for several weeks, with headgear, just like any other Brooklyn Gym war. Hernandez was worried about his hands, but they didn't cause him any problems. He was worried about building up his weight to 135 pounds—he almost never weighed more than 133, even when he wasn't training. But some work in a swimming pool built up his shoulders nicely, and he didn't think 135 pounds was going to be a problem.

Things were going well. "At the time when he was suffering from the hands a lot," Lilliana said just days before the nose injury, "I would question, 'Why is he in there?' I just didn't want to have to see him go through so many surgeries. But, now, he's been okay, he hasn't been complaining. I don't know if it has to do with God, but maybe He made him feel better about his hands now that he's getting this fight. I guess it's time to heal. And he's doing okay. I'm not worried. It's like this is meant to happen."

Genaro was beginning to feel more sure than he had ever felt: He was going to win. For once, everything was falling his way.

For this camp, Rudy wanted to be extra careful—he wanted Genaro to wear extra heavy headgear, just in case.

"You're going to go in there with all the protection in the world for your training," Rudy told his brother. "You're going into it at 100 percent that day. We're going to kick his butt, man. We're going to kick his butt, and then we're going to finally get the money you deserve. Make big, big chunks of money."

But Genaro didn't like the heavy gear that crawled over his nose. It was hard to see, and it made his head bob, because he wasn't used to so much padding. Rudy argued with him for a while, but, as always, Genaro won out.

"Genaro wants to do what Genaro wants to do," Rudy said.

Several sparring sessions went by, then several weeks, and there were no problems.

Then, two weeks before the fight, in a hot exchange in the last thirty seconds of the eighth and final round of sparring—on Mosley's last scheduled day with Hernandez—Mosley sent an overhand right that crashed into the bridge of Hernandez's nose. And immediately he knew that something had gone awry.

"It was a freaky accident," Genaro recalls. "From nine years old all the way to twenty-nine years old, all that time, twenty years of boxing, I never had a broken nose. Nothing like that. All of a sudden, this fight comes up, biggest fight, for two months, I'm doing things that I never did before for any fight. I was getting up to run every morning at 5:30, going to swim. Man, I was ready for this fight."

Then, pop.

"I didn't even feel it," Genaro remembers. "I felt it hit, and then..."

They thought about asking for a postponement, but knew they couldn't. There was too much money involved, too much history. Genaro might never see $500,000 again if he backed out now. Plus, Arum had already paid him an advance that would have to be returned if the fight was pushed back.

"If we didn't take that fight then, who knows, they probably would've never fought Genaro again," Rudy says.

Genaro took a couple of days off, then returned to work with giant headgear, including a long brace that crossed over his nose. Though the doctor told him he would be fine for the fight, Genaro knew that the doctor had never been hit on the nose by Oscar De La Hoya—with or without a fractured bone in his nose.

"Up to that time, I was doing real good with Shane Mosley," Hernandez said. "But you know what, after that, everything just crumbled. Everything was just shattered completely. I couldn't move. The headgear was so heavy. When you're wearing big old headgear like that, and it's heavy, you feel the weight on you, you get frustrated, and you're sparring with a guy who's quick ... and before that, you weren't getting hit as much and now you're getting hit. It was just frustrating. It added up. That kind of wore us down. That kind of beat us. Not taking anything from Oscar, but if it hadn't been for the broken nose, it probably would've been a different story. I thought we would've beaten him.... But bad luck struck."

After watching his brother in his first few sessions after the injury, Rudy grabbed him and spoke sadly. It wasn't the way to motivate him, but it was reality.

"The way you're working out right now, I don't see you beating Oscar," Rudy told him.

A few years later, Rudy was philosophical: "It's funny how things work. Gosh, whoever or whatever power in the sky worked it where Oscar would be the fighter of the '90s. And I think he's a great fighter for this era. But what would have happened if he was in there with Sugar Ray or Tommy Hearns? I mean, he would not be champion of the world right now. At 135 pounds, it was just his time. . . . I've always said luck has a lot to do with everything."

And his brother interjected: "And he got luck."

With the left-right combination to the heart of Hernandez's most vulnerable bone, De La Hoya shattered Hernandez, and X rays would later reveal that Hernandez's nose was broken into more than twenty pieces.

De La Hoya, though, did not try to finish him off, perhaps worried that he was being duped. And Hernandez still was a marvelous defensive fighter, blocking shots with arms and shoulders, twisting and rocking back and forth.

"It was very difficult to get inside of his defense," De La Hoya said later. "He's a tall, lanky fighter who knows how to use his jab."

But as the bell sounded, Hernandez fiddled with his nose—he could no longer breath out of it. Through two rounds, Hernandez had thrown sixty-nine jabs, De La Hoya only twenty-four. De La Hoya looked tight, but Hernandez was in trouble. He needed a knockout, and he wasn't a knockout fighter.

"I didn't even notice it was broken," Rudy recalls. "My thing was, 'Go for broke!' One more round and just go for fucking broke. Fuck it, just go wild and shit. Hit him low and hit him high. . . . I don't care what you do, but hit him. But Genaro said. . . . I remember Genaro telling me that even his jab hurt the shit out of him. Genaro had gone through pain before with broken hands and he's always continued on. So it was definitely more than that."

In De La Hoya's corner, they knew something was bothering Hernandez, but they weren't quite sure of the extent of the problem. They just wanted De La Hoya to keep hitting him—and avoid the Hernandez panic punches, as he tried to rally himself into a knockout.

"The fight was going on and he was leading, but I wasn't thinking. 'This is over,'" Alcazar remembers. "I didn't think [Hernandez's nose] was broken in twenty different pieces. Oscar was controlling the fight. And I think Genaro was frustrated. Because Genaro was the one on the attack. And he knew that Oscar was too smart for him. At that particular moment in the ring, he started getting frustrated. He started feeling frustrated."

Once the third round began, with all hell streaming out of Hernandez's fragmented nose, De La Hoya started exerting some control—even though his right side still hadn't loosened up. In between rounds, he had Pajar try to rub out the stiffness, but he didn't have power in his right hand for the rest of the night. It was like the old days, when he blew out amateurs with just his left. Left jab, left hook, left uppercut.

About forty-five seconds into the third, Hernandez tried to duck through De La Hoya's jabs, and powered forward for an attack, but once again De La Hoya bent away and backpedaled away from danger.

"He never let you get close enough for you to damage his body," Rudy told his brother years later. "Because he knew that you had a good fucking body shot. So he stayed away from you as much as possible.... He was so focused on his game plan, he wasn't going to change that. Even if Genaro hadn't gone into that fight with a broken nose, he would've done the same thing: Jab and move, jab and move. And not fight you, especially against the ropes. You go against the ropes, he threw several punches and missed about nine of eleven. And then walked away, the hell with it."

Later in the round, De La Hoya exhibited a classic Rivero move— aping the old techniques of Willie Pep, one of the greatest defensive tacticians ever. De La Hoya extended both arms and sort of popped Hernandez away, giving him a sense of space and a feel for the distance.

With that, the Hernandez corner sensed that De La Hoya was not going to be beaten this day—or maybe ever, by anybody. De La Hoya was a better fighter that day than he'd ever been, and he had always been extremely dangerous.

"In the third round, I told [cornerman] John Montes, 'Man, the motherfucker's good,'" Rudy recalls. "He's really good. I have nothing but respect for him. What I do respect about him is that he goes up into that mountain and he doesn't waste his time. He's up there working and learning. . . . That's why I give him a lot of credit. He did exactly what he needed to do against Genaro. He never left his game plan."

But Genaro still harbored hope. If he could just gut through the pain, he thought, he could catch De La Hoya, if he ever stopped moving.

"He was almost leaving his game plan, though," Hernandez said. "It was just a matter of time."

A Hernandez left hook missed a few seconds later, and De La Hoya responded to the opening with a left-right combination that brought another Hernandez smile. With forty-five seconds left in the round, De La Hoya pumped a left hook to the chin that sent Hernandez's body into a quick contortion and momentarily caused his legs to noodle.

"You're much stronger," Alcazar told De La Hoya at the end of the third. "That was a beautiful round."

De La Hoya kept up the pace through the fourth and fifth, landing hard, accurate shots and sending shock waves through Hernandez's body anytime he came near his nose. By the time the fifth ended, De La Hoya hadn't exactly dominated the fight, but he was in control. Entering the sixth, Hernandez was trailing on one judge's card by one point and by three on the two others. He still had a chance.

This is where the Hernandezes thought the fight would start. But, with the nose puffing up and his eyes watering, it's where it ended.

"Oh yeah, I knew," Hernandez remembers. "Couldn't breathe through the nose. In the sixth round. In the beginning of the sixth round. I just kept fighting . . . but I started to think, 'You know what, I can't. I can't go no more.' I could see, but there was no sense in gambling."

De La Hoya, by now aiming for the nose, started it off with a right that glanced over the top of Hernandez's nose. Hernandez was gasping for air now. Ten seconds into the round, he couldn't stop swiping his nose with his gloves, to clear it out, make it better. And it hurt. All Hernandez did now was try to avoid shots, to keep De La Hoya from touching his nose again.

Hernandez got his shot twenty seconds later, as both fighters moved in, shoulder to shoulder, and fired hooks—Hernandez's connected first, and it sent De La Hoya bouncing backward into a corner. Hernandez ducked and charged, right into the fateful fusillade from De La Hoya.

With Hernandez bobbing his head low, De La Hoya caught him with a short left perfectly on the nose, splattering blood several feet, jolting his head up. A split second later, De La Hoya crashed another left against the nose, stopping Hernandez's own counter-right in midflight. By then, Hernandez's nose was in shards.

"The guy is a little different, he's a little cuckoo," veteran trainer Emanuel Steward would later say, trying to describe De La Hoya's ability to finish off wounded opponents. "You look at him, he's so sweet, so polite, so nice and classy. Then once the bell rings, after about forty-five seconds, you see him transform into a cold-blooded killer, one of the worst I've ever seen."

The end was near, and a little panic began to set into Hernandez's mind. It was so hard for him to get air, his labored breathing was audible from ringside. As the sixth round was ticking down, Hernandez already was planning his exit. Then the bell rang.

As De La Hoya turned back to his corner, Hernandez took three steps to his corner and spit out his mouthpiece as Rudy was busy bringing up the stool. Quickly, Hernandez said, "That's it," in the general direction of his brother, then immediately pivoted and walked to referee Richard Steele, who was standing twenty feet away in a neutral corner.

"No more," he said, as Steele blinked back his surprise.

Hernandez's eyes were wild and his nose was crushed. Back in his own corner, Hernandez's father yelled desperately: "Come here!" Rudy was just confused.

Then Steele understood and waved his arms, ending the fight.

Rudy sagged in his corner, as Genaro walked back. De La Hoya leaped on the ring ropes and threw his fist in the air, screaming: "East L.A.!"

Hernandez walked over to De La Hoya's corner to touch gloves. There, he told De La Hoya, despite all their inflammatory public statements: "You know, I've never been hit that hard in my career."

Rudy later said that if Genaro had let him tell Steele that he couldn't let his brother fight anymore, nobody would have ever called Genaro a coward for quitting. But Genaro did it his way and was called a coward.

Genaro: "He wanted the fight so bad, I wanted the fight so bad. I didn't want to sit down. Because he might've talked me into going another round. He might've . . ."

Rudy: "Genaro didn't want to take that chance. I thought Genaro might never hear the end of it. I just wish he had waited. I would've never made him do anything."

Genaro showed up at the postfight press conference in severe pain, but sensing that he needed to explain himself to all those in the crowd who had booed his surrender.

"I feel bad I let down a lot of people, but I have to give up," Hernandez said, his face distorted and his mouth wrinkling in pain. Then he started to cry softly into the microphone. "There's been a lot of serious injuries in boxing lately, and I've got a daughter and a beautiful wife. I don't need to end up like those other fighters. It's better to say *no mas* than not to say another word."

For his part, De La Hoya realized that this was a much more important fight for him mentally than the Ruelas blowout. Ruelas was tailor-made. Hernandez had to be figured out, then broken up. Beyond that, De La Hoya had adjusted to his own sore back and shoulder and still came out with blistering power.

"I was barely warming up," De La Hoya said after the fight. "But tell you the truth, since the first round, my back was killing me, my shoulder. I guess the wind hit me. I was so warmed up. . . . After the first round, something went wrong with my back and it's killing me right now. It hurt so much. But I got him with a great shot right on the nose, right on the button. And he felt it. I felt very strong. I'm ready for the big boys. I think I'm ready. I guess my trainer will say maybe two more years, maybe three, to go after the big guys."

That meant, really, only one big guy. The ultimate big guy in Latino boxing, really, in nonheavyweight boxing overall. Julio Cesar Chavez, who was sitting with the WBC super-lightweight belt, just five pounds up from where De La Hoya was.

After knocking out Hernandez, making him surrender, Team De La Hoya felt ready to make the big step.

There wasn't any more need to take on personal rivals.

"Oscar knows the money he can make at welterweight," Mike Hernandez said, already looking two steps ahead. "So, if he's ready and he feels he can beat Chavez, he's going to go."

Said De La Hoya: "I know I'm ready for it. He's made for me. His style is made for me. It should be no problem. In boxing, alone, he's a hero to everybody, because he's a good fighter, he's a tough warrior, but that's as far as it goes. If I were to say he's my hero because he's a great person and has a great personality, I'd be lying. It was over for Chavez a long time ago."

It would come in September of 1996—the fighter of the year (De La Hoya was named 1995 Fighter of the Year by the Boxing Writers Association) against a fighter for the ages.

Hernandez, meanwhile, endured. And, true to his survivor's spirit, eighteen months later he got his redemption in the eyes of a skeptical boxing public. For weeks, Hernandez heard mumbles when he entered gyms, and felt the wrath of the fans who thought he quit too quickly, that maybe he had taken the money and taken a dive.

The people who respected him most also wanted to see De La Hoya beaten the most. And Genaro Hernandez had failed. Failed by quitting.

But in March 1997, Hernandez faced WBC champion Azumah Nelson, a day after Roy Jones lost to Montell Griffin on a disqualification. In his fight, Hernandez was controlling the veteran Nelson. Then moments after the bell signaling the end of the seventh, Nelson threw a egregiously late left that splattered into Hernandez's throat. He could've stayed down and taken the title by disqualification, as Griffin had done a day earlier even when it seemed that he could've continued. But Rudy said: Remember champions are made by fighting and not by laying on their backs!

Hernandez took his allotted time to recover, and, with his other cornermen screaming for him to stay down and take the victory, Hernandez resumed the fight, and defeated Nelson to regain a world title.

"I do believe it cleared up a lot of things for people who called me a coward with the Oscar fight," Genaro said. "I guess I proved to the people . . . they realized that it's not the way they saw it. It's different going in injured than going in there 100 percent, no injury, and still getting up to fight when you could've won the title if you stayed down. I think that happened for a reason. That cleared up what happened with Oscar."

The Hernandez fight, though, had a fascinating postscript. After the press conferences and the victory dances and the Chavez talk, the two met again, a couple of hours after the fight.

The meeting was at University Medical Center, the nearest hospital.

Hernandez could barely breath. De La Hoya could barely move his shoulder. Hernandez was there with his brother and his wife. De La Hoya was there with his publicist and Alcazar and Peralta. And quietly the two groups mingled, and hugged, and thanked God that there weren't any more serious injuries, ending the rivalry quietly, at last.

"To this day, I have nothing but praise for him. Everybody tells me, What do you think of De La Hoya?" Rudy Hernandez says. "I think he's a great fighter. At the hospital, I told Oscar, 'Hey, for two fighters who barely hit each other, they both ended up in the hospital.' And he starts laughing, and he had to catch himself, because you could see he was really in pain bad."

Says Alcazar: "That was a great experience, because we're closer than ever. Now we're friends. We ended up with deep respect for each other. When you're at the hospital, finally, you realize the dangers of this sport. And you come to respect the other people."

chapter nine

Blood on His Hands

Nineteen fights, almost that many millions of dollars earned, and Oscar De La Hoya was becoming a giant in boxing—a Latino Lancelot dressed in Italian suits and $400 shoes, a bright and shallow knight riding amid a field of villains.

How big was he? He had already carried two major pay-per-view cards, the fights against Ruelas and Hernandez, and combined the two shows grossed more than $20 million—serious cash even in the big-money world of boxing. Here was a commodity more bankable than Roberto Duran ever had been, more fiscally reliable than Roy Jones Jr. or Pernell Whitaker—De La Hoya's two contenders for the mythical crown of best pound-for-pound fighter in the world—more bankable than anybody not in the heavyweight division. And more bankable than all but a handful in that division, too.

He was twenty-two years old. He was handsome. And he did more to protect his image in the U.S. marketplace than any fighter since Sugar Ray Leonard. He did the commercials. He smiled at the corporate outings. And he knew how to earn brownie points. Once, when he was filming an interview with several Caesars executives nearby, De La Hoya halted the questioning and quickly put on a Caesars T-shirt, to the great satisfaction of his benefactors.

"He has a knowledge of the bigger picture and what's going on and saying the right thing," said Caesars sports chief Rich Rose. "All in all, he is the most astute since Ray, and is as good as any athlete I've had the opportunity to work with since Ray."

In an unpublicized but remarkable event, Arum brought De La Hoya to the 1995 national convention of the Associated Press Sports

Editors for a round of schmoozes and back-patting. Could anyone imagine a Tyson or a Whitaker sitting at a panel before editors from every major American sports section, smiling through ninety minutes of questions, then going to dinner with Arum and a select few of the elite editors? Not possible. But De La Hoya gladly performed the duty, for wise reasons. These editors controlled what America would read—if they liked him (and, wholeheartedly, they said they did), they could surely find room for glowing features and fight coverage that they carved out for no other fighters.

Good coverage meant more money. More money meant more exposure. And the cycle turned and turned. After the Hernandez fight, De La Hoya signed a multiyear deal with Anheuser-Busch. Other major deals were on the horizon.

In a sport of screams and unvarnished larceny, in the sport of Don King and the other harrowing personalities of the time, De La Hoya, as long as he won fights and maintained his public appeal, was nearly perfect: polite, Latino, born in the U.S.A., consumed with making money—and history.

"I don't think there's any question that Oscar's going to be a major sports personality," said superagent Leigh Steinberg, who had been hired by Hernandez to help shepherd De La Hoya deeper into the mainstream of the U.S. sports celebrity culture. "He'll be a major marketing force in this country."

If there was something less than vibrant about him out of the ring, the corporate executives only loved him more, because he smiled, didn't he? He didn't make a fool of himself or them as Tyson had. He just showed up for the charity events and the golf tournaments and shook the hand of everyone he needed to. Duran was feared, but never was imaginable as a commercial spokesman. Hagler was revered, but never emerged from his blue-collar persona. Ali was transcendent, but by the time he lorded over the scene, he was more about politics and glory than he was about moving merchandise.

De La Hoya was a man for the new marketplace, moving more

swiftly and more successfully than any other Latino athlete ever had from the traditional Latino audience to the U.S. market at large. There had never been a true crossover Latino athlete. De La Hoya was poised to be the first.

"Oscar has charisma, which is very hard to find," Arum said. "And part of charisma is that, like Ali, like Leonard, he knows instinctively what to say. He could've gotten up and run his mouth and said bad things about Genaro Hernandez, but he took it on himself to tone the rhetoric down. Now that's something that really appeals to people. People don't like hot individuals, they don't like people who lose their temper, say aggressive things. I'm guilty of that myself. On television, if you see a news broadcast and they're arguing and fighting, the guy who makes the best impression is the guy who has a slight smile on his face and says things in a calm, cool way. Now, he can be as tough as he wants when he says it—he doesn't backtrack on his ideas. But it's the way he does it that makes the difference.

"People like cool personalities. You can get your message across in a cool way. And Oscar knows how to do that. He's absolutely perfect. I mean, it's amazing how he handles himself on television, handles himself with the press. It comes out the way he wants to say it, but the manner in which he says it is really brilliant. He has that quality, you can't teach it. He's a great communicator. We've got a lot of Tyson out there, who gets so much of the attention. He's almost like an anti-Tyson."

He wasn't rude. He wasn't stupid. He wasn't an embarrassment. He wasn't unpredictable. If you had to find faults, and he was making so much money that there were bound to be observers eager to find faults, he was criticized far more for what he wasn't—colorful, passionate— than what he was.

Well, really, what was he? He was a winner, and always had been. He was a champion. He was incredibly talented, fast, and strong, and he wasn't self-destructive in any of the usual clichéd boxing ways. But in the boxing world, he was still undefined as a fighter. His distinction was that he was making money—not that he was making history.

Everything was so different with De La Hoya. Usually, the experts spotted, elevated, and then dropped stars quickly, skipping about from fighter to fighter in a fickle search for the greatest of the great. From Sugar Ray Robinson to Sugar Ray Leonard to Thomas Hearns to Mike Tyson to . . . there was always somebody else. The embrace of Oscar De La Hoya, though, took time.

"He's just not very experienced," said Hall of Fame trainer Eddie Futch. "I'm not comfortable predicting anything for him until he gets more experience."

Everyone appreciated his abilities, but even the fighter himself didn't seem to quite know where it was all headed, or why. Which is why he needed a foil. Ruelas was his breakthrough. Hernandez was his personal rival. But neither was a milestone—they were just steps.

There was only one milestone fighter for De La Hoya, and that was clear from the very beginning of his career. It was, and could only be, Julio Cesar Chavez, who was aging, arrogant, and abundantly willing to chop down De La Hoya.

For years, well before De La Hoya fought Hernandez, De La Hoya versus Chavez was the holy grail of nonheavyweight boxing. With the Latino audience establishing itself as the most reliable in the sport, and the pay-per-view universe expanding by the day, Chavez–De La Hoya was a monster, even before it was a reality. Young versus old. Warrior versus teen idol. Mexican hero versus crossover Latino.

For a while, though, it looked like their paths would never cross. In 1994, De La Hoya was twenty and fighting at junior-lightweight (130 pounds). Chavez was fighting at 140 and fading. Chavez had carried promoter Don King through several tumultuous years—when Tyson was on trial, then sent away for a rape conviction. But by 1994 he was over thirty. In January 1994, the night before the Super Bowl, he had lost for the first time, in a staggering decision to journeyman Frankie Randall that included a stunning eleventh-round knockdown.

That was not the beginning of the slide. Five months before that,

Chavez had faced Pernell Whitaker in the biggest fight of the year, and escaped with one of the most generous decisions in the recent history of major boxing. Whitaker bounced around Chavez, whirled combinations across his face and body, and attacked the champion for twelve rounds with a ferocity no one had previously dared. Chavez was lost, stumbling, and his face was bloody. So thorough was Whitaker's dominance of the fight that when it was declared as a draw, the crowd of 53,000 in San Antonio's Alamodome—raucously pro-Chavez—sheepishly accepted the decision, and, like Chavez, quickly got the hell out of there. They knew a travesty when they saw it.

After those two deflating fights, maybe Chavez wasn't worth the trouble—or worth the money—for a meeting with De La Hoya. He had slipped too far and been reduced too much. A few days after the Randall loss, De La Hoya sat up in Big Bear and said good-bye to the Chavez dream.

"Chavez was a great, great champion," De La Hoya said. "I called up my father right after the [Randall] fight, and he said, 'It's over for him.' I believe it, too. Now he's going downhill and I'm picking up more experience and coming up. It would've been a big, big, huge fight."

Too big, it turned out, to let fall away.

While De La Hoya fought Paez and Ruelas, King, who still needed a marquee player with Tyson serving out his jail term, maneuvered Chavez into a rematch with Randall in May 1994, four months after the disastrous loss. For seven rounds, Randall whacked Chavez, who was just as slow and just as hittable as he had been in the first bout. But this time fate, and the Byzantine rules of boxing, intervened.

In the eighth, Chavez was badly cut in a clinch by a Randall head butt. After consulting with the ringside doctor, Chavez protested he could not continue, as blood streamed down his face. Flip Homansky, the doctor, looked at Chavez, shrugged, and said the fight was over.

Which is when things got truly convoluted. Logically, Randall thought the fight would either be given to him (Chavez quit, didn't he?) or would be ruled a draw, and Randall would retain his title. But

Randall did not have Chavez's political heft, or Don King in his corner, or luck on his side. Due to arcane WBC rules (Chavez was a favorite of WBC president Jose Sulaiman), the fight was scored through seven rounds, and, counting a penalty point given to Randall for the head butt, Chavez was given the decision, and the title back.

Chavez, protected but still regal, was back. The Mexican fans still flocked to him. The legend was still alive. And once again, De La Hoya popped up on the horizon.

There was one gigantic problem, though: Chavez was still under contract to King, and De La Hoya was an Arum fighter. Neither aging promoter was willing to do the other any favors, or sign any fights that would make the other even richer. Chavez implored King to get him the fight, but his influence on King was not what it once had been. First, Chavez was overextended financially, and had yet to pay back $1.5 million King had loaned to him. But there was much more to complicate the relationship.

In September 1995, with King on trial in New York federal court, Chavez was the prosecution's star witness, testifying that King had falsified insurance claims for a Chavez fight against Harold Brazier that was canceled. King, who had promoted every one of Chavez's fights since 1983, was enraged. Reportedly, in the days before his testimony, someone from King's office sent Chavez a copy of his contract with the word "Judas" written on it.

Chavez, in deep financial trouble, needed De La Hoya, and figured out a way to get the fight: He'd go straight to Arum.

Surprisingly, King didn't fight the approach—King needed the money, too, and with Tyson coming out of jail and getting ready for a huge comeback, if Chavez wanted to sacrifice himself against the younger, bigger fighter for a big payday, that was fine with King. Arum gave King a 50–50 promotional split, and paid $1.8 million for the right to promote Chavez. This fight was too big to mess up. It was time for De La Hoya–Chavez.

"It's time for him to have a marquee fight," Arum said of De La

Hoya. "If we waited, Chavez might've retired or gotten beat. This was the time to do it. I was paying big stakes, but if he wins, Oscar becomes, next to Tyson, boxing's biggest superstar."

Chavez was ecstatic—and already getting in his early shots.

"That fight will break a lot of records," Chavez said through a translator in the summer of 1995. "Two Mexicans. Well, I don't know if De La Hoya is Mexican or not."

And Chavez smiled after that, as the reporters around him laughed. If De La Hoya is not Mexican, Chavez was asked, what nationality is he? "Portuguese," Chavez said, chuckling.

Then he got to serious talk: "But this will definitely break Mike Tyson's record [for the highest-grossing fight ever]."

Chavez and De La Hoya, as quickly became obvious, had a history.

When De La Hoya was a red-hot amateur in East L.A., when he couldn't find many amateurs to spar with him, and was working mainly with tough professionals (against amateur rules but largely accepted as necessary by USA Boxing), the most famous professional to enter the ring with the young kid was none other than Chavez himself.

It was the summer of 1991, and it was supposed to be a secret meeting, in a makeshift ring set up in Jack's Restaurant in Huntington Park, an enclave in the heart of East L.A., as Chavez wound through town before heading to Las Vegas to defend his title against Lonnie Smith. Despite the secrecy, hundreds of people showed up for the session, and several video cameras recorded the scene: The lanky, mustached De La Hoya nervously bobbing and flicking at a smiling and comfortable Chavez—both in headgear and heavy gloves.

De La Hoya, egged on by the small crowd, flew at Chavez a few times and landed several hard lefts that Chavez barely acknowledged. But as the crowd whooped it up for the eighteen-year-old, Chavez gradually became more interested in the activity. In the second round, De La Hoya kept pressing Chavez, who pawed back tentatively. Was De La Hoya that good at eighteen? Midway through the second,

Chavez answered that question. As both pulled back their right hands to punch, Chavez beat De La Hoya by a flicker and connected flush on the teenager's jaw as De La Hoya's fist misfired.

Suddenly, De La Hoya dropped straight down to one knee. Chavez smiled when De La Hoya got right back up, shook his head, and continued on. But that was the end of that, and the sparring ended with the second-round bell.

"We hit each other with two rights—I even have a swollen knuckle because of it," Chavez said five years later. "He did fall, but it was in training."

Said Alcazar: "I've still got the tape. I brought Oscar, Pepe Reilly, Shane Mosley . . . to the same workout. And they made me sign this paper: 'If Chavez hurts De La Hoya, we're not responsible.' I said okay. I signed the paper. So did the other people. So they started sparring. Oscar did real real good against him. He went down to a knee, but then he got up and he really started fighting back."

As the real Chavez–De La Hoya fight neared, Chavez giggled quickly when he was asked if he had a mental edge from that sparring session knockdown more than five years before.

"Yes [the sparring is significant], because it gave me an idea that I can knock him out," Chavez said through a translator. "It gave me an idea of his punch. At the time, the one who was trying hard was Oscar, not me."

De La Hoya's memories of Chavez, however, reached back much farther than the sparring session.

"He was my idol growing up," De La Hoya said repeatedly, but not quite honestly. It was Arguello he idolized. Chavez was just the man he wanted to replace.

When De La Hoya was a teenager, each time a big Chavez fight came up on pay-per-view or HBO, Alcazar took De La Hoya to a friend's house to watch it. "You'll be there," Alcazar told him repeatedly, pointing to Chavez on the screen. "You can get there."

Chavez wondered about that. Even after De La Hoya had beaten Paez and Ruelas and Hernandez, Chavez couldn't help rolling his eyes when interviewers compared him to De La Hoya. Chavez was measuring De La Hoya for signs of greatness, and convinced himself that it was not yet there.

Was De La Hoya his proper successor? "It's very difficult to say now," Chavez said. "He hasn't fought that many fights. He hasn't fought that many true boxers. He hasn't been hit a lot. He's gone a good road and he's got a big future." Then Chavez laughed again and looked at his interviewer sharply.

"You're always asking me about De La Hoya," Chavez said, making it clear that he did not consider De La Hoya his equal, "and I'm tired of talking about him. Whitaker is much better. De La Hoya hits hard, and he's fast, and he comes in with a lot of force. But he has to learn how to fight, and Whitaker is very difficult. That's why I want to fight De La Hoya soon, before he learns. . . . Oscar De La Hoya looks good boxing, but you have to consider the opponent. Chicanito Hernandez certainly is not an opponent in my category. Fighting me will be a much more difficult opponent. Chicanito doesn't know how to move in on a fighter. . . . He needs more heart."

But Chavez saw that his time was not going to last forever. The Whitaker fight told him that. The Randall fights surely told him that. Chavez could be stubborn and vain and purposely ignorant of reality at times. But his shoulder hurt, his knee was sore, and he wasn't immortal.

"There are people coming behind me, pushing me very, very strongly," Chavez said. "That's why I want to retire. My time has now come. . . . I don't know if I'll get to one hundred fights because I'm a little bit exhausted with boxing. I've had a lot of problems with my arms, with my knees. I really don't want to extend myself much longer. After so many years of working out, it all builds up. I am not giving what I used to be able to give. I will fight De La Hoya for a lot of money, and then retire."

Chavez was no Olympic hero. He was not hunted for Hollywood roles. His life story was a fight for survival, and he had long relationships with the drug lords of his hometown, Culiacán, Mexico. Chavez was worth millions, but he'd never left Culiacán. Chavez could've opened up the U.S. market for himself, but he never chose to learn English. He was stubborn. In the ring and out, he was a hard head—he could wear you down, and he could wear thin. But everything Chavez was was right in front you. Nothing was hidden about Julio Cesar Chavez.

The contrast to De La Hoya, then, was luminous. It was the selling point of the whole endeavor. De La Hoya said the right things, did the right interviews, wore the right clothes, then vanished, off to his own hideaways and far from the streets of the barrio.

Chavez embraced the barrios—and the people embraced him right back, fervently. On a walk with Chavez down Olvera Street in downtown Los Angeles one afternoon, through a narrow corridor lined with outdoor booths, it seemed like arms and hands were everywhere, reaching out to him and touching him and chasing him. Chavez soaked it all up, jubilantly yelling to the crowd, and the crowd rapturously chanted back to him: "May-he-co!"

Chavez was exactly what Mexicans loved in fighters—to hit you, he would allow you to hit him with everything you had. Then he would batter you, body part by body part, until, at the very end, you were swallowing your own blood and dizzy from the experience. To the people of those streets, to the immigrant Mexicans and the fight fans of the Latino populace, Chavez stood for Mexican pride. When Chavez bled, they believed, he bled for them.

The everlasting and essential Chavez experience came in March 1990, when he faced Meldrick Taylor, a powerful, fast fighter from Philadelphia, in the biggest nonheavyweight fight of the year. Taylor tattooed Chavez for eleven rounds, and was fifteen seconds away from winning an easy decision when Chavez's slow, steady attack finally reached its climax with a couple of hammering lefts to Taylor's cheek.

Taylor went down with ten seconds left in the fight, got back up, but was so woozy and had swallowed so much of his own blood that his dazed look convinced referee Richard Steele to stop the fight only two seconds before the final bell.

Chavez had performed the perfect warrior's drama: When all is lost, when the opponent is moments from celebration, reach deep into your soul and make your last charge. Win, despite the wounds. And become stronger for it. Taylor never seemed to recover from that loss, and five years later, showed up for a rematch against Chavez as a shell of his former self. He slurred his words, and his punches were loose and ineffective. Chavez knocked him out in eight rounds.

In direct and delicious contrast, De La Hoya was what Americans loved in fighters—thunderously powerful, elusive, and handsome. It did not escape Mexican boxing fans that De La Hoya was building his name by defeating Mexican or Mexican-American fighters—Paez, Ruelas, Hernandez. Chavez was next.

"We've got to stop fighting our own people," Alcazar said at the time. "It's not good for us or for our people."

Rivero approached it from a larger perspective. If it was De La Hoya versus Chavez for the hearts of the Latino people, the choice should be obvious, he said. Chavez, Rivero noted, was a close associate of and received favors from the disgraced former Mexican president Carlos Salinas, part and parcel of Mexico's corrupt past and present.

"Why does the Mexican public favor Chavez and boo Oscar? Why?" Rivero asked. "Chavez has embraced a corrupt government, he has dedicated every one of his fights to the president Carlos Salinas. How is it possible that a boxer gains prestige by serving a government that steals from its people? Why does the Mexican population of Los Angeles favor him instead of Oscar? If he beats Chavez, nobody can stop from recognizing him."

Chavez did not take Rivero's criticism lightly. "He is a traitor," Chavez said bitterly of Rivero, then he said no more.

De La Hoya, meanwhile, had just commissioned the design of his own private bus, painted with his face. And he wouldn't even comment on the hot-button issue of the day—the California proposition that, if passed, could severely limit Mexican immigration into the state and was widely viewed as part of a slightly veiled anti-Latino movement. De La

Hoya didn't think about such things, and he surely never talked about them. If De La Hoya ever bled, the people of the barrio never saw it, and they knew it wasn't for them, anyway.

Where was De La Hoya from? With the Chavez fight approaching, this became an issue of contention. For his earlier fights, De La Hoya's hometown was announced correctly: It was Montebello, then Whittier. Then, with the Hernandez fight, Arum decided to switch the announcement to say East L.A., even though De La Hoya hadn't lived there for years.

For all honest purposes, De La Hoya was by now of Whittier and the golf courses and Hugo Boss and Mennen and whatever other corporate sponsors his marketing gurus could cobble together. He made about $250,000 a year from his endorsements alone. He was from anywhere but East L.A., and the people of the neighborhood knew it. Long before any fight was even negotiated, Oscar De La Hoya and Julio Cesar Chavez were polar opposites of the same world, increasingly and inevitably headed toward each other, for one of the most lucrative and anticipated fights of the decade.

They both were Mexican, but was that where the similarities ended?

Chavez was wanton and wild outside of the ring, happy with a beer in his hand and at least one girl by his side, most of the time not his wife, and another flying in tomorrow.

Inside the ring, Chavez was a warrior, lacking in size and athletic skills but capable of enduring the punishment of a Brahma bull in order to bash his way to victory.

De La Hoya chose the Mexican preference for Chavez as grounds for contemplating retirement. He complained that he wasn't being appreciated by his own people. He felt sorry for himself, and further inflamed the emotions of those who hated him.

"I've been thinking about retirement a lot," De La Hoya said. "So many fans boo me. I don't get hit. I don't have a lot of cuts and bruises. For that reason, I don't think the young people appreciate me. If I was all beat up, they might appreciate me more. If I looked like a fighter, they might think of me as a warrior. It's time to catch up on my personal life. As each day goes by, I see more and more bad things about boxing. The politics and everything else. It takes me away from the sport and makes me think about retirement."

De La Hoya was passive in public, with his strained smile and high, sometimes faltering voice. Even by his father's reckoning he was an incredibly light drinker—"One beer and he's drunk," Joel Sr. said. "He has one drink, and he's throwing up," said one De La Hoya friend. "He gets so sick, it's unbelievable. But then he just wants to drink some more."

Said Peralta: "If we go out, he has to drink. If he drinks, he has to get drunk. If he gets drunk, he's going to get sick. That gets real tiring."

But in the ring, he was literally head and shoulders above everybody else, so fast and skilled that once he struck cleanly, the fight was usually over. He had proven that against Ruelas and Hernandez (and a few months later, former champion Jesse James Leija) and almost everybody he had faced.

Against Leija in December 1995, De La Hoya finally staged his New York debut, and it was trumpeted across the town as a rebirth of boxing. With a huge promotional push, De La Hoya versus Leija (who was dwarfed by De La Hoya) drew an impressive crowd of 15,000 (translating to a $1 million gate), at Madison Square Garden, which hadn't hosted a major fight in years. A few months later, a Roy Jones Jr. fight put only 8,000 in the Garden.

"The rap on him is he's just another West Coast fighter, but he's come here and he's grabbed people's imagination," said HBO's Lou DiBella. "This is the most successful Madison Square Garden bout in years because of Oscar."

De La Hoya finally played the big town, and he loved it. It was Christmastime in New York City, the snow fell softly, and De La Hoya roamed the city with Veronica, Pajar, and his closest friend among his bodyguards, Arturo Galvan. Arum was pleased enough by the ticket sales that he paid for a $15,000 De La Hoya shopping spree—to Barney's and Bloomingdale's. On Wednesday night, two days before the fight, De La Hoya and his friends ate dinner twenty feet away from Gene Kelly (neither noticed the other) at a theater-district Italian restaurant. And everywhere he looked, his arrival was heralded: in the tabloids, on billboards, by people walking past him, thanking him for coming.

"I think if you don't go to Madison Square Garden, you'll never be really big," Mike Hernandez said. "This is very good for Oscar. Let's face it, if he was facing the toughest fighter in the world, it'd be better. But just to be there, it's good. Madison Square Garden is number one for boxing. I know Madison Square Garden has been the best—where Sugar Ray Robinson used to fight."

Said Arum, a New York native: "This is huge for De La Hoya. His last two pay-per-view fights had trouble getting coverage in the newspapers in the East. Sports editors said they were just regional fights. Oscar had never campaigned outside the West, but the fact he can draw here at the Garden the way he has and the way it created such a fuss in the papers and on TV here is going to help make him a national celebrity. Boxing in New York legitimizes Oscar."

The fight was called "Return to the Mecca," and New York just seemed happy to have big-time boxing back at the Garden. A few years later, big-time boxing would provoke a riot in the Garden, after Andrew Golota was disqualified against Riddick Bowe, and the Bowe entourage attacked Golota's people in the aftermath. But there were no riots for De La Hoya–Leija, only the crackle of De La Hoya's fists against the five-foot-five Leija's head. He wanted to put on a show—with Walter Cronkite, Mel Gibson, most of the New York Knicks, and Donald Trump sitting ringside. And he did.

"This is the most important fight of my career since the Olympics," De La Hoya said in the days before the bout. "It can take me to the next level. This fight in New York gives me the chance to expand myself to people in general. People outside of boxing don't know me yet, but after this, they will begin to. I've been on the West Coast all my life. I understood what coming to New York and being successful could do for me. I've even changed my style for the fans here. I need to box a few rounds to show them my skills and then I need to take Jesse James out."

After dispatching the mismatched Leija in two rounds, De La Hoya was done with the 135-pound division, and everything pointed to fighting for Chavez's World Boxing Council 140-pound title. It was time to move up to 140 pounds, to Chavez's division, and start the real rumbling.

What he left behind was another fallen opponent.

"This kid breaks careers," DiBella said of De La Hoya.

"He should be a middleweight," Leija sighed.

"I'm still just a baby in this sport," De La Hoya said. "It might be two-three years, but if I keep learning and learning, I'll be able to be with the big boys pretty soon."

At HBO's postfight party in the Garden, Arum squirreled away with Chavez and his business people, loudly and happily signing a two-fight contract: De La Hoya and Chavez would fight separate fights on the same card in Las Vegas in February 1996, then meet each other at Caesars in June. Chavez drank some wine, shook Arum's hand, then giddily wandered through the party crowd, hugging every female he saw.

Chavez would earn at least $9 million for the fight, and another $1 million for the tune-up in February. De La Hoya was guaranteed $8.95 million, in deference to the Chavez legend. That was the only sign of deference, though, on De La Hoya's part.

"I think Oscar is ready," Mike Hernandez said in 1995. "I really do. I was way ahead of Bob Arum on this. I told Oscar right after the Ruelas fight, 'Your next goal is Chavez. The rest is easy.' I talked to him a couple days ago about Chavez. He said, 'I don't see any problem with that.'"

Chavez got $2 million up front to help with his taxes, and Arum had himself the Latino dream fight.

Meanwhile, De La Hoya exulted in the moment, and promptly dropped any retirement plans.

"I know I talked about taking a year off after Chavez," De La Hoya said. "But that depends on the fans. They're the ones who make it possible. With this kind of response, it makes me want to stay on in boxing a long time. I was honored to be a part of it. The expectations of the people of New York were high, but I gave them a great show."

Back home, the warmth of the New York reception only served to highlight De La Hoya's estrangement from Los Angeles—most particularly from the Mexican and Mexican-American boxing hotbed. A few weeks later, at a parade celebrating Mexican Independence Day in East L.A., several tomatoes were tossed at De La Hoya, who was serving as a marshal. De La Hoya ducked the incoming and laughed off the jeers.

But the taunts persisted. One person carried a sign that read: WHAT'S OSCAR DOING AT A *MEXICAN* PARADE?

Said Erasmo Granillo, a local fight fan: "Chavez is real, and he has a lot more power than Oscar De La Hoya. I don't want to see any cowards. Oscar is a coward. You can tell, because De La Hoya talks too much sometimes. I don't like that. Chavez is 100 percent Mexican. And Oscar's half-and-half. *Mise-mise*."

Another face in the crowd put it more harshly: "Oh, Oscar, that *white guy?*"

If the jibes stung, De La Hoya tried to brush them off. He could afford to.

"They love me everywhere but L.A.," De La Hoya said.

What had happened between him and his town? De La Hoya saw it as both the price and the natural result of his popularity. Sugar Ray Leonard experienced something similar during his rise from the blue-collar towns of Maryland, but it was not nearly as volatile a relationship between homegrown superstar and angry populace. He never had eggs thrown at him during a visit to his own high school, and he wasn't booed at a parade through his home base.

"I think it's all about the perception here that Chavez, with his background and his culture, really is blue-collar," Leonard said. "And Oscar is a white-collar fighter. I kind of went through a little bit of that with Tommy Hearns. The way it was for me wasn't on this grand of a scale. But tell you what, depending on who wins this fight, and how impressive it is, there's room for change."

Rivero, for his part, blamed the image-makers. To sell De La Hoya to the corporate barons, Arum and Hernandez packaged him as a product, and packaging did not sell well at home. The fights were too easy, the money was too fast, the home base was forgotten. Oscar was a sterile figure—and a mystery to his own hometown.

"The image that they have created is negative," Rivero said. "He's a young man who lives the fast life, plays golf. . . . He left his place of origin and he's had easy fights. Those are the images they have of him, of a boxer who hasn't faced anybody who has challenged him. Another is the image that because he plays golf, he has money. That's all negative. In boxing, I have to admit he hasn't had a difficult fight, at least not since Chicanito. The rest have been mediocre fighters. But see, the Mexicans in California, they always go for the poor, for the weak. But it's not justified in Chavez. Oscar is a good person, he's not arrogant. Chavez is arrogant."

As the Chavez fight approached, on the streets of East L.A.—and El Monte and Monterey Park and Huntington Park and even Montebello—the irritation moved beyond something De La Hoya could possibly ignore. The contrast with Chavez heightened the gap between De La Hoya and East L.A., between the ideal and the reality.

The loudest parts of the community wanted De La Hoya beaten. He had been handed talent, looks, and a gold medal . . . the least he could do was suffer a little. To feel life the way they lived it. For once.

"What was the first thing he did after he came back from the Olympics? He moved out of here and went to the Montebello hills," said Gladys Martinez, sitting in a Monterey Park restaurant weeks before the Chavez fight. At the counter, the restaurant kept a running tally of pro–De La Hoya and pro-Chavez fans, and Chavez was ahead, with nearly twice De La Hoya's count. "He couldn't drive that Corvette or whatever fast enough out of here," Martinez said. "All the people that I know, they want Julio to beat his butt."

"Why don't we like Oscar? He's conceited," said Garfield student Christina Avilla. "He thinks he's all that. We do like his body, but still, I go for Chavez."

It was an exasperating situation for some of the established figures of the community, who knew and supported De La Hoya and watched sadly as the rift opened wide. East L.A., or at least every part of it that was loud and attended fights, didn't like its most famous son.

"Oscar's got two big problems: He's attractive and he's damned near perfect," said comedian Paul Rodriguez, also a product of East L.A. "Which makes for a lot of petty jealousy. But Oscar is absolutely the best thing to come down the pike. He's the real deal—trains like a monk, is absolutely clean, has no skeletons in the closet. And he will go down as the first superstar celebrity who can totally cross over."

Rodriguez, who knew De La Hoya well, said De La Hoya's docile personality was being unfairly held against him. It wasn't that he disliked where he came from, it's just that he rarely showed emotions of any kind, Rodriguez argued.

"A lot of my Chicano friends misunderstand being shy for arrogance," Rodriguez said. "Oscar is not a very talkative guy. Oscar is reserved and shy, and he's not the kind of guy to go out to Lincoln Park and have a Budweiser with the boys. That's what they want. But he can't do that. It's not in his system."

Peralta, who was working as a student teacher in a local high school at the time, said she sometimes would turn her back in the classroom, and hear one or two of the students shout: "Chavez!"

To ease the tension, Mike Hernandez decided he needed to fashion a base for De La Hoya's good works in East L.A. Something big, something very public, something with his name on it that he could point to—that's what I'm giving back, De La Hoya could say. Oscar wasn't ever going to live there again—he was already thinking of moving farther away, geographically and socially, from Whittier, maybe to Malibu, or even to Beverly Hills. But he could build something. Hernandez focused on the kids of the community—they were more likely to cheer De La Hoya than their teenage brothers and their fathers.

The solution: Buy the old and decaying Resurrection Gym and transform it into a youth center. As the Chavez fight neared, De La Hoya and Hernandez were arranging to purchase his old gym from the man who owned it, former congressman Ed Roybl, who was weeks away from shutting it down. For $250,000, De La Hoya funded some desperately needed refurbishing, cleaned it out, and turned it into the home of the Oscar De La Hoya Youth Center. Along the way, Hernandez noted, De La Hoya paid for scholarships at Garfield, and made scattered donations—worth tens of thousands—throughout the community, including the Hollenbeck Youth Center, where he had trained with Stankie.

But to many these were viewed as merely public-relations gestures from a multimillionaire guarding his image, not the honest reinvestment of a hometown hero.

"He says he does these things," said Jesse Castellanos, eating at the Monterey Park restaurant. "But how come we never see him? All he's got is a big head."

Said Joel Jr.: "It does get tiresome. It pisses me off, that's what it does. First of all, they say, 'Oh, Oscar doesn't come around.' What is he going to do? Shake everybody's hand in the community? Go around East L.A. and shake everybody's hand? People don't appreciate him, what he does for the community. He puts in a lot of time talking to children, donates a lot of money. People expect him to be walking the streets of East L.A. They say he was born with a silver spoon in his mouth. . . . If they only knew."

Alcazar just waited for the outcome of this fight. The fans, he said, won't be able to resist De La Hoya much longer. Beat the biggest Mexican fighter alive, and they will come running to the best Mexican-American fighter ever.

"Julio Cesar Chavez is like the king of boxing for every Latino," Alcazar said. "By Oscar beating him, all the people who support Chavez will move to the new king."

Most of the time, De La Hoya himself brushed off the antipathy. He was making enough money, and was popular enough around the world, that it didn't matter, he said. Those who hated him would never like him, no matter what he did. Those who loved him would love him no matter what, too. He was a symbol, and people saw in him what they wanted to see, about themselves and about their community and about their sport.

But in more thoughtful moments, when he was at Big Bear, in his new cabin (which was completed in time for his Chavez training camp), De La Hoya allowed frustration to creep into his voice, and let the wounds of his expatriation show.

"I never thought that would happen, never in my life would I think that people would be against me in my own community, never, ever," De La Hoya said. "I realized it after a few pro fights, five or six pro fights. When I started getting endorsements, that's when I found out. 'Oh, man, why?' Like when I started doing English [-speaking] endorsements, it would hurt me first. But then I realized, 'Hey, the more critics, the better.' Why not?

"I'd say, 'I'm going to quit because the fans don't love me here.' But after a while I got over it. It's not everyone. I would say now it's proba-bly like maybe 2 percent of the people here in L.A. who don't like me. Everywhere I go, those 2 percent follow me. What can I do? I can't do anything. I thought I was doing everything perfect, representing East Los Angeles. . . . To this day they announce me as being from East Los Angeles, and still that 2 percent doesn't respect me. They respect failure, yes. That's what they want to see. When I lose . . . I *won't* lose, but let's say I do lose. Then they'll respect me. If I get cut up and bruised up and knocked out, then they'll respect me. Because I'll be what they want, a warrior. My father's bothered by it, my brother, too."

Even if De La Hoya didn't understand how it happened, he said there were some very real results. He was not welcome in his own neigh-borhood. He could feel it. Did it say more about him or the community?

"I'm scared to go back to East L.A. because of that group," De La Hoya said. "Because I don't feel welcomed. I don't. I just don't feel wel-comed. If I want to go back to my favorite place to eat tacos, King Taco, I always hide. I'm always hiding. If I'm in a car with a bunch of friends, I'll stay in the car. I don't feel welcomed. It's an ugly feeling. I just don't feel welcomed. They're driving me away. It's their fault, not mine. They're driving me away.

"I'll go anywhere around the world and I'll guarantee you they love me. Anywhere except East L.A., and it'll never change. Never, never. I know it won't. There's always going to be that jealousy, always. And it's that younger crowd, that crowd that has the pretty girlfriend and, 'Oh, we're afraid that Oscar's going to take her away.' Maybe it'll change when I get married. Maybe they'll respect me then."

In a convenient coincidence, the heat for this fight was building just as Arum was engaged in a public relations battle with the pay-per-view distributors for fiscal control of the big events.

Arum, whose recent non–De La Hoya pay-per-view shows had been disappointments, screamed that the pay-per-view companies weren't policing the illegal distribution of so-called black boxes, which gave homes free access to the pay events. Meanwhile, the promoter had guaranteed almost $18 million in purses to De La Hoya and Chavez (and a million more to the undercard fighters), and if they weren't going to cut off the black boxes, he wanted the assortment of pay-per-view distributors (who did the actual selling of the fights, home by home) to put up a big chunk of that outlay up front.

"Pay-per-view is flawed," Arum said. "If this fight was on pay-per-view, it would do two million homes," Arum said. "Maybe 500,000 would pay and 1.5 million would steal."

What really bothered him wasn't the black boxes—it was that the pay-per-view businessmen weren't willing to be partners in his promotion. Quickly, Arum negotiated a deal with closed-circuit exhibitors, who were excited to be back in the big-time boxing business and guaranteed him $12 million. Add in Caesars' $6 million guarantee to host the fight, and Arum had his $18 million purse expenditure covered. Everything else would be profit off the top.

Arum threw himself into promoting the fight, setting up a crazy, chaotic twenty-three-city barnstorming tour with both fighters, using separate planes, traveling across the nation in eleven exhausting days. The promotion was called "Back to the Future," and it evoked the old days of boxing, of Dempsey and Marciano and Sugar Ray Robinson.

The plane tour kicked off on March 4 in Los Angeles—at the Olympic Auditorium, coincidentally—with a flourish and ragged symbolism. Several hundred locals showed up for the event and raucously razzed De La Hoya (and chanted "Cha-vez! Cha-vez!") when the two fighters were introduced. De La Hoya ignored the reception, and Chavez laughed his way through it, making sure to comment, "I have never been booed in my hometown."

Said Arum: "This is like a Super Bowl, except you get a Super Bowl every year and you get a fight like this once a decade. This is what you live for."

One interested observer, barely noticeable in the ruckus, was Bobby Chacon, the great former featherweight champion from Los Angeles, who lingered in the back of the arena as the show went on, mumbling to himself. In 1974, Chacon beat Danny (Little Red) Lopez at the Sports Arena in the greatest L.A. fight of the era.

But twenty-two years later, Chacon was a weary man. The first of his four wives, Valerie, committed suicide in 1982, and his son Bobby (Chico) Chacon was killed in a gang confrontation in 1991. And Chacon, who served jail time for domestic abuse of his second wife, also suffered from weak kidneys and *pugilistica dementia,* which, in layman's terms, meant he was literally punch drunk.

Chacon watched the goings-on with a particular interest, and heard the crowd roar. Then, when the press conference was over, and the double entourages sped toward the airport and to the next city, Chacon wandered back to work as the arena emptied—wading through trash to collect cans.

As a show of his serious focus for the fight, Chavez took a deep gulp of champagne at the kickoff of the March plane tour, then swore he wouldn't drink again until after the De La Hoya fight. So what if he stole away for a few beers here and there throughout the trip? So what if he was forty-five minutes or more late to almost every one of the tedious press conferences? So what if he was irritating De La Hoya more and more every day? Chavez was enjoying himself—flirting with his stewardess, with girls he met on the tour—and he was confident that the young fighter wasn't ready for him.

In the middle of the trip, Arum had to place a call to a young girl's family in Orange County, asking her parents if she could travel with Chavez. They said yes. Chavez had a new friend for a night or two.

In El Paso, the tour reached its crescendo—thousands of fans blocked the fighters' vans' path into the hotel, and screaming girls threw themselves in front of the De La Hoya entourage. Chavez's van wisely detoured to the back entrance, but De La Hoya emerged amid the throng, inciting a near riot. His clothes were torn, his hair was mussed, his publicist, Dena duBoef, was tossed to the ground helplessly trying to maintain order, and his conditioner, Andy Shumway, was shoved aside. De La Hoya made it through to the hotel, beaming.

"That was great!" he said to no one in particular. "I love El Paso!"

At last, by April, the fighters set to training for the bout. For Team De La Hoya, it was time to clear the decks before the biggest fight of his life.

In Big Bear, there wasn't even any attempt to pretend that Alcazar was the main trainer anymore. By the time the Chavez fight rolled around, Alcazar didn't even go to Big Bear—except for the days when he knew the media would be watching. This was Rivero's camp. His plan, his responsibility. For the first time, Rivero was publicly acknowledged as at least an equal of Alcazar's, and also for the first time, Rivero was scheduled to be in De La Hoya's corner for the fight, giving the orders.

"This is your fight," Hernandez told Rivero when the Chavez fight was signed.

To soothe Alcazar, Mike Hernandez lengthened his contract, with a modifier. Instead of taking 10 percent of each purse, as he had in the beginning, Alcazar's earnings were capped, so the most he could earn on any one fight was $100,000. Rivero was also paid about $100,000 per fight, not including bonuses, which, for the Chavez fight, reached $50,000. Alcazar told the media that he was the one paying Rivero, and stayed down below, busying himself with his new El Monte restaurant.

"There will always be a place for Roberto," Hernandez said. "I think everybody knows where their place is. I hope so, anyway. Because I'm the one who has to take the heat from each of them. It wasn't easy. But I think Robert's a very reasonable guy. He's going to be around Oscar for a long time. Oscar always felt Robert was part of it. But we're going through a transition to a higher level of boxing, and Robert knows that."

Alcazar wasn't at camp, but he wasn't letting go. He insisted on keeping his title as head trainer. Rivero, he decided, was not going to last. Alcazar always had.

"We've been getting more and more experience as time goes by," Alcazar said. "And now, with this adjustment, with this move and this new deal we've put together, it brings peace to everybody on the team. Everybody knows who's working in which area and everybody's supporting everybody. All this has been planned almost a year ago. And finally, it's here. We've been getting ready for this specific fight for almost a year."

This time, a full year into their relationship, Rivero stayed in a downstairs bedroom in De La Hoya's cabin. De La Hoya had the entire upstairs to himself. De La Hoya already trusted Rivero's boxing sense, and his advice. But in this camp, in closer proximity and without Alcazar's interference, the two were inseparable, mentor and pupil. Rivero held long videotape sessions with the fighter in the evenings, after training. Sometimes the two took long walks into the woods, talking about fights and about life. Everything was directed, Rivero said, to having the will and the skill to defeat a legend like Chavez.

"Since the Ruelas camp, I was thinking of a fight with Chavez," Rivero said. "The first time I met with Mike Hernandez, I asked him if Oscar could not only be a champion but a great champion, like Sugar

Ray Robinson. Was he going to be distracted by all these different things, by the movies?"

Nobody had ever really asked De La Hoya that question straight out before: Are you going to be great? And De La Hoya loved the challenge. Joel Jr. described Rivero's influence as bringing "a light to this camp," and called him Mr. Miyagi, playfully referring to the mentor figure in the movie *The Karate Kid*. Oscar just called him Don Jesus, as if he were a wise man.

"Don Jesus is opening my eyes, you know?" De La Hoya said. "There's so much to learn and such little time. This old man is atheist— I don't pay attention to that. I like listening, because it's funny, the things that he talks about. We discuss religion a lot, but I don't pay attention to him really on it. It is interesting to talk about. I've never had discussions like this before. He doesn't want me to be just another boxer. He wants me to expand my mind into things other than boxing."

Since his mother's passing, De La Hoya's life had been entirely about boxing: training, conditioning, winning, earning. No one around him, with the exception of Veronica Peralta, thought about anything else, or wanted him to think about anything else. And Peralta was easily shunted aside in the rush to keep him in shape and winning.

There was a void, and into it walked Rivero, who eagerly acted as a guide for the development of De La Hoya's soul away from boxing. It was all related. Unless the fighter also became a fully rounded man, Rivero believed, there was no way he'd be a great fighter.

"I want to awaken him," Rivero said.

Rivero pointed to history for a comparison, back to the golden age of sports, to the Roaring '20s, when Jack Dempsey was as popular as Babe Ruth, a towering man dominating the heavyweight division with his fists and his personality. Dempsey romanced actresses, gambled wildly, starred in movies, and burned as brightly as any American sports figure ever had. And, as De La Hoya went through flings with actresses like Elizabeth Berkley (of the movie *Showgirls*) and envisioned movie stardom, Rivero saw the parallels.

"Dempsey was the number one idol in North America," Rivero said. "He made millions of dollars in his fights, did movies, dated stars. And he had problems, being put in another world. I want Oscar to learn from Dempsey's life. He could be a good example for Oscar, what could happen to him—being put into the movies, living that kind of life. He can be more careful about what he does. There is plenty of time to be in the movies. It's an adventure. But there's time for that. If he beats Chavez, there's some big fights that can make good money, then, he's twenty-five or twenty-six, with good good money, he can quit. And when his career is over, he can do the movies."

What did Rivero see? De La Hoya had his girls, he had his toys, and he had golf. But what else? What would De La Hoya have once his boxing life was over? The same aimlessness, the same boredom. Unless something was cultivated inside.

"A boxer is a human," Rivero said then. "He needs to destroy his enemies, but he can't always think about money and fame. A boxer has to understand things like music and literature and history and politics. He needs to concern himself with the great problems of society, of life. He needs to learn about history and economics. It's very important to understand the full world that's around him. Listen to good music, read Shakespeare. I'm trying to wake him up and see another world. There's a whole other world out there he hasn't seen."

These were huge steps to take for a fighter who missed many of his high school classes for boxing tournaments and who barely passed the GED. "I don't like to read, I like to listen to you better," De La Hoya told Rivero.

Said Joel Jr.: "He's a real intriguing man. We sit and listen to him. We may not agree with whatever he talks about, but we'll listen to him. Because it's real interesting. He teaches us more about the history of the sport, not just the opponent you're going up against, but the history. Oscar's never done this before—he's never picked up a book outside of school. And what the old man is trying to do is just trying to educate him a little. You can't be a boxer for the rest of your life."

But he would have to be a hell of a boxer to beat Chavez on June 7. Rivero was determined that De La Hoya would be ready. The old De La Hoya, even the fighter himself admitted, might not have held up against the force of Chavez.

"Obviously, my style has changed a lot," De La Hoya said. "Now I'm just a smarter fighter. I don't get hit anymore. Back then, it was like if they were to hit me, I would stay right there and just go at it with them. See who falls first. It might've worked against Chavez, who knows? But knowing that Chavez is a dangerous fighter, of course, this style is going to work better."

The corner was going to be a little crowded—Alcazar would join Rivero in the corner for at least one more fight—but Rivero made it clear that there was only one person in charge during the fight.

"He will be in the corner, too," Rivero said of Alcazar, "but he will be quiet, and I will be the only one talking. It is my game plan, so why would he say anything?"

De La Hoya had to be ready for Chavez at his best, hammering at anything that stayed still in front of him. De La Hoya had to be ready for the Chavez who cut down Meldrick Taylor and blasted Hector Camacho.

"Chavez is not finished like everybody says," Rivero cautioned. "He isn't the fighter he was years ago, but he still is a dangerous fighter. He's a strong fighter, he's got a lot of experience, and he's got great pride. Despite the problems that he has, with his family, his money, there's no way you can take him lightly, no matter what. It's my obligation to get him ready for this."

Said De La Hoya: "I think every boxer needs a man like this—a professor. This guy brings out the best in you. Him being in the corner just gives me so much confidence, because he knows what he's doing. What he tells me, I do up in the ring. This is a man who knows what he's doing. He knows the game plan, he knows what Chavez will do, he knows what I have to do to beat him. Everything is in order now. It should've been like this for my first pro fight. Finally, we have the perfect camp—perfect timing."

Tragically, things were not so smooth for Julio Cesar Chavez, in the camp for the richest fight of his life, the hundredth of his career.

Chavez, as was his custom, started his training in the mountains of Toluca, Mexico, with loose plans to head to Lake Tahoe for the final weeks of training. Chavez was comfortable in Toluca—the food was prepared right, his entourage was happy, the sparring partners didn't have far to travel, and the air was thin.

Chavez was comfortable, until April 9, and then he took off as fast as he could.

That day, Jesus (Bebe) Gallardo, a close friend and regular sparring partner of Chavez's, took his five-year-old son to the bathroom of the Holiday Inn restaurant. Everybody in the camp, including Chavez, stayed at the Holiday Inn—it was the base of the camp. As Gallardo walked into the lobby, a gunman jumped from behind a row of plants and fired, striking Gallardo three times and killing him. A state government official, who suspiciously received a cell-phone call to distract him just before the gunshots, also was shot and killed.

Immediately, the investigation focused on drugs. Gallardo had been released from a Tijuana prison in February, his second jail term for drug possession. Chavez was rattled and angry. Rumors persisted that he was closely associated with the drug lords of his hometown, Culiacán. Was Chavez perhaps involved, either as a target or otherwise, in this cold-blooded murder?

"Look, I wasn't there when Bebe was killed," Chavez told reporters after the incident. Then, a few days later, he was gone to Lake Tahoe, with the rest of the camp, without any plans to participate in the investigation. "What am I going to testify?" he said. "I was there for four days after the assassination and they never asked me anything. Please. What am I going to tell them?"

Ensconced at Caesars Tahoe, in unfamiliar territory, Chavez was in a fitful mood—and seriously worried about reprisals or follow-ups to the murder of his friend. To make things worse, his estranged wife, Amalia, was loathe to bring his children to see him. Chavez doted on his boys, especially his middle son, three-year-old Christian, who was as rowdy and impetuous as his father.

Some days, Chavez completely skipped his workouts. Some days, he went through the motions distractedly. A few Mexican reporters who were allowed to watch him train wondered if Chavez thought he could beat De La Hoya by force of personality alone. De La Hoya was five inches taller, faster, almost eleven years younger, and Chavez hadn't looked sharp in four years.

"I have demonstrated what I am already," Chavez said. "I have had thirty-four championship fights. The younger one, the favorite, has to demonstrate what he has. I'm coming in without any pressure at all. We'll see what happens in the ring."

Chavez scoffed at Rivero's influence on De La Hoya. "The fighter is born," Chavez said. "He cannot be made."

But being away from Mexico did help Chavez in one area—he was able to, for the most part, stick to his alcohol- and fat-free diet. He was, as he repeatedly said, in the best shape of his life. At least he looked good.

"I want to be the Julio Cesar Chavez you have seen in the good fights," Chavez said. "I am not going down like everybody says. Oscar De La Hoya has never fought anyone like Chavez. I haven't prepared myself like this since Rosario [whom he beat in 1987]."

But there were further embarrassments. With Chavez in Tahoe training, a reporter from a San Antonio newspaper went to Culiacán and interviewed several Chavez friends and relatives. Almost every single one of them said he should retire.

Chavez wasn't retiring. Not with a $9 million payday straight ahead of him and debts to pay. Chavez needed this fight more than he wanted to admit. For pride, and for money, Julio Cesar Chavez desperately needed this fight to happen. So when disaster struck again, there was no backing out.

About a month before the bout, right after a sparring session in the hotel, Chavez and three or four of his closest associates disappeared for a time from Tahoe. Nobody knew where they'd gone, just that Chavez wasn't training at the hotel, and that hopefully he would be back. Then, when he returned, the windows that looked into his workout room were covered—nobody could look inside.

What had happened? During a workout in May, sparring partner Lalo Mendoza had opened a cut above Chavez's left eye—the same area that had opened up against David Kamau and Randall before that. It had to be kept secret, though, because a postponement or cancellation of the bout would push back that payday. And Chavez needed the money. In supersecret meetings with his private doctor, apparently in Mexico, Chavez was told he could fight, but that he had better be careful not to open it up again in training.

Chavez went to enormous lengths to keep the cut a secret. At the fight's final press conference in Las Vegas, the normally fastidious dresser (Versace was his favorite) showed up in shorts, a T-shirt, and a big baseball cap—the better to hide any visible signs of damage.

"It was very peculiar," said someone who had spent a lot of time with him during the camp. "I had been with him for twenty, thirty press conferences, and he never dressed like that. It was always Versace, Versace, Versace. And for the final big press conference, he looked like a mess."

Later that day, appearing on a Spanish-language TV show from Las Vegas, Chavez sat with Christian on his lap, chatting away with the host. Then, suddenly, he leaped up from his seat, and darted offstage. As he would later admit, Christian had bumped his head into his father's new wound, reopening the cut.

Only in television close-ups before the fight is there a visible, telltale sign: a thin dark line, about one inch long, above his left eye, only partially obscured by what appears to be makeup.

But in the final days, Chavez bragged that he had trained so well he was actually faster than he had ever been, and surely would be able to keep up with De La Hoya.

"Chavez has had ninety-nine fights, and now he's faster?" De La Hoya said. "What does that mean? Is he trying to psyche me out or something? Chavez says he's in the best shape of his life. That's good. I don't want there to be any excuses."

De La Hoya was a 7–5 betting favorite the night of the fight, but that was down from 3–1, after waves of mostly Mexican and Mexican-American fans poured into Vegas and put bets down on Chavez. According to the casino sports books, about $30 million was wagered on the fight, breaking the record of $22 million bet on the 1987 Sugar Ray Leonard–Marvelous Marvin Hagler fight.

Don King, who had maintained a low profile (until he sued Chavez two days before the fight, for a piece of the purse he said he was owed), loudly boasted that he had bet $600,000 of his own money on Chavez.

"This fight is very special for me," Chavez said. "The chance to have this fight is like having a beautiful woman in front of you. Win or lose, this is going to be one of the greatest fights. If I were to lose, I wouldn't be frustrated. Even if I lose, I'm going to be very, very proud of this. I will not lose easy. I will give my life for this fight."

The crowd roared during the fighter introductions—overwhelmingly loud for Chavez, mostly boos for De La Hoya. In the closed-circuit theaters across Southern California, many observers estimated that the crowds were 95 percent pro-Chavez.

Did De La Hoya know about the cut? He swore he didn't. Either way, his strategy going in was perfect. De La Hoya opened the fight determined to put as many tight jabs on Chavez's face as possible for as long as possible. It was a long and lethal jab, what boxing people call a "jackhammer jab." De La Hoya threw it four seconds into the fight, and never stopped pulling the trigger on it.

He scored several times in the first few seconds, but Chavez, as expected, just kept walking into and through De La Hoya's punches, peering in for his own attack. When Chavez leaned in, De La Hoya bent backward, side to side, and then lashed a few shots back at Chavez, who didn't have the speed to fire back. The two circled in the center of the ring for thirty seconds—De La Hoya firing the jab through Chavez's gloves and into his face, and Chavez moving slowly, but certainly.

"Frankie Randall had the perfect game plan for Chavez," De La Hoya said earlier, "but he didn't have the power to stop Chavez. A fighter who stays in front of Chavez and tries to stop him, that'll stop him in his tracks."

The crowd stayed relatively silent, waiting for something meaningful to happen.

Then, fifty-one seconds into the fight, De La Hoya whipped two more jabs on top of Chavez's left eye, the last one with a little twist at impact, to increase the friction. Chavez blinked a couple of times, nodded his head, and kept going.

The blood didn't start flowing for a few seconds. It looked like a smudge at first, a pink film above Chavez's eye. At the first trickle, Chavez instinctively pawed at the incision, not because the blood was in his eyes, but because he knew there was something wrong.

A few seconds later, his face was a red river.

A minute into the fight, De La Hoya was staring at an old, bleeding man, frantically and hopelessly wiping blood out of his eye, onto his nose, all over his body. Chavez took a few steps backward, to give himself time, to give himself air, as the blood poured down in front of his mouth. The blood came streaming, dampening De La Hoya's trunks and flickering to the canvas. Eight or nine jabs had done *that*?

For a time, both fighters were frozen by the development, and neither engaged the other. De La Hoya stayed away, and Chavez regrouped and wiped. But he was in shock. Then, thirty seconds after the first flow of blood, De La Hoya singed Chavez again, faking a left jab then bombing a right hook into Chavez, who was already dazed. Gruesomely, that punch actually served to clear Chavez's vision some, spraying blood across the ring.

But the bleeding wouldn't stop. Halfway through the first round, Chavez's face was bright red, and De La Hoya's gloves glowed a liquid crimson. The crowd by now was in shock, too.

"I was very surprised because Julio Cesar Chavez, he's known to get cut, he's known to have a very tender nose," De La Hoya said, "but I really didn't think that my stiff jab was going to cause a big gash over the eye."

Two minutes into the round, referee Joe Cortez called time and took Chavez over to see Flip Homansky, the doctor who had stopped the bout when Chavez was bleeding against Randall two years earlier. As Chavez twisted his neck to lean closer, Homansky toweled away the layer of blood and immediately decided that the cut wasn't deep enough to halt the bout. Not yet, at least.

For about five seconds, Chavez's face was clean. He waded back into action and threw a few punches at De La Hoya. After De La Hoya took a vicious swing and missed, Chavez had enough inside of him to taunt De La Hoya, sticking his chin out and daring De La Hoya to cut loose again. De La Hoya did not. But a moment later De La Hoya touched the cut again with a jab, and Chavez's eyebrow was a gash again.

At the end of the first, Chavez stalked back to the corner, his mouthpiece popping out of his mouth and blood pouring down his face. "Are you okay, Julio?" one of his cornermen yelled to him. "The cut is pretty big. We're going to have to play it by ear."

The blood didn't start flowing again until fifty-five seconds into the second round, and this time De La Hoya let more than the jab fly. He landed two big hooks and an uppercut, and Chavez was blinking away blood, De La Hoya barely visible in front of him. In a clench, he wiped his face on De La Hoya's right shoulder and face, smearing blood all over De La Hoya's body.

As the round wore on, the crowd implored him with a chant: "May-he-co!" But De La Hoya was in rhythm now, and less and less wary as the fight wore on and more energy oozed from Chavez's body. Chavez tried a few shots, and landed one solid shot to the body, but De La Hoya waved away the punch and moved quickly away from any real danger.

At the second-round bell, the toll of the bloodletting was clear: Chavez staggered two steps toward a neutral corner, wiped his eye distractedly, and kept heading the wrong way until Cortez yelled, "Julio, over there!" and sent him to his own corner. Through two rounds, De La Hoya had landed forty-one punches, most of them lashing jabs. Chavez had landed only seventeen, and maybe only one or two of those that had any hope of knocking De La Hoya offstride.

For the first minute of the third, it seemed that Chavez might grind his way back into the fight. He had done it against Taylor in 1990, and, when he was cut, against Kamau. The blood flow had slowed, and Chavez looked like he was honing in on De La Hoya, who hadn't yet flown in for a real deadly attack. De La Hoya was content to wreak his damage from the outside, and Chavez was bouncing in a little here, a little there, finding his way as the fight wore on. Finally, with ten seconds left in the round, Chavez flashed a hard left hook to De La Hoya's chin, rattling the challenger and rousing the crowd.

But through the noise, the most important moment was missed: De La Hoya had been hit hard and hadn't taken a step back.

At the round break, Rivero was calm. "It's no problem," he told De La Hoya. "Just keep doing exactly what you were doing."

Chavez made the crowd roar once again in the early moments of the fourth, cuffing De La Hoya against the ropes with a hard left hook, bending De La Hoya slightly backward for the first time. Again, twenty seconds later, Chavez fired a left hook at De La Hoya's chin, and the challenger wavered. Had De La Hoya lost his chance to put Chavez away?

In reality, this was a panicked Chavez, bulling and charging recklessly, and not with the precision and power of his better days. He knew that if the blood started flowing again—and it would, with the way De La Hoya was jabbing—he would not have a lot of time left. If the blood flowed again, he couldn't see De La Hoya's best power shots, and if you couldn't see them, you ate them.

One hundred seconds into the round, another deadly accurate De La Hoya jab ripped into Chavez's left forehead, and, inevitably, the blood ran again. And it was a gusher this time, more blood than before, more blood than anyone imagined could come out of a relatively thin cut. At the feel of it, Chavez flailed at De La Hoya, desperate for one massive shot, praying to duplicate his Taylor moment. But that came in the twelfth round of a war, when he wasn't bleeding and when he was six years younger. This time, as he barreled at De La Hoya, his face was a sheet of red, and the opponent bowed away easily from the attack.

Chavez stumbled into De La Hoya and waited for a clinch. But De La Hoya angrily shoved Chavez backward—had anyone just pushed Chavez back like that?—flared his eyes, and started dropping bombs. The first one was a left hook that crumpled Chavez's body, and De La Hoya followed that swiftly with a left-right combination to Chavez's swollen face. Another left to the cut area tore open the cut, and by then Chavez was teetering, blind and helpless.

Instead of defending himself, Chavez pawed at his face, trying to see through the red curtain. De La Hoya conked him on his head, then went to the body, like a machine gun. But Chavez did not fall. That much pride, at least, he still had.

With twenty-three seconds left in the round, Cortez stepped in again and took Chavez to Homansky. Could he continue? Homansky touched Chavez's face, and his hands were instantly coated with blood. Chavez's face was liquid. At the ropes, Chavez visibly sagged.

"That's it," Homansky said loudly.

"That's it?" Cortez asked.

"That's it."

Chavez did not protest, instead, he took a half-step backward and slumped into Cortez's arms, as the referee waved his arms to end the fight. De La Hoya had conquered the Mexican king, in Chavez's first-ever knockout loss.

He had the power ... the power to blast Ruelas off of his feet, to break Genaro Hernandez's nose ... to send Paez into a fetal position ... and to cut Chavez to pieces.

George Foreman, analyzing the fight on the closed-circuit broadcast, shook his head at the circumstances. "Reminds me of Clint

Eastwood in *The Unforgiven*: 'Well, I've always been lucky at killing people.' De La Hoya seems to be a little lucky at doing this stuff," Foreman said.

Not that it was particularly relevant once the cut yawned open, but De La Hoya won all three rounds on all three judges' cards, and averaged a very impressive thirty jabs per round.

"We knew his nose was tender," De La Hoya said after the fight. "Once you attack him, once he knows he can't back up a fighter, he's in trouble. He's lost."

Even while arguing that De La Hoya's victory was tainted, Chavez verified the completeness of the defeat: He was vulnerable, but had continued on in the fight because he needed the paycheck. He had to come to the fight on De La Hoya's terms.

Then De La Hoya's power and precision had driven straight into the weakness and torn him open. Which is how champions win.

"I was already hurt over my eyebrow," Chavez finally revealed after the bout. "I really didn't want to postpone the fight because of it. You guys noticed it was just a minor punch and it opened up a cut. Oscar De La Hoya really doesn't have a big punch. I just couldn't see because of the cut. It was three months of preparation for this and I didn't want to cancel this. . . . I couldn't see. I just could not see."

At his lavish victory party at Planet Hollywood in Caesars late that night, De La Hoya sat next to Veronica Peralta, greeted Charles Barkley, and laughed off Chavez's excuse before heading out to the crap tables.

"It shows that he's a crybaby," De La Hoya said with a huge smile. "I'm happy, because that means he can't take losing. He has to come up with excuses for losing to me. I beat him in the ring, and if he wants a rematch, I'll fight him any time, any place, anywhere. I'll fight him in Mexico if he wants, and the next time it won't last four rounds. I wanted to show I had control of the fight early, and I did. I knew right away that I was going to knock him out, because he felt my punch and that was it. . . . Actually, after it was over, I was thinking, 'Man, this was an easy fight—easiest fight I've had. Didn't get touched, four rounds against a legend.'"

Oscar De La Hoya was on the summit: A champion with blood on his hands.

The next day a wilted but defiant Chavez denied that his nose was fractured in the fight, and said he deserved the chance to fight De La Hoya without blood flowing into his eyes.

"You never saw that Oscar De La Hoya was superior to me," Chavez said. "His punches never really hurt me. Oscar De La Hoya is not the best fighter I've encountered. He was just lucky because of the little cut. If De La Hoya had knocked me down, I would've retired last night. But he didn't hurt me enough to knock me down."

A few days later, back in L.A., De La Hoya was less satisfied. Chavez's complaints convinced too many people, he thought, and already he felt like the victory was diminished. And nothing had changed in East L.A., De La Hoya could already sense that. Chavez's cut gave the critics every reason they needed to keep booing him, to keep braying that De La Hoya hadn't beaten anybody without having it handed to him.

"They'll never accept the fact that I beat their hero," De La Hoya said.

Then, with Pajar encouraging him, De La Hoya cut loose, speaking as honestly as he could about the rift he felt with the boxing fans of his hometown.

"You know, I'm learning how these people are," De La Hoya said. "We call them *La Raza*—ignorant. They don't know what boxing is, they don't have the slightest idea what a boxer is. They just want to see blood and guts, and that's all it is."

The Chavez fight gave them blood, but not satisfaction. De La Hoya didn't find it, either. "I wasn't satisfied with what happened," De La Hoya said. "I was very happy. Hey, I beat him. But I wasn't satisfied. But I knew that '*La Raza*' was going to say, 'Oh, he was cut already.'"

Those two words—*La Raza*—hit the paper and electrified the dialogue. To many in the community, it was as if De La Hoya was separating himself forever from his community, on purpose, and with derisive language. To them, using *La Raza* (literally, the race) in such a fashion was like a black fighter saying that he wasn't being supported by his community because they were all "stupid n———s."

Hernandez's dealership, home of the fan club, received death threats after the article, and Hernandez angrily called a reporter, saying that De La Hoya was misinterpreted. "He never said that," Hernandez said. No, he had. Pajar had even spelled the words out on the paper menu.

"You should have said what I told you, the '*maldicion de las Aztecas*' ... the ill feelings of the Aztecs," Hernandez barked. "He never said '*La Raza*.'"

But he had. And he had meant it.

Meanwhile, Arum hunted a Chavez rematch, because he could smell the money. Though the fight didn't reopen the path to closed-circuit millions, Arum never really intended that, despite his boasts. He just wanted to scare the pay-per-view distributors, and he did. Full totals for the closed-circuit experiment were nearly impossible to tally, but the best estimate was that about 500,000 tickets were sold—and about 300,000 of those in Southern California, where seats were at such a premium that the L.A. Coliseum had to be opened up at the last minute for spillover.

But Chavez suddenly seemed uninterested in a fast rematch, demanding a ridiculous $10 million, and resigned with King.

That meant the best move was also the one that might truly start establishing De La Hoya with the Mexican people. Why not go after Pernell Whitaker, the fighter Latinos disliked more than anyone? Arum already was in negotiations with Dino Duva, Lou Duva's son, for the fight, and once Chavez fell by the wayside, the Whitaker fight was on, set for April 1997.

"There's going to be a point," De La Hoya said. "It's going to take for me to beat non-Mexican fighters. When I fight Whitaker, I think everybody's going to be with me from the community. The fact that I've been fighting nothing but Mexican fighters, people don't like that. So when I fight a Whitaker, they're all going to be with me. I guarantee that. That's Bob Arum's idea, been his idea for the longest time."

Or, as Joel Jr. said: "When he fights Whitaker, who the hell are they going to support? They don't have anybody but him."

De La Hoya had resigned himself to the fact that many of the loudest members of his own community would never embrace him. So what? That just meant more money when they paid for the pay-per-view to root for his opponent. When they booed him as he walked in with a phalanx of bodyguards to watch Chavez's next fight in Anaheim, De La Hoya acknowledged the noise and chuckled.

"I raise my arms and wave at them," De La Hoya said. "Keep on paying, keep on paying. Shit, buy my fights. I mean, I understand now that I'm going to work with both crowds. I mean, those people came so they could boo me. More than half of those people were there to boo me. But I was thinking, 'Shit, if these people hate me, then I'm going to make them hate me more!' I was thinking like a businessman, right? Maybe they'll pay me more to see me.

"I learned. I learned throughout the years that it's a business, it's a job. You have to come out on top and think money. Because once I retire, what am I going to have? Just the money I made in boxing and the strategies I learned to get that money."

For De La Hoya, beating Chavez triggered another turning point. Finally, after all the fights and breakups, he decided to break up with Veronica for good.

His father and Mike Hernandez and his brother had lectured him for years about her ... and finally, after Chavez, De La Hoya was worn out. He stopped arguing. He was too big to be fighting with his family about something as simple as a girl. Was she a gold digger? No, probably not. But why fight the argument anymore?

"I got tired . . . not tired, but I didn't feel the same anymore," De La Hoya recalled. "I saw little things that would catch my eye. Like she started getting obsessed with money. She loved the attention. I could see that right away. I'm aware of it. I'm very careful about that. My father hated her. My brother hated her guts. They would always see what she was trying to do to me, and I didn't want to believe it."

At about the same time, Joel Jr. broke up with his longtime girlfriend, the mother of his child.

And Oscar was hoping the De La Hoya breakups didn't stop there. His father was having trouble with his second wife, and that was causing problems with the whole family.

"That's the problem with my father's wife—too much friction," Oscar said. "Oh man, and it's hard on my sister, you know? My sister has grown up so fast that she realizes that my father has to be happy, too. But we see that she's not right for my father. She's not. We can see. I can truly really say that she's a gold digger. I can see it. We all see it.

"My brother was blind—he finally broke up with his girlfriend," Oscar said. "I was blind. So I hope my father realizes he's blind, and breaks up with her. We're the De La Hoya boys . . . the breakup boys, eh?"

But Joels Jr. and Sr. eventually would get back together with their women. Oscar De La Hoya would not be getting back together with Veronica Peralta. Like the list of fired trainers, Veronica was just someone else Oscar De La Hoya had moved coldly beyond.

"It seemed like as the years went by his true colors started coming out," she said after the breakup. "Little remnants of what I fell in love with would kind of try to come out. But it seems like . . . sometimes all around him they wouldn't let him. They were always telling him, 'Oh, she's a gold digger, she's just after you for your money. . . .'

"I think that if he ever really was gentle and genuine and kind and sincere and naive, all those things he was before, they brainwashed him so much that he no longer at any point trusted me or anybody around him. He doesn't trust anybody. He's a very, very insecure person. From what

I know of his childhood, he always had his mother's support. His dad was very forceful in making him choose boxing as his career. Then as he grew up, he lost his mother, so that was a huge sense of insecurity for him.

"I wanted to give him the love he didn't get from his mother. I wanted him to feel like he was loved. Maybe he wasn't trying to hurt me, maybe he loved me but he was just so insecure, he didn't know how else to show his love. Maybe if he felt too attached to me he might lose me like he lost his mother."

chapter ten

The Icon

He was traveling so fast and so far, there had to be a crash and casualties somewhere along the line.

In the summer of '97, not much more than a year after his Chavez triumph, De La Hoya was twenty-four, and racing toward a whole new realm of celebrity, creating tumult and financial bonanzas wherever he went.

The money? In 1997 alone, De La Hoya would make $38 million, third behind only Evander Holyfield and Michael Jordan among American athletes. For one noncompetitive fight against washed-up Hector (Macho) Camacho, in September of that year, De La Hoya collected a staggering $10 million, and drew 650,000 buyers for the pay-per-view show.

The popularity? According to an in-house HBO survey, the legendary George Foreman was the most recognizable fighter in its stable, with 90 percent of those polled knowing who he was. De La Hoya was next, at 78 percent. Formidable fighters such as Pernell Whitaker (45 percent) and Roy Jones (30 percent) languished far behind. Advertisers from the National Milk Advisory Board to Florsheim Shoes were lining up to do business with him.

Professionally? He fought five times in 1997, as he moved into the lucrative welterweight division. He started the year with Rivero, whom he still called his mentor. Then in May, after a frustrating victory over Whitaker, he fired Rivero. He hired Emanuel Steward. Then, two fights later, after Hernandez was displeased with Steward's methods for the Camacho fight and for letting De La Hoya go Las Vegas soon afterward to watch an Evander Holyfield title fight, he fired Steward. By

December, his fifth fight of the year, De La Hoya was back to Robert Alcazar as his main trainer. And he kept winning.

Personally? Early in 1997, De La Hoya was introduced to an eighteen-year-old girl, Cassie Van Doran, by her parents, who took her to an autograph session at Hernandez's dealership. A few months later, De La Hoya proposed to her. She accepted. While all that was happening, a girl he had known for years claimed (without challenge) that she was pregnant with his baby. Suddenly, the marriage was off, and he was about to have a son.

Things were moving quickly.

On a particularly happy night in June, before the proposal, before the baby news, De La Hoya was speeding back home after dropping his girlfriend—soon to be fiancée—off at her parents' house. De La Hoya was alone in his brother's brand-new Mercedes, in the fast lane of Interstate 605, an exit short of his condominium in Whittier. It was only eight days after he had walloped David Kamau—the same fighter who had pushed Chavez to near defeat in 1995—in a crashing knockout, picking up $4.5 million and stirring up a festival in San Antonio, where his every move was a piece of news and drew scores of screaming Latinas.

On this night, though, after the Kamau fight, he was in a tuxedo— he had been attending a posh awards banquet in Century City. Now he was racing home, at seventy miles an hour, on the tight freeway. He was happy. But, an exit short of his turnoff, the Mercedes, a $70,000 car, stalled out, the steering wheel locked, and De La Hoya was on a dark road, with no acceleration or ability to maneuver to safety. As he jerked at the steering wheel and pounded on the accelerator, the car slowed down, sixty, fifty, forty... as other cars flew past in the night.

De La Hoya's heart raced. He started sweating, then flipped on the hazard lights, fearing a rear-end collision. He turned on an interior light, too, so he could be seen from behind.

Please, let them see me....

Then, wham! As his car continued to slow, someone hit him from behind, veering to the right, too late, and accelerated away. A hit-and-run. The Mercedes jerked forward and continued down the fast lane. De La Hoya was helpless.

"Oh, man, I'm dead here," De La Hoya told himself.

Finally, his car stopped. The traffic kept flying by. For a long moment, De La Hoya was lost. "What should I do?" he asked himself.

De La Hoya couldn't just jump out to the left to avoid the cars, because on that part of the freeway there was no median, only a white retaining wall between the northbound and southbound lanes. He was four dark lanes away from safety—at least thirty feet, dodging speeding cars.

So he turned around and fumbled for his cell phone, "which I always bring with me into the car," De La Hoya recounted, to call for help. But there was no cell phone there. What now?

"You know what? I'm going to get out of the car," De La Hoya told himself.

He got out of the driver's side, slowly waited for a break in the traffic, then sprinted across the freeway, four lanes of fear. "I was just happy I was in shape," De La Hoya recalled, "because I was running fast."

He stopped for a breath, then started looking for a roadside call box. Almost immediately, he heard rather than saw the collision—a truck ramming the Mercedes at sixty miles an hour. In an instant, there was an eight-car pileup, and the Mercedes was destroyed. The impact was so great, two sets of golf clubs—his own and Joel's—were cracked into bits. De La Hoya froze. If he had been in the car, if he had been talking on his cell phone, he would no longer be alive. He would be cracked into bits, too.

"Oh, man," De La Hoya thought, "I just hope nobody's dead."

Nobody was dead. Then he started shaking. "If I would've had my cell phone and I had stayed in the car, I would've been history," De La Hoya recalled later. "Easy as that. History."

Even after the police arrived, De La Hoya was shivering and unable to put coherent words together. His sister came a little later, and she just grabbed him tight and cried, imagining that he could've been a ghost. "I was shaking so hard I couldn't talk," De La Hoya said. "I mean, I get nervous for fights, but I was shaking so hard. . . . I literally was kind of jumping up and down the whole time."

He talked to his publicist, Dena duBoef, later in the morning. "He'd never been through anything like that," duBoef recalled days later. "I've never heard him like that before." At the scene, during the cleanup, De La Hoya saw one man bleeding from his nose. De La Hoya went to talk to him, thinking the man was going to blame him for the crash and the injury. Instead, seeing who started it all, the man smiled.

"Man," he said to no one in particular, "I got a broken nose from Oscar De La Hoya!"

Peering from the flames of a near-disaster, the rest of his life came into clearer view. Even before the accident, De La Hoya had either instigated or accepted several major alterations in career and life. But the accident—and his shaken emotions in the aftermath—would serve as a fulcrum on which everything else turned.

He *wanted* things to be different.

"The accident just changed everything," De La Hoya said later. "I kind of saw how, if it was all over right there and then, what is my family left with, how is my family going to live? I've got some big fights ahead. I've got to make the most of this."

But the people who now guided his career had some very different ideas about how he was going to accomplish his goals—and even if he should accomplish them at all. His closest friends, Joe Pajar and bodyguard Arturo Galvan, encouraged him to take more responsibility. They helped him accept the fact that he was going to be a father, and to embrace the idea.

Hernandez, however, rejected their input. Oscar De La Hoya didn't sell as a father, and he didn't sell as a married man. A baby meant more responsibilities, and maybe less focus on the fighting career. A wife meant another voice in De La Hoya's ear, a voice that might not be in tune with Hernandez. And just as he did with Peralta, Hernandez campaigned against any ties, against any new major relationships. Mike Hernandez wanted Oscar De La Hoya for Mike Hernandez.

The last thing Hernandez wanted was a mature, grown-up Oscar De La Hoya, an Oscar De La Hoya with a purpose in life beyond the swiftest possible accumulation of money. How could Hernandez control his image then?

"We're all growing up," said Pajar, who was married in 1996 and had twin babies. "I mean, we still go out together, and everything's still the same. But we have responsibilities now. And he's going to have one soon. He's going to realize how everything is. He's going to go through everything I went through with the kids . . . and I feel happy for him. I hope everything goes well for him like it's gone well for me.

"He needs that. He feels lonely sometimes, so he needs somebody to be with him a lot of times. He needs a baby . . . someone he could be with all the time. So he can be doing it *for* something now—for himself and his family."

When he heard those words, Hernandez raged, and called Pajar "retarded." For years, Hernandez had worked to lessen Pajar's influence with De La Hoya—eventually removing him from the Big Bear camps, ostensibly to help run the Oscar De La Hoya Foundation at the former Resurrection Gym. But Hernandez's abrasive wife, Cindy, claimed she ran the operation, and that Pajar was barely a presence there. She said Pajar was scared of her, and that he couldn't even read. She said she endured him for the betterment of the foundation—to get Pajar out of De La Hoya's hair in Big Bear.

"Oscar doesn't want Pajar up there anymore, you can ask him," Mike Hernandez said.

De La Hoya resisted the move when it was first suggested. He wanted Pajar up there and didn't like it when Hernandez said Pajar was useless. Pajar was his oldest, best friend. His clown. His golfing partner when Joel Jr. wasn't around. Maybe he was useless to Hernandez's grand plans and Cindy's machinations, but he wasn't to the fighter.

"That's being too harsh on people," De La Hoya said. "I mean, each person has their own job up here. I have them up here for a reason. Little Joe, he's been my best friend forever, and he still is my best friend.

Just little things, he helps me out. Even if he washes clothes for me, he helps me out. You can count on him and I can trust him."

After the accident and the baby news, Joel Jr., like Pajar, was glad. This could be a turning point, he said, for his restless little brother.

"He only wants to box for a couple more years," Joel Jr. said. "And I think he's ready. I would love to see him settle down myself. I've got my woman and I have my kid. And then I see him, and he's with his buddies . . . and there's something missing. That's like a void in his life right now."

Hernandez, though, called Joel Jr. "an addict" after those words were spoken, and said that nobody in the camp should be talking about retirement or settling down.

"He has no credibility," Hernandez said of Joel Jr. "Talk to the father. He will tell you. The brother is nothing."

All these conclusions and conflicts were beginning to bubble to the surface right after the Chavez victory, and straight into the beginning of 1997—what would turn out to be one of the most eventful, controversial, and lucrative years of De La Hoya's life.

The man who beat Julio Cesar Chavez wanted some time off. He deserved time off. He wanted to get to Cabo San Lucas, play golf, and just play, period. He was negotiating to buy a piece of a resort, and he was investing in a brand-new golf course there. He was also having the time of his life socially, and his list of girlfriends grew and grew and grew.

Rivero wanted some time off, too. He'd been away from Mérida for most of the two years he was with De La Hoya, and he missed his ranch and his books. He felt a little tired. He had his girlfriend back in the Yucatán, and he missed her, too. Take three or four months away from boxing, he urged De La Hoya, refresh your mind. Then we'll jump back in, hungry again. Then we'll fight Whitaker or whoever else is out there for us.

But Arum and Hernandez wanted to rush him back out into the arena. He was too hot to take a breather—coming off that bonanza, it made no business sense to push the pause button. With a Whitaker fight signed for April 1997, Arum booked a fight against former lightweight champion Miguel Angel Gonzalez for November 1996—the last high-profile Mexican De La Hoya needed to knock off. De La Hoya wasn't enthused, and for a while balked at the fight, asking for a guarantee of $10 million. Hernandez had to mediate with Arum, and got a grumbling De La Hoya to accept a $5 million guarantee.

Fate, however, intervened. While in light training, De La Hoya felt a twinge in his left shoulder. For a few days he tried to work through it, but it wouldn't go away. Eventually he went to a doctor, who said there was no option but to shut down his training and wait out the flare-up. That meant postponing the Gonzalez fight, at least until January 1997, and backing away from golf.

"I'm retiring from golf," De La Hoya said at the announcement, "until I retire from boxing."

He didn't wink when he said it, but those who knew him best knew he was only saying the right thing, not intending to do any such thing.

The injury gave De La Hoya a whole winter to relax, and he relished it. Predictably, he enjoyed it a little too much—but it was worth it.

At a Christmas party thrown by Arum in Reno, De La Hoya stood up in front of the hundred or so guests and grandly presented Arum with his Olympic gold medal, saying that he "owed it all to you." Taking the medal, Arum seemed startled, then said he'd only accept it if De La Hoya promised to take it back the day he retired from boxing. Oscar agreed, and the party-goers applauded wildly.

Give away his Olympic gold medal? How could he do that? "Aww," one close friend of De La Hoya's said a few weeks later, "he only gave him a copy. He's still got the real one over his doorway at his condo." Did Arum know? "I don't know," the friend said. "But Oscar knows."

Before the training started for the Gonzalez fight, De La Hoya finally accepted a long-standing invitation from Rivero to visit his ranch in Mérida and spend some time around the Yucatán. De La Hoya brought Mike Hernandez, Joel Sr. and Jr., and a few others—a group of eight—for a few days with Rivero. There, Rivero introduced Oscar to Miguel Canto, who still lived in Mérida.

"Tell him about boxing," Rivero urged Canto, who nodded his head and turned to De La Hoya.

"I am very happy that Mr. Rivero is with you, because he is an honest man, he will tell you the truth," Canto told De La Hoya. "It may hurt, but he's going to tell you the truth. Don't trust your family, don't trust the parasites. That's what boxing is. It happened to me."

De La Hoya didn't reply, just nodded his head. His father said nothing.

When it was time to reassemble for the Gonzalez camp again—the fight was rescheduled for January 18—De La Hoya weighed well over 150 pounds and no longer had the taste for lectures. Plus, Rivero came to the camp with his girlfriend, which meant that he didn't live in the cabin—putting a little distance into his relationship with the fighter.

De La Hoya, though, felt great. The seven months between fights, he said, were exactly what he needed, especially after the grueling camp to get ready for Chavez.

"I have a love for the sport now like I had when I was six years old," De La Hoya said. "The layoff was tough to handle. I missed fighting. I've never been away from boxing for seven months. How I felt surprised me. I wanted to be in the limelight again. I missed performing. But I needed the break, too. It gave me an opportunity to rest, which I needed. . . . Boxing is my number one priority now. I need to focus on boxing right now. Before the injury, I thought I was already on top of the world. I'd beaten everybody and I thought I had nothing more to learn. If I'd kept going the way I was, I probably would have lost already. I didn't think I needed to learn anymore."

Against Gonzalez, he showed how much he needed to learn. Gonzalez was a nice, solid fighter, thirty years old and considered a poor man's Chavez. But he was no superstar, and he wasn't particularly sharp himself. He had just brought in Emanuel Steward to lead his corner, but wasn't quite meshing with the Steward emphasis on rhythm and footwork. De La Hoya at his best could have walked right through Gonzalez. De La Hoya, if he had been as sharp as he was against Ruelas or Hernandez or Chavez, could have knocked Gonzalez out, no question. Too much speed and power.

But, for the first time since the Molina fight—since Rivero had become his trainer—De La Hoya looked beatable, tentative, and incomplete. Though De La Hoya dominated Gonzalez for the first eight rounds—raking lefts across Gonzalez's face—he didn't have the finishing kick. Gonzalez managed to work his way inside, as Chavez couldn't, and did damage to De La Hoya's rib cage and to his left eye, which was swollen almost shut at the end of the fight.

De La Hoya landed 67 percent of his jabs—a tremendous accuracy rate, especially for a jab as powerful as his. But he threw and landed very few rights, fighting basically one-handed against a skilled former champion. Part of that occurred because he had to keep his right hand up to protect against Gonzalez's left—and De La Hoya had never had to sacrifice a part of his offense to protect himself from another fighter before. He did wobble Gonzalez with two hard lefts in the twelfth that almost put Gonzalez to the canvas, but he couldn't put him down.

At the end of the fight, his eyes peeping out from the swelling, De La Hoya shouted: "This is what boxing's all about!" But that was P.R., you could see it in his expression. He was unhappy. Everyone who watched the fight knew that he was flat.

Said veteran trainer Teddy Atlas: "He looked like a model when he walked into the ring. I know he's a good-looking kid, that's what they say. But I had never seen him look that way, like his hair was moussed before he got into the ring. To myself, I said, 'He's into that.' And if he gets into that too much, that can stop a real good fighter from being a great fighter. I think it's all there for him to be a real good fighter if he doesn't get caught up in himself along the way."

"My boy was just too slow," Steward said of Gonzalez. "But if he could've gotten his head out of the way of that jab, he might have won the fight. It will be different when [De La Hoya] gets in there with Pernell. Oscar is a different fighter when he starts to get hit. Then he's bouncing around all over the ropes, here and there. We told Miguel, 'When De La Hoya throws the right hand, roll with it and come back with your own right.' He did it and landed and De La Hoya never threw it again. He got hit a couple times with those overhand rights and he never threw his right hand again. You can't beat Whitaker with one hand."

But the fight plan was dictated by Rivero, who knew that De La Hoya was not in good shape. To counteract the physical problem, Rivero wanted De La Hoya to look like Willie Pep—flick the body, feint with the right, but most importantly, stay away from Gonzalez's right hand. The result was a listless performance and a swollen black eye.

And most worrisome to the De La Hoya camp, no knockout. Not even a knockdown. As De La Hoya got set to move up in weight yet again, was there a chance his power would be less and less a factor against the bigger fighters? Fans wanted to see knockouts. And Rivero wasn't providing them.

"I don't know if Rivero did the right thing," said Rafael Mendoza, Rivero's friend. "He was showing off a little bit: 'Let me show the world what I'm doing with this kid.' And it hurt him for this fight. In my opinion, that was Rivero's ego. He wanted to teach, he wanted to show the world through Oscar. He didn't want him to just go there and kill the other guy. He wanted to show that Willie Pep is *here*. He told him about Pep, about Bob Foster [an underappreciated light-heavyweight champion from the '60s and '70s], all the classics. And I know that because I am the one who gave him all the tapes.

"And then that time he got hit. And I think that Oscar got insecure when he felt the punch of the other guy. And then he tried to knock him out in the last part, which was not the plan. He couldn't knock him out, but he almost did."

De La Hoya won the decision fairly easily on the judges' cards, but, once again, a less-than-perfect performance rattled the fighter. He came out of it with a huge welt, and he never reacted well to marks on his face. The last time his vanity was wounded like this, he spent the whole night in his hotel room after the Molina fight, moaning in pain and frustration.

And after the Molina fight and the marks on his face, Alcazar was pushed aside for Rivero.

The Gonzalez fight reinforced the complaints that Alcazar—and, gradually, Joel Sr.—had with Rivero, who was exerting more and more control over De La Hoya. Rivero was stubborn. He clashed with Joel Sr. and, sometimes, Hernandez. Rivero was getting on their nerves, and Hernandez was tired of dealing with it.

In a telling moment, Joel Sr. compared Rivero to another famous L.A.-area bigmouth. When another passenger in a car traveling up to Big Bear for the Whitaker camp mentioned that former Dodger manager Tommy Lasorda was knowledgeable, but spoiled it by talking too much, Joel Sr. jumped into the conversation: "That's like Rivero. He knows a lot. But he also talks too much."

Nobody was going to make a move on Rivero with the all-important Whitaker fight just months away. This wasn't a milestone fight like Chavez, but it was a respect fight. The New York–based boxing establishment still hadn't completely bowed down to De La Hoya. The stylish Whitaker—a five-foot-six man with the moves of an NBA point guard—was a thinking man's fighter, their favorite fighter. Of course, by this time, Whitaker was four years removed from his dominance of Chavez and fading fast.

More than anything, Whitaker wanted a rematch with Chavez. But he couldn't get one. And, as he sat and waited, he watched De La Hoya rocket past him in earnings and on the mythical lists of best pound-for-pound fighters. De La Hoya made $8.95 million to beat Chavez. For all his plaudits and titles, for all the fealty HBO had paid to him through the years, Whitaker had never made more than $3 million. His training habits were eroding, his spirit was sagging. He didn't want to fight mediocre fighters for mediocre paydays. He was thirty-three years old, he was a 1984 Olympic gold medalist, he was a champion. Whitaker wanted big fights for big money. De La Hoya was his only hope.

Around him, rumors swirled that Whitaker was drinking too much, that he was dabbling in drugs, that his work habits were gone.

"Sweet Pea is just different than he was," cotrainer Bob Wareing said. "He's not the hungry kid from the projects anymore. He's got different motivations. You can't keep going from mountaintop to mountaintop. You've got to hit some valleys in between. There aren't any shortcuts in this business. You can grow a little fat and contented. That's human nature."

Said Whitaker's friend and 1984 Olympic teammate Mark Breland: "What kills me—and I'm sure it kills him—is that he was always the underdog. I don't understand why he never had a name. The guy's been champion for ten years. He's fought everybody, beaten everybody, and they won't give him his just due. I mean, this Oscar kid, he beats Chavez and he's king. But the guy who started the Chavez beatings was Pete."

A few weeks after De La Hoya's less-than-stellar outing against Gonzalez, he sat ringside as Whitaker looked like he was fighting with his feet stuck in cement against an inexperienced Cuban named Diobelys Hurtado at the Foxwoods Casino in Ledyard, Conneticut. The only time his feet left the floor was when he was knocked down, twice, by Hurtado.

Going into the final two rounds, Whitaker was on the verge of losing his WBC welterweight title—he trailed Hurtado on all three judges' cards—and just about to blow the biggest fight of his life. De La Hoya, at ringside, was sweating: "Oh my God," De La Hoya would recall thinking later. "I'm not sure he's going to win this thing. I really wanted him to win, because I knew I could beat him."

Then Whitaker did something even more out of character—he surged forward in the eleventh round, connected with a gigantic left, followed it up with a dozen unanswered shots, and took a knockout victory. Before that, Whitaker had never knocked out any opponent after the sixth.

Whitaker pulled it off, and De La Hoya and Arum sagged in relief. Then, having delivered the miracle, Whitaker pronounced himself ready to make De La Hoya vanish, too.

"There's not a hard part to that kid," he said. "Look in his eyes. There's something there that says he's soft."

In camp, Rivero worked to counteract what he figured were Whitaker's two most dangerous aspects: his left-handed stance, and his flickering ability to make his opponents tumble off balance when they attacked him. As part of the game plan, Rivero encouraged De La Hoya to spend time using a left-handed stance for the first time since Joe Minjarez turned him around when he was six years old. If De La Hoya switched from a right- to a left-handed stance in the middle of the fight, he should be able to send his left at a more comfortable angle, Rivero reasoned, and eliminate much of Whitaker's advantage.

This, among many other issues, generated a degree of stress in the camp that had not been present since the Ruelas fight. De La Hoya had never fought at 147 pounds before, and Joel Sr. and Mike Hernandez worried that he needed to use his power as a welterweight—not continue working Rivero's defensive schemes.

But the De La Hoya camp, other than Rivero, consistently downplayed the difficulty of facing Whitaker. "It's just that he's left-handed," Joel Jr. said a few weeks before the fight. "Everybody gets confused by that and loses. But if you know how to fight southpaws, there's no trouble."

Slowly, probably too slowly, Rivero was working in more offense with De La Hoya. And even De La Hoya himself was getting antsy. He felt he was sound defensively. He wanted to attack Whitaker and answer back Whitaker's jeers and taunts with his fists. Some of Whitaker's strategy—getting the young fighter to press—was working.

"Everything he's been saying has been totally negative," De La Hoya told the *Boston Globe* before the fight. "It makes no sense. He's talking about how he's going to break my arm and break my shoulder

and cut my chin. He just doesn't want to accept that he isn't in the limelight the way I am and he never was. He knows he's going downhill. It's
all jealousy. He is one of the best fighters in the world, but I've studied
him at his best—against Chavez, and Azumah Nelson, and Freddie
Pendleton. And he didn't impress me.

"He says I haven't fought black fighters, but to tell you the truth, the
Afro-Americans I fought, they don't have heart. They can't take it to
the body. I use my speed and my power punches on them and they give
up right away. No Afro-American fighter can take my punch. That's
what I've seen."

De La Hoya knew that he'd made a public-relations blunder by
responding to the racial issue with further inflammation. But even when
he was asked about it later in interviews, he didn't dispute the remarks.
He only said it came out wrong, that he just wanted to beat Whitaker.

He already was a well-oiled publicity machine. De La Hoya was a
miniconglomerate by now, appearing in national advertising campaigns
and taking meetings with Hollywood producers. Though the relationship with Leigh Steinberg had run into trouble (Steinberg complained
about Hernandez's interference and De La Hoya not showing up at
several booked events; Hernandez complained that Steinberg didn't
spend enough time with the fighter and that another agent, Leonard
Armato, would be a better fit), other business contacts were flourishing.
While flirting with taking some time off for acting classes and trying to
land a movie role, De La Hoya met with high-powered Hollywood
attorney Jake Bloom. De La Hoya wanted career advice, and Bloom
gave it to him: Don't quit your day job.

"He really listened to what Jake Bloom had to say," Hernandez
said. "Jake Bloom said, 'You're going to earn more in boxing now than
you would in movies. Stay in boxing, earn as much as you can, finish
that—then, go to movies.'"

The math was fairly easy: He could make $25 to $40 million a year
for the next three or four years in boxing, and, short of being cast in
Titanic, no amount of acting classes was going to net him that.

All De La Hoya had to do was look over at his thirty-three-year-old opponent and see how lucky he had been. In Whitaker, De La Hoya saw the career he had avoided, thankfully. Too many fights, to few major-dollar victories, too little reward. Whitaker talked too much, De La Hoya felt, and he ruined his image. Whitaker—who only had been on pay-per-view once, against Chavez—shouldn't be complaining about all these years without $5 million paydays, because he brought it on himself. The $6 million Whitaker would make against De La Hoya doubled his best purse. De La Hoya was raking in $10 million for the fight—or about as much as Whitaker had made in his whole career up to then.

"I wouldn't have gone through that, that's for sure," De La Hoya said. "You have to be smart with what you do in boxing. Fighting all those years and not having a big, big super fight, that's a shame. But he could've presented himself better. Whitaker says crazy things. He's weird. When Whitaker talks on TV and has all these interviews, it seems like he's a cocky fighter, like he can beat anybody he wants. . . . He was saying he was going to break my arms and break my chin. People don't want to hear that, they don't like that. Maybe the die-hard boxing fan gets a kick out of that, but the regular person is like, what kind of guy is this? Whitaker [almost] never fights on pay-per-view because he won't draw."

De La Hoya pointed to the numbers of his last fight, against Gonzalez, which was his fourth main event on pay-per-view. That fight elicited an amazing 395,000 buys, and grossed $20 million, incredible numbers for a fight against a midlevel opponent. And De La Hoya analyzed the numbers like a movie executive studying weekend grosses.

Who needed the L.A. crowd when he was pulling in numbers from across the world?

"In that fight, we noticed that we didn't draw the most from the Mexican-American crowd," De La Hoya said. "We drew more of the American crowd, which is something I've always been hoping for. Now, I know that if the Mexican-American or Mexican fans don't support me, it doesn't matter, because I have fans all over the world. I didn't think there would be that many this time, but we were surprised we had Louisiana, Nebraska."

In the week of the fight, set for the Thomas & Mack Center in Las Vegas, two loud and familiar irritants popped up in De La Hoya's face: Lou Duva, ranting about De La Hoya's abandonment of the Duvas and Shelly Finkel at the beginning of his career, and peppery eighteen-year-old Fernando Vargas, the hot young prospect out of Oxnard who flopped in the 1996 Olympics but was drawing a fan base in Southern California with his street attitude and swagger.

Duva, De La Hoya was used to—he'd been hearing it off and on from Duva for most of five years. But the medalless, mouthy Fernando Vargas challenging De La Hoya . . . that was another matter. Any attention that Vargas received only pricked at the old De La Hoya scab: The L.A. fight community loved just about anybody but him. At one recent Mexican-American Independence Day parade, Vargas and several of his friends heckled De La Hoya, and De La Hoya believed that one of them tossed tomatoes at him.

"Oscar's a phony, and everybody knows it," said Vargas, who had recently joined the Duva stable of fighters, alongside Whitaker. "He says he does all these things for the community, but I say it's too late now. What did he do when he first had the chance? Nothing. All he cares about is himself. I hate fighters like that. And I've sworn that I'll never be like that. I never want to be like Oscar De La Hoya. I hate being compared to him. But I do want to fight him. That'll be the biggest fight, and I'll knock him out."

The response was icy.

"He tried to be like me and win a gold medal," De La Hoya said of Vargas. "But he was too cocky, he was too overconfident. He wasn't focusing on his career, he was focusing more on me. I think he is obsessed with me. He might be in love or something. I don't know, he just doesn't leave me alone. People ask me if I'm going to give him the opportunity to fight me, but I'm never going to give him that opportunity, ever, ever, ever. . . . I would never, ever give him a good payday."

Said Finkel, who managed Vargas: "I honestly believe he's a lot better fighter than Oscar is. He has a lot more desire as a fighter, not just as a pretty boy. And time will tell. I also feel like he's different in a lot of ways. He is more toward his Mexican roots. He doesn't want to be, quote, white."

For Arum, this was a fight about restoring De La Hoya's credibility within the Latino community, and he set about the mission with typical vigor. Before the fight began, Arum held things up by putting a mariachi band into the ring and having them play several songs.

Then respected HBO analyst Larry Merchant, calling the fight, inadvertently thrust himself into the fray by calling Arum's ploy for what it was. It wasn't wrong, but it was a little less than sophisticated. At Whitaker's expense, Arum was whipping up Mexican loyalties for De La Hoya, where not much had stirred before.

"You know guys, it really doesn't make any difference what kind of music they play before a fight," Merchant said on the telecast as the music played. "But I'd like to remind you and everyone out there that both Pernell Whitaker and Oscar De La Hoya are born and bred American. This is a gesture to the great American, er, the great Mexican fight fans who support the promoter. But in a way it slights the fans of the champion, whose title is at stake, Pernell Whitaker. In other words, in my view, as wonderful as this music is—and it is—in this setting, it sucks. Unless they follow it with some soul music, which I don't think they will. This is a marketing ploy, using music to get Mexican fans, not Mexican-Americans, but Mexican fans, to support De La Hoya."

There was no soul music for Whitaker. And before the fight was over, the HBO phone lines were jammed with protests from Latinos who had heard, or heard about, the Merchant comments. Arum loudly and proudly implied that Merchant was a racist and said he never wanted Merchant to work another De La Hoya show.

After he apologized to De La Hoya for any offense he might've taken from the comments, an aggrieved Merchant was pulled off the next HBO telecast of a De La Hoya fight, but was back on for the fight after that. De La Hoya didn't say much, only parroting that he didn't like anybody in the Mexican-American community being offended.

It was a proper framework for the actual fight.

When De La Hoya–Whitaker finally arrived, it was a fight that was all about preconceptions and perceptions: What kind of boxing did you prefer, sleek and defensive, or straight ahead and stalking? Did you favor the aggressor or the fighter who made his foe look bad? Would the ten thousand girls screaming for De La Hoya have any effect on the scoring? Since neither fighter provided much in the positive, everything viewed was from a negative angle: Who didn't do what he wanted, and who didn't get the benefit of the doubt.

Once the fight started, it fell into a pattern that neither fighter could, or apparently wanted much to, avoid. Whitaker had no interest in engaging De La Hoya in a firefight, and De La Hoya had no idea how to cut off Whitaker's escape routes. Whitaker was fast and sharp, but it was all strictly defense, twisting away from De La Hoya's lead left and tying up the tall fighter with swift but stingless dives to the body.

De La Hoya showed off some of his own athleticism, bending from side to side, but that wasn't what was going to get Whitaker hurt. Not only did Whitaker's southpaw stance help erase De La Hoya's ability to find an angle to throw his own left, it also eliminated De La Hoya's jab, which had become by far his most effective punch.

Early on, De La Hoya looked confused and frustrated. He wanted to land combinations, but just as he touched Whitaker with the first punch, Whitaker would be gone, and the second punch would catch only air.

The soul of the fight was captured in an exchange in the third round—after two rounds of general fistic purposelessness. With both men flashing feints at each other and landing nothing of significance,

De La Hoya maneuvered out of a clinch and finally caught Whitaker with a left uppercut halfway through the round. Whitaker tossed his right jab into De La Hoya's face a few times to regain his legs, then irascibly flung his palm into De La Hoya's nose and pushed. A few seconds later, Whitaker ducked inside, then drove his head up and into De La Hoya.

Referee Mills Lane immediately penalized Whitaker a point for the move, but Whitaker smiled about it while De La Hoya fumed and rubbed his right eye. When the fight restarted after the penalty, De La Hoya made a bull run at Whitaker, who dropped his left shoulder, caught De La Hoya against the ropes, then let him tumble to the canvas. It was a slip, not a knockdown, but it was ugly. De La Hoya couldn't get to Whitaker without tripping over himself, it seemed.

And Whitaker couldn't hurt anything but De La Hoya's feelings.

In the corner, Rivero was frustrated. De La Hoya wasn't following his game plan, or any game plan. He was letting Whitaker dictate the terms of the action. "Don't get into a roughhouse with him," Rivero told his fighter at the break. "Don't be fighting his fight. Let's get a lot of distance."

In the fourth, the crowd roared as De La Hoya finished up with a flurry of punches, missing most of them as Whitaker bobbed away. After the bell, Whitaker mocked the crowd and his opponent by wiggling his body frantically as he walked back to his corner.

In the last few moments of the fifth round, De La Hoya showcased his secret strategy—he switched to a left-handed stance, but looked awkward, and Whitaker evidenced very little discomfort with the tactic. De La Hoya tried to paw at him with his right, then come over the top with his left, but it was an unnatural movement, looking more like desperation than real boxing. Whitaker just shook his head.

De La Hoya switched back and forth from left- to right-handed stances in the sixth and the seventh, and was off balance for most of the time, with almost no obvious benefits. Whitaker seemed content to wobble away from any real danger. Their heads clashed again in the seventh, and this time De La Hoya emerged with a bloody nose. Then, in a sign of rage and frustration, after the seventh-round bell, De La Hoya pumped his arm and gestured mockingly to the crowd.

What was happening? Had he lost his mind?

"Tell me the truth," Rivero asked insistently before the eighth, "are you tired?"

"No," De La Hoya answered.

Rivero: "Let's see if we can dominate him now."

It wasn't dominance, but De La Hoya regained his focus in the eighth and tapped Whitaker hard enough to shake his whole body. It was De La Hoya's steadiest and most damaging round, and Whitaker wasn't doing much scoring of his own. And his corner saw the fight slipping away—even if many at ringside were overimpressed by Whitaker's slyness (and overlooking his inability or unwillingness to actually try to hit De La Hoya).

Before the ninth, Ronnie Shields, Whitaker's cotrainer, told him: "You're behind in this fight, babe." Whitaker did not want to hear any such talk. He thought he was winning, and to Shields he said: "Why are you telling me that? It's okay."

Duva said, "We're one round down."

Whitaker then spoke the truest words of the night: "To tell you the truth, if I am, I'm going to lose."

Whitaker was either going to win this way—by eluding De La Hoya, by making him look bad, and then zinging one or two punches off of his face when De La Hoya was off balance—or he was going to lose. It was up to the judges, because Whitaker wasn't about to jump in there and rumble with the kid. He was doing the only thing he could.

But just as he seemed to be gaining control, De La Hoya's balance problems led to a strange knockdown in the ninth. As De La Hoya lunged at Whitaker, Whitaker skittered to the side, and De La Hoya's momentum caused his right glove to touch the floor after a light Whitaker left. It could have been ruled a slip, but Lane said it was a knockdown, costing De La Hoya a point. De La Hoya jumped up, glared at Lane, then gestured angrily for Whitaker to come and get him. Everything now was too close to call.

"Oscar, how come you're not dominating from the distance?" Rivero shouted after the ninth. "Are you tired? Then, what? You need to dominate from distance! Let's not get into a dogfight here. You're not feinting him at all!"

As the last rounds arrived, neither fighter looked good—or looked particularly much like a champion. Blood flowed out of De La Hoya's nose from the head butts, and his face was worn and worried. Whitaker's right eye had begun to swell—too many taps by De La Hoya's left jab— and he blinked in pain every three or four seconds.

"Let's win!" Whitaker shouted to his corner before the twelfth and final round started.

But any thoughts Whitaker might have had about finishing the fight with an attack melted away forty-five seconds into the twelfth, when De La Hoya connected with two solid shots to Whitaker's chin. That sent Whitaker flying away backward, and he never leaned in again. Instead, Whitaker started doing his clown act, bicycling side to side, ducking down below De La Hoya's belt and craning his neck forward in an exaggerated gesture: Go ahead, hit me.

Whitaker's corner knew it was a close fight. His trainers screamed for him to take control of the decision. Whitaker knew he probably had to win the twelfth going away to win the fight. And he still stayed away from De La Hoya, who at least was attempting, if awkwardly, to throw shots at Whitaker.

At the final bell, De La Hoya crumpled with relief. It was over. And he knew he had won. As Whitaker grimaced in frustration, the final tallies were announced: Chuck Giampa had it 115–111, Jerry Roth 116–110, and Dalby Shirley 116–110.

In a quiet moment, De La Hoya huddled with Rivero in the ring and whispered something Rivero remembered with an ache a few days later. De La Hoya hadn't followed instructions. He wanted De La Hoya to move to the right, to cut off Whitaker's evasions. He told De La Hoya to throw his right hard and often. He told the fighter to keep some distance between himself and Whitaker, the better to use his reach advantage and force Whitaker to try to step inside.

"He never listened," Rivero said later. "Oscar was disobedient with a lot of my instructions. I think he was frustrated. Somebody must've told him before the fight that he had to knock out Whitaker. But it was dumb to expect a knockout of Whitaker because he's not that easy to knock out."

Amid the madness, with Whitaker's handlers screaming in protest and the girls in the crowd warbling for De La Hoya, the fighter moved to his tiny trainer and pulled him close.

"It was my mistake, forgive me, Don Chuy," De La Hoya told Rivero, using his nickname. "I'm sorry, it was my fault. I will knock him out in the rematch." Rivero hugged him back, and said, yes we will. "At that time," said Rivero's friend, Rafael Mendoza, "he didn't know they were going to fire him."

Later, De La Hoya said he knew that Rivero's strategies were all wrong. "I think like in the third round, I said, 'Man, this game plan is not right.' It was hard for me to change," De La Hoya said. "I won that fight on heart and talent alone."

Which is exactly what he said about Alcazar in the Molina fight.

An hour after the fight, as the arena cleared, veteran trainer Emanuel Steward, on hand as a commentator, left with Arum, and they were both talking quietly and intently. The wheel was about to turn again.

For Whitaker, this was the cruelest moment.

The Chavez decision was more flagrant, but Whitaker could almost understand it. That decision was outright thievery, a thuggish coup de boxing designed solely to prop up the Mexican legend for a few more years. The Chavez decision was obvious. It was all about Chavez and his legacy.

This one, though, was a direct slap at him, at his style of boxing and his attitude. This decision, Whitaker protested, was about judges who punished him for not being as glamorous or crowd-pleasing as his opponent. Nothing more.

"This was worse than Chavez," Whitaker said, "this one was the worst."

"Tell you what," Whitaker said at the postfight press conference, which was broadcast on the public address system to the thousand or so fans still in the arena, "Oscar ought to thank every one of those girls who were screaming for him the whole fight. He missed, they screamed. And those judges reacted. '*Oooooh*, Oscar!' And he never hit me."

Whitaker did land more punches (232 to 191) and more accurately (40 percent to 34 percent), but he landed almost no significant blasts, while De La Hoya landed twice as many power shots. And when it came time to try to pull out the fight, Whitaker danced and jiggled instead of coming at De La Hoya.

"I would rather see him do more punching than showboating," Lou Duva admitted after the fight, "but the whole theme was to frustrate him. Look how many punches the other guy missed. Could he have done better? Sure. I tried to motivate him to do more, but when he's in the rhythm of showboating, it's tough."

Finkel, Whitaker's manager and the man spurned by De La Hoya all those years ago, was disgusted.

"At the end of the fight, when I was listening to those judges' scores, I said, 'He's like the Ali of today,'" Finkel said of De La Hoya. "Because there were several decisions that Ali shouldn't have gotten the decision on. I remember Jimmy Ellis in Baltimore. . . . Oscar didn't deserve those scores. Those flurries, pitty-pats at the end of a round. But people wanted to give him the round. And they did. It's hard. It's a hard sport. It's not like there's exact rules. . . . People's judgment gets in the way."

By arguing their point, Whitaker's handlers conceded something amazing to De La Hoya: He was a superstar, the kind Whitaker would never be. At twenty-four years old, De La Hoya, like the megafighters before him, entered the ring with the benefit of star charisma—and the benefit of the doubt.

"This fight makes me know I can beat anybody," De La Hoya said early Sunday morning amid the clatter of his $20,000 postfight party, complete with a live band, paid for by his father. "Whitaker had a difficult style, and I beat him easily. And I can fight fifty times better than I did, that's for sure."

This was the boxing reality: Judges and fans respected fighters like Whitaker; they *craved* the power and pervasiveness of De La Hoya. What could Whitaker's handlers do but protest De La Hoya's popularity?

"Unfortunately, here in Nevada, the attitude of Las Vegas is money talks," said Whitaker's promoter, Dino Duva, campaigning hard for a quick rematch. "And the more glamorous fighter, the guy who means more to the future of the local economy, he's going to be, perhaps subconsciously, favored by the judges. You could compare it to a couple of Sugar Ray Leonard fights—even he admitted he got the close decisions. Let's face it, De La Hoya's seen as a money machine for this town."

By the measure of anybody who wasn't financially biased toward either fighter, it was a tight fight—a point here or there, and it would have been hard to complain about Whitaker retaining his title or De La Hoya claiming it. According to a *Las Vegas Review-Journal* poll of writers who covered the fight, fourteen scored it for Whitaker, eleven for De La Hoya, and one scored it as a draw.

But were those who scored it for Whitaker reacting to anything he did—or to their overblown expectations they had for De La Hoya to knock out Whitaker. How could he meet those expectations against an opponent who was only concerned about not getting knocked out? Up close, listening to the roar of the crowd and the sound of his punches—whether they landed squarely or not—De La Hoya was the dominant player in the ring.

"I know De La Hoya, how tense he is, and how he stiffens up when you just talk about him," Lou Duva said.

But Whitaker didn't rake De La Hoya with body shots, as he did against Chavez, and he tasted enough De La Hoya power shots to leave him leery of anything more than a backpedal.

"Everybody's saying that he couldn't hit Pernell, but Pernell couldn't hit him, either," said Steward, who by then already was having informal talks about taking over De La Hoya's training. "Every time Pernell tried to open up on him, Oscar was too quick. I don't know if I've ever seen a fighter with that kind of quickness, not in a long time. And remember, Whitaker's a great defensive fighter, maybe the greatest defensive fighter in boxing history. I don't want to see a rematch, because it's going to be the same thing. Both of those guys have the reflexes so neither one of them is ever going to get hit."

Dino Duva offered Arum a $10 million guarantee (split between Arum and De La Hoya) for a second fight. "I want to fight him again, because I know I'll beat him. But the price has to be right," said De La Hoya, who made $10 million (and Arum about $3 million) for the first fight. How much would Duva have to guarantee to get a rematch? "Twenty million," De La Hoya said.

Arum shot down any thought of a rematch with a derisive wave of the hand. He heard the boos for Whitaker, and he saw how frustrated De La Hoya had looked for most of the fight. Who wanted to see any more of that?

"If the fight had been a great fight, one of these real classic Leonard-Hearns battles, then I would certainly think differently," Arum said. "But it wasn't—it was a stinky fight. And the public isn't going to buy a stinky fight again. I made a ton of money on this fight and I ain't losing it back on a rematch. It's Whitaker's own fault; he didn't fight."

The purchase numbers, though, were astounding once again. The fight broke the Chavez-Whitaker record for a nonheavyweight fight, drawing 865,000 pay-per-view buys and grossing about $45 million.

"We knew that we were setting the record, and we knew that a new day in pay-per-view boxing had occurred," said Mark Taffet, vice president of TVKO, HBO's pay-per-view arm. "It was the first time that I believed that there was a nonheavyweight that consistently rivaled numbers the heavyweights had generated. Chavez did it with one fight, with Whitaker. But Oscar has the potential to consistently draw higher numbers than Chavez because of his crossover appeal. . . . Other than Evander Holyfield in a marquee matchup, Oscar De La Hoya is likely to generate more pay-per-view business in a single night than any other boxer today."

And there was one huge, demographically obvious reason why De La Hoya was scoring the monster box-office numbers. Women. Thousands of them who had never even thought of watching boxing made sure they watched De La Hoya.

"In our focus groups, we've seen numbers that have us believe that 40 percent of the homes buying Oscar De La Hoya fights are influenced by females desiring to see the fight," Taffet said. "That's very big numbers, it really is. Oscar De La Hoya is a pay-per-view franchise, and the industry treats him as such. . . . His magic is being able to combine his skill as a boxer and his marketability as an athlete and his crossover appeal and his Mexican-American heritage."

By comparison, the heavily promoted Lennox Lewis–Andrew Golota heavyweight title bout later in 1997 totaled only 250,000 buys. The big Holyfield–Michael Moorer heavyweight bout registered 500,000 buys. The difference in the numbers, a growing number of boxing and television people were realizing, was the women. Nobody else brought them in. De La Hoya got them in hordes.

Which raised a fascinating, and totally unique, question: If his allure meant that he could draw 200,000 buys (about $9 million) to a fight no matter whom he faced, what was De La Hoya's motivation to fight anybody who could threaten him? Big fights against Ike Quartey or Felix Trinidad—also young and fast and powerful—were on the horizon, but what compelled De La Hoya to fight them if he could pick up $5 million to $10 million by knocking out handpicked fall guys?

"He's only going to get bigger if he fights someone," Finkel said, eyeing the situation. "If he doesn't, then it's going to be tough. But I've pointed out to Arum—I said the difference in this kid and everyone else is the girls come to see him. And Arum never realized that. Even for Ray Leonard, the girls didn't come. And that's huge. Because not only can girls watch him, they also can influence their boyfriends to watch him. It's at least 20 percent or 30 percent more, especially for the littler fights. We've never seen anyone else do that. When I was with him on the press tour for this fight, in San Antonio and Houston it was shocking. The screaming and the girls. . . . I joked with Oscar at the time. I said, 'Look, why don't you quit boxing and we'll start a band and I'll promote you.' And he said, 'I can sing a little.'"

There was relief after the Whitaker victory, but there was also a casualty: Someone had to pay for the perception that De La Hoya struggled. Someone had to pay for the superstar looking frustrated and confused.

Joel Sr. was deeply disappointed that his son couldn't get a knockout in his last two fights. Though the Whitaker fight was De La Hoya's first at the welterweight limit of 147 pounds, and he was going to need some time to adjust to the greater weight, Joel De La Hoya wanted knockouts. And he was the one with the ten-year contract, and he was the one who, ultimately, was the father of the son.

Nobody could blame the fighter, of course. At least nobody who wanted to stay on board. And no one on Team De La Hoya was going to give Whitaker credit. So the blame was easy to pinpoint—Alcazar had been pinpointing it to Rivero for almost two years.

"Watching the fight hurt my feelings," Alcazar said. "If I was in the corner. . . . If that fight happens today, I can guarantee you Oscar knocks out Pernell Whitaker in no more than five rounds. If I work in that corner and Oscar fights Miguel Angel Gonzalez tomorrow, I promise you Oscar knocks out Gonzalez in no more than three rounds. That's embarrassing those guys went the distance with Oscar. There was no game plan. This guy was trying to teach Oscar a different style, and he was not making any game plans. He forgot how this kid fights. Here Oscar was coming into the ring, he didn't know whether he was coming or going. That's the problem in those two fights."

So two years of pressures left Rivero in just about the same position as Joe Minjarez, Manuel Montiel, Al Stankie, and Alcazar before him. He was with De La Hoya for two years, and five fights, and then he wasn't anymore.

Two years of Joel Sr.'s complaints that his knockout machine was turning too defensive and of Alcazar's constant nudging brought the relationship to its inevitable breaking point. And Oscar wasn't about to intercede—he never interceded.

Rivero wasn't fired so much as he was just left behind.

He didn't get a phone call, he didn't even talk to the fighter. He went home to Mérida, then a few days later got a call from a reporter who said that De La Hoya had hired Steward, and that was that. Rivero knew, though, exactly what had transpired: Joel Sr., Alcazar, and Hernandez had taken this opening to remove him from the scene.

"Afterwards, he didn't even have the courage to call me," Rivero said. "To come and say, 'Señor Rivero, thank you very much for all that I've learned.' He hasn't told me anything. But it's clear what happened. Oscar said he feels alone, he feels he doesn't have any friends. He's afraid of retiring, he's afraid of losing, and the person he's afraid most of is his father. He's a young person. He has a lot of problems. He's traveling, he's doing publicity . . . and he doesn't have a woman who loves him, to help him, to support him through this. There's no one there to stimulate him, so it's natural for him to feel alone.

"Boxers are surrounded by vultures, a bunch of parasites. They are the ones that take advantage of others' hard work. I was introducing things to him slowly, involving offense, the counterpunching. . . . All that technique of bending and moving and punching was postponed for later, because we could not do that against Whitaker. But now there is no later."

To Rivero, the firing was a triumph for the isolationists in the camp: They didn't want Oscar to connect with anything that could lead him away from his father, his trainer, and Mike Hernandez. They wanted him up in the mountains and tethered to no one and nothing but themselves. They wanted him alone, and making money. They didn't care so much about boxing history, but about making money for themselves and protecting their precious treasure.

De La Hoya just went along with it.

Rivero, with his wild talk and fancy moves, was a serious threat to all of that. Veronica, another serious threat, had, of course, already been dispatched.

"Mike was afraid," Rivero said. "I thought Veronica was magnificent and independent and exactly right for Oscar, but they pushed her away to keep exploiting him. I call them *saganos,* like the bees who don't do anything but eat. They are a bunch of leeches, parasites that surround him. His dad is a parasite. He gets 9 percent for every fight. Yes, they're all a bunch of snakes. They're thieves. And I would always tell Oscar that. I would tell Mike that, but I didn't realize until later that Mike was the same way. Mike Hernandez would record what I said, I found out later.

"Oscar gives Joel [Jr.] $400,000 for every fight [if it's a $10 million purse], can you believe that? All that does is feed Joel's addiction. And he doesn't do anything. He has his addiction, and that's one of Oscar's worries. And Oscar giving him money doesn't solve anything."

De La Hoya, for his part, conceded that he hadn't handled it totally properly, but shrugged and said it was part of the boxing business. Five trainers come, five trainers go. . . .

"He's hurt about the whole situation," De La Hoya said of Rivero. "Yeah, it was a big mistake on my part, not personally calling him. But hey, I was on vacation. I didn't know all this was going on. I mentioned to Mike Hernandez that I wanted Emanuel Steward and everything just happened so fast. I didn't have the chance to call Rivero in time, to apologize. This is all business, we've got to move on. It's like golf, if something's wrong with your game, you're going to get a teacher. If that teacher's not teaching you, you've got to get another one, until your game is right, until your game is perfect. Just like boxing."

It was important for De La Hoya to keep it all about boxing—because if he started analyzing the personal issues, he knew he'd have to admit that he had been too weak to overrule his father and his old trainer. So the decision was all about boxing, De La Hoya said. Steward was a knockout trainer, famous for facilitating the power punches of Tommy Hearns and Lennox Lewis. Steward, who started up the legendary Kronk Gym, was probably the busiest trainer in the business, a straightforward, genial teacher with a taste for producing devastating knockouts.

Rivero had been brought in to tighten up the defense, and now it was time to move on.

This had happened before.

"Too much defense," De La Hoya said. "Even before Whitaker, my father would tell me, 'Hey, you're losing your power, you're losing your offense.' And with having Robert back and then the experience of Emanuel, I think it's going to work out perfect. You see the way we get along. I feel I'm getting back the confidence to go in there. These last three fights, even though we were working so much on defense, I was getting hit more than I used to. The bruise against Gonzalez. . . . That's because I wouldn't get the respect that I deserved from the fighters. They weren't fearing me."

Said Arum, handling the P.R. chores for his fighter: "Oscar's not a fickle person. But he's also a very highly intelligent person, and if it's not getting done, you've got to get it done."

Though Steward was the main man in the corner, the Rivero firing redeemed Alcazar and brought him back into the good graces of the camp. Alcazar knew that he had been laughed at and written off. He had suffered. But he had a huge smile his first weeks at Big Bear, yelling as De La Hoya did his work and laughing at anything Steward said.

Rivero was gone. Alcazar was back. He had been through this before. This time, he wasn't ever going to let go of his prize, not even a little.

"Since he was an amateur, a lot of people have tried to steal the kid away from me," Alcazar said. "My full-time job actually was to try and keep them away. That particular experience was real tough for me.

I figured it out myself. I know one thing for sure, they're not going to take this kid away from me. If I really want to help this kid, I think I should give him the opportunity to see and try it with somebody else. And that's what I did. And what happened? In his last fight, he was resting in Mexico and he asked himself, Why am I getting hit more than I was hit before? So that's why he decided to fire Rivero."

Steward rushed into service with De La Hoya and welcomed Alcazar beside him. And for a while, the team worked. Steward was terrific at loosening Oscar up and getting him to unleash his power in the ring. Oscar was happy, Steward was happy, Joel Sr. was happy, Arum was happy. Everything was fruitful.

Oscar wanted to feel dominant in the ring again, and Steward was there to help him rediscover it.

"Oh yeah, that's my time there," De La Hoya said. "That's my spotlight. It's like I transform into a different person. The ring's my stage, you know? It's about really beating a guy. Seeing him surrender or knocking him out. I miss it. Man, do I miss that. That's why for this fight...I don't have the pressure of having to go out there and knocking him out, but I feel that I'm going to knock him out, because this camp's been good."

Up at Big Bear quickly after the trainer change, De La Hoya flourished in Steward's relaxed tutelage as he prepared for a minor fight against David Kamau, scheduled for June 14 in San Antonio's Alamodome. (It would be De La Hoya's first fight in the state of Texas.)

Wednesdays were a day off, and sparring was reduced to a minimum—maybe ten to twelve rounds a week, at most. De La Hoya felt refreshed and frisky. Steward liked to have fun, and the whole camp enjoyed long dinners and longer nights at the karaoke bar.

On most afternoons after the ring work, Steward hung around before going back to his own gym, and he and Oscar shot hoops on the makeshift basketball court in the compound's driveway. "He thinks he can play," Steward said then, "but I've got to bring Lennox over here to show him how to play."

"This camp here has been the best training camp I've had," De La Hoya said. "We're going to spar fifty, sixty rounds. I feel as fresh as ever. Even with Robert, we'd spar 120 rounds. I love sparring, but Emanuel makes sense. I've been fighting all my life. I'm not a person who takes forever to get in shape. I'll be up here for a week, ten days, and I'm in perfect shape."

In order to take care of his other fighters—and still cater to De La Hoya—Steward set up a gym, Kronk West, near De La Hoya's private compound. And Lewis, the WBC heavyweight champion of the world, cooperatively moved his camp to Big Bear to suit Steward and De La Hoya.

"Oscar," Steward said, not even trying to hide the contrast, "is my number-one priority."

Emanuel Steward wasn't the only reason De La Hoya felt loose and lively that training camp. Just a few weeks earlier—right after beating Whitaker—De La Hoya was introduced to Cassie Van Doran, a self-possessed, beautiful eighteen-year-old girl who lived with her parents in Orange County.

When he saw her at an autograph session at Hernandez's dealership, De La Hoya said he was instantly floored. Cassie didn't throw herself at him. She didn't look stupid. She came over with her parents, shook his hand, and stared into his eyes. And De La Hoya decided immediately that he had to see her again.

"Now I've found my señorita," De La Hoya said. "At the end of the day, I go home and I live by myself. And it is lonely. That's why I'm looking for the right woman. And I think I found her. I think I may get married in a couple years. If that's what's going to make me happy, I'm going to do it."

Why Cassie, out of the thousands of girls volunteering to be his girl-friend every day? "She's a virgin," he said with a conspiratorial smile.

But when that question was asked among several of his closest associates—why an eighteen-year-old, why her, why now?—there were knowing smirks. "Cassie looks like a baby Veronica," said one. "It's really obvious."

About the same time, De La Hoya found out that Veronica was engaged. He remembered telling Veronica that she could never marry anybody but him, and that he'd storm the church on her wedding day to make sure of it. But he laughed about that now. He had Cassie now, and, with Veronica on his mind, he started thinking about getting married. It was time, he thought. That way, he might be able to free himself from some of the niggling details of his father and his brother and all that chaos.

What would getting married do to his family? He smiled at the thought. His brother was making 4 percent of every purse. His father was making 9 percent, and had opened his own restaurant. (Though, in what Oscar blithely described as "a miscommunication," the famous son failed to show up for the grand opening, to Joel Sr.'s obvious disappointment.) Alcazar already had his restaurant. Pajar was making a bundle. Mike Hernandez's salary as president of the De La Hoya Foundation and De La Hoya Enterprises made sure he wasn't ignored, plus Hernandez collected a nice rent check for the office of the De La Hoya fan club, still operating out of his dealership. An aunt was set up with a new restaurant. The family, maybe, didn't need him forever, he hoped.

"Actually, the pressure is less every day," De La Hoya said. "My father has his own restaurant. So now he has his own business he can take care of, his own investments. So now that I've established that, it takes pressure off of me. My brother, he's going to have his own place. I've opened up some restaurants for my aunt in Fullerton. So little by little, there's less pressure for me. I don't feel like I have to keep on fighting. For a while I did. I always would think, man, if I stopped fighting, what's my family going to do? Money...is spent and it just slides by just like that. But if you have that responsibility and worrying about you have to fight because you're supporting your family, it doesn't make it fun."

De La Hoya contentedly left the family finances up to Hernandez

—and the planning for his future beyond boxing. "He overlooks everything," De La Hoya said. "That's a big responsibility for him. If I don't succeed in something other than boxing, it'll be on him."

Yes, he thought, maybe it's time to get married. It felt like such a grown-up thing to do.

"I think so. I think so," De La Hoya said. "If that's what's going to make me happy, I'm going to do it. I think it'll make it different. It'll make me more of a responsible person. I look forward to it. Because I call the shots up here. And I can just move my wife up here, that's all I have to do, no problem."

De La Hoya's family and friends didn't know what to make of him talking so freely about marriage, but they didn't say anything to him. Maybe it would just go away, like other serious issues had gone away, they thought. Most importantly, De La Hoya was training well under Steward, Alcazar wasn't causing any problems now that he was up at camp again, and David Kamau looked like a goner.

San Antonio screamed for De La Hoya when he arrived for the Kamau fight. The local paper treated him like a visiting head of state. Or Elvis. Or if Elvis were a head of state. The teenage girls of the city— just a short drive from the Mexican border—gobbled him up and chased him through his hotel.

This was what he'd always wanted out of his celebrity: lines of girls, unbridled heat, and the chance to making millions for it. Leaving Las Vegas and L.A., the moment and the mania suddenly seemed perfectly suited for him. In other places at other times, De La Hoya sometimes sounded as shallow and callow as anybody might suspect a twenty-four-year-old multimillionaire to be, somebody who was just named one of *People* magazine's fifty most beautiful people and recently posed for a *Playgirl* cover shoot.

But as he wandered through the river-banked streets of the mariachi-drenched downtown Riverwalk, or packed 150 screeching females into a sweltering gym for a quick workout, it was obvious: Oscar De La

Hoya was boxing's living idol and its greatest hope. You knew things were looking good for De La Hoya when Kamau's two managers, Frank and Al Ronzio, pushed their fighter aside at the final press conference to pose for a picture arm-and-arm with De La Hoya.

At his workout (which had to be canceled the next day for fear of a stampede), he tossed sweat-stained towels into the crowd; he threw his underwear out of the ring, and there was wild roaring, and a giddy tug-of-war. Almost a year to the day of the slaying of the ragingly popular Tejano singer Selena, from nearby Corpus Christi, a tall Latino from Los Angeles tapped into the heart of the phenomenon.

"He's so beautiful," said a girl there named Monica. "He's perfect! He's like Selena. He's the boy Selena!"

He earned $3 million for a walkover bout, two rounds, twenty solid punches, one easy knockout over Kamau. Though he drew less than the 20,000 expected at the Alamodome (Chavez-Whitaker had drawn 53,000, in admittedly a much more significant matchup), De La Hoya was in his glory that whole San Antonio week.

"Boxing's in a sad state. The only young man out there who's doing a thing is Oscar De La Hoya," Sugar Ray Leonard said. "Oscar De La Hoya is the only one I think making a difference in boxing."

Said Steward: "He's perfectly placed to do something. Look at him: He doesn't look Mexican, he doesn't look white, he doesn't really look anything . . . but he's beautiful. Look at that face. Everybody thinks he's part of them. He appeals to everybody."

They wanted a hero?

"The timing is just perfect, everything is perfect," De La Hoya said. "Boxing needs a new hero, and I think I'm the one."

There was no other fighter who could have stirred what he stirred in San Antonio—just by stripping off his shirt, or flinging fists into a willing foe. This was his audience, his alone: The women of San Antonio were just responding to what every other woman in America understood. "I felt comfortable because there were a lot of women out there," De La Hoya said. "This is my field."

Under Steward, De La Hoya looked stronger. Kamau was slow and had no defense, but he also was the man who gave Chavez fits in a fight several years earlier, and a man whose right hand held some degree of power. Kamau tagged De La Hoya once with his hard right in the first round, but De La Hoya didn't even hesitate. He smiled, then took a step forward and rocked Kamau until the Kenyan dropped for good.

"I feel the power," De La Hoya said. "It's back."

Both the pupil and the new teacher were thrilled. Steward hadn't exactly gone poor the previous few years, but he had gone through a handful of fighters, always looking to find himself the perfect situation with the perfect fighter.

He had trained with Hearns, Evander Holyfield when Holyfield roared back to upset Riddick Bowe, and Chavez. Steward found the magic inside Oliver McCall for a brief moment—time enough to choreograph the stunning knockout of Lennox Lewis in 1995—but was bounced from the McCall camp quickly enough that he was in Lewis's corner when Lewis beat McCall in the rematch.

Steward was still with Lewis—but Steward saw something burning brighter in De La Hoya, something Steward had hoped to find his whole career.

"Oscar's biggest asset I think is the unbelievable intensity and viciousness that he brings into the ring," Steward said. "He's totally transformed once the bell rings. And I have never in my life seen a fighter who does that the way he does it. I've noticed all along. He looks so sweet, talks almost like a little girl, a little boy. Then when the bell rings, he moves around, and after about forty seconds, it's like a Jekyll and Hyde. He totally wants to destroy the person. That is so impressive . . . and to be liked, those qualities are going to take him over the average fighters. I just don't see him losing to anyone."

Steward admitted that even after watching De La Hoya fight for years, he was surprised at the ferociousness of his training.

"In his sparring, in the gym workouts, he's so intense," Steward said. "His eyes are just so ferocious. He's just totally transformed. Very seldom do you see a guy who's not aware of anything that's going on outside of the ring or anything. . . ."

What Steward wanted was to see De La Hoya reach for the heights—a desire that was not necessarily 100 percent encouraged by Hernandez and Arum, who had a money machine to protect. Steward was already rich. He wasn't around De La Hoya to get rich. He was around De La Hoya to be a mentor to greatness. To see him fight huge fights, against men like Felix Trinidad, the young welterweight rival aching for a shot at De La Hoya, or even a Whitaker rematch. These were the fights that could make De La Hoya a Sugar Ray Leonard, or bigger. But Hernandez wanted sure things.

"He has set records, won titles, beat champions, but he has not been in big fights," Steward pointed out. "He has been in with big names, but at the time he fought them, they were not really all there, you know what I mean? Chavez was at the end. Genaro Hernandez said his nose was broken. He's fought the best of his era, but those guys have not been that big with the American public, except for Chavez, and Chavez's reputation since he lost to Randall hasn't been that strong. Until he beats a guy like a Trinidad . . . like Leonard and Hearns, you know? They had to fight each other."

When De La Hoya survived the accident in the Mercedes after the Kamau fight without a scratch, Steward sounded as if he were John the Baptist, proclaiming a new era in boxing.

"I'm telling you, a child of destiny," Steward said. "He's got a special glow over him. Those type of kids, like Ali, when a guy might be beating him, all of a sudden the other guy's eye will get hurt. Something will happen to the guy. These come along every once in a while. The last one we really had, a child of destiny to come in like a savior, was Muhammad Ali. And with these type of kids, all kinds of strange things will happen, even in fights. Strange things will occur that will always bring them through. I've always felt that about him. It's just like something will protect Oscar. I really believe that. Like when he fought Julio Cesar Chavez, what happened? Chavez came in with a cut eye. Genaro

Hernandez? He came in surprisingly slow. These children of destiny, they come along every thirty or forty years. And he's the one. He's the one.

"Listen, I'm not afraid to drive with him. That accident, the more he gave me a complete description of it, I said, 'That was God taking care of you, Oscar.'"

De La Hoya had a slightly—only slightly—different interpretation of the crash and the survival. "After I got out and I saw the accident," he said, "I knew my mother was looking down on me for sure."

And what else did she see? After the accident, De La Hoya started thinking about that, about what his mother must think of his life. He already had brought Cassie close to him, and since the crash, it all seemed right. It was weird, enlightening symbolism: Cassie was still a virgin, Oscar felt like he was chosen, and it was time. He asked her to marry him. She said yes.

"I'm ready and this is the one," De La Hoya said in August. "Yep. I've lived the life. Man, I've lived it. I have lived it. . . . But what's opened my eyes actually has been my father. He told me, 'Something can happen to you, you know? Messing around and having all these women can end your life just like that. Women will take your money, all that party scene, it'll mess you up.' And my brother actually told me, too.

"I was surprised. When I told them I was going to marry her, they were, like, 'Man, you do it.' I thought my father would be the last one to want me to be married. My father would always tell me, 'You're not getting married until you're thirty or thirty-one, just like me.' But when I announced it to my father, he was like relieved and happy. Because he knew all the women I would have. When I finally introduced my father to Cassie, my father told her, 'Well, I hope you don't like Oscar for his money, and for his fame. I hope you respect him and like him for him.' And she said, 'Well if he doesn't respect *me* and if he doesn't love *me,* I'll just leave him. I don't care for his money.' That's what really caught his ear. He adores her.

"I don't think I can marry a girl my family doesn't like. I don't think so. I would want my family to also love the person that I marry. I don't think I could have that friction between anybody in my family. . . . It's time. It's time. . . . I'm the happiest when I'm with her. She's very religious. I go to church with her like twice a week when I'm down there. The values she has are the same as the ones I had growing up. And that's special. She didn't grow up poor, poor, poor, but the way her father's strict with her and the way her mother wants the very best for her, it's very touching."

The hardest part of it all, De La Hoya recounted with amusement, was summoning the courage and the words to tell her parents that he wanted to marry their daughter. She was eighteen. They were deeply religious.

What were they going to say to him?

"Asking *her* was quick and easy," De La Hoya said. "It took me about an hour to try to ask her parents, though. I was just trying to break the ice, trying to say something. . . . 'Well, I've known your daughter for a while now, and I really love her. . . .' This and that. I couldn't say it, I couldn't break that ice. . . . But finally, when I asked the parents, her father got up, came behind me, I was, 'Oh, shit, he's going to coldcock me or something.' Then he started crying and I thought, 'Yeah, he's going to say yes.'

"I haven't even touched her. I don't want to touch her until we get married. That's what kind of girl she is. And oh man, her parents . . . they believe in me so much, I won't let them down."

Then, a few weeks after that, practically on the eve of his $10 million fight against Hector Camacho in September, De La Hoya was called into a meeting with Hernandez and Joel Sr. and a few others of the inner circle.

"There's a problem, and we shouldn't even be telling you this," Hernandez said, as Oscar sat still. "There's a girl who says she is having your baby."

Hernandez wanted to fight the girl's claims—she was already saying that she would go to the media. There had been a few claims in the past, some true, some not, and they all had taken care of themselves—

or Hernandez had taken care of them. There was at least one miscarriage and several abortions that Hernandez helped arrange, including two that involved the younger sister of one of De La Hoya's closest friends. Also, several De La Hoya intimates point to twin babies that were born to another girl, in late 1997—though that girl apparently never sued for child support.

"Do you know how many times this has happened?" Hernandez said a little later. "They've all gone away. This one will go away, too. They all do. I'll make it go away."

But this time, the girl was serious. She was hardly someone De La Hoya could deny knowing—he had seen her off and on for years, all the way back to Barcelona. She was keeping the baby, and it was De La Hoya's. Oscar nodded and said there was no problem here.

"If it's my baby, that's it," Oscar said. "I'll take full responsibility."

Hernandez wanted no part of that . . . but how was he going to fight it? Oscar had always wanted to have a child. Despite the uncomfortable circumstances, Oscar rooted for the baby to be his. Something inside of him felt fulfilled. A little boy, he thought.

"It's going to change my life," De La Hoya said in an interview that drove Hernandez into palpitations, "but it's going to be for the better. If it is mine, I would want to be around the baby twenty-four hours a day—full custody. Because I know I can take care of a baby. I know she can't. . . . I know I will. We would have to hire a nanny, you know? No big deal. Get a bigger home, extend the home. It'll make it better. He'll say, 'Poppy, I want to fight!' Oh, it's a lot of responsibility, but I'm willing to do it. We need a change up here in camp. We need a new face. At first, I was surprised, then I thought, 'Wow, it's going to be good.' My brother has a kid, and every time I'm around him, it's the best feeling."

Said Pajar: "He's going to be a good father—because, well, having a father like him, that kid's going to have everything he wants. Oh yeah, he's going to be a spoiled kid because he's always wanted a baby. He loves babies so much. He wants to be part of it. He wants his own babies now. He wants to be happy like us."

"It's all happening now," De La Hoya said with a smile as he finalized his preparations for Camacho. "Things always happen to me for a reason."

De La Hoya and Cassie quickly broke up, though De La Hoya never said why. A friend close to De La Hoya said the fighter had quickly grown bored with Cassie, after the excitement of the proposal. Plus, he wanted other girls.

All De La Hoya would say was: "I'm not engaged. No, no, no. Not engaged. I'm single. Siiiiin-gle!"

Steward loved that De La Hoya was becoming freer and looser with his thoughts and boxing. After the maturing Rivero years, now there was less caution, more power.

The next fight for De La Hoya, though, was all about cautious calculations.

Arum and Hernandez booked him a left-hander, but it wasn't Whitaker. It was Hector (Macho) Camacho, a tough veteran of many, many top-bill fights and a proven showman. But Camacho was way past his prime, even at thirty-two, and had never been considered an elite fighter even when he was young. His last fight was a knockout victory over an embarrassingly benign forty-two-year-old Sugar Ray Leonard.

Camacho talked a loud and brassy game, and Arum and Hernandez figured that putting the young Mexican-American in against the mouthy Puerto Rican–American would set up a good-versus-bad matchup that finally placed De La Hoya in the former role.

Camacho did his best to play the part. At the same time as the press tour for De La Hoya–Camacho, Mike Tyson took a bite out of Evander Holyfield's ear during a fight, raising a world-class media conflagration. Asked about Tyson on CNN, Camacho mumbled something, then referred to Tyson acting like "a n———. You know how they act."

Camacho was equally shrill about De La Hoya, and De La Hoya was listening.

"If I'd have met him when we were both 130, I'd have killed him,"

Camacho said. "On the streets, I'd have kicked his butt. But he'd never go to Harlem, anyway."

Added his wife, Amy: "He's more exciting than Oscar will ever be. Bottom line: He's the more exciting person, and fighter. He's not trying at all, it's just natural. He was not molded to become a fighter like they did with Oscar. He was born to be a fighter. And now Oscar's in his prime and Macho's about to make an ending to his story. I think this is a perfect ending."

Trainer Teddy Atlas, watching the 8–1 underdog bark at De La Hoya, said the emotions were hardly surprising.

"Camacho must feel a little resentment for De La Hoya," Atlas told the *New York Daily News*. "He has to be thinking, 'This is what I could've been.' He has to look at De La Hoya and think, 'I've been through tougher things, I've met tougher fighters, and I may have blown a lot of days, but I'm not blowing this one.' This is his last shot at being considered a special fighter—and you know what, it might mean something."

Meanwhile, De La Hoya wanted to knock out Camacho in the worst way. He hated his taunts and his little smile. He wanted to do something that Chavez, Edwin Rosario, and the other great fighters Camacho had faced, including Trinidad, could not do. None had even knocked Camacho down.

"I'll play with him for six rounds," De La Hoya said, "and then I'll knock him out in the seventh."

At a press conference in Las Vegas, De La Hoya—set to make $10 million versus Camacho's $3 million—went to the podium and dared Camacho to accept a bet: If De La Hoya won, he would get to snip off Camacho's dangling forelock in the ring; if Camacho won, De La Hoya would pay him $200,000 out of his own pocket. Camacho laughed, and said fine, let's do it.

For De La Hoya, training was complicated after he suffered a slight dislocation of a knee caused when he slipped on a wet floor in Big Bear. But with Steward already toning down the work, De La Hoya wasn't overly concerned about Camacho.

The fight itself was uninspiring. De La Hoya looked sharper than he had against Whitaker, but he also facing a less talented foe—and the left-handed stance was far less confusing to De La Hoya the second time around. Camacho showed up early, but, like Whitaker, tasted a few De La Hoya rockets and went about trying to hang on for dear life.

De La Hoya dominated the fight, but with Camacho clutching at every chance, he couldn't put more than one or two punches together. He punished Camacho (landing 340 power shots in the twelve rounds, at a 51 percent accuracy rate), but other than a ninth-round knockdown, couldn't put him away.

Derided for his performance, Camacho defended his tactics.

"Let me punch you in the face a few times and see what you do," Camacho said after being booed. "If you can't stop a guy from punching you in the face, you better hold him. . . . Oscar is the best fighter I've ever fought."

After the overwhelming decision was announced, De La Hoya moved toward Camacho and grabbed a pair of scissors. "Be a man," he said to Camacho, "you made a bet."

"The bet could be paid off," Camacho said. "But I think I'll be the bad boy of boxing and since he said he'll knock me out in seven rounds and he didn't, I ain't going to give him shit."

Said Steward: "Camacho was just tricky. Camacho just went into a survival mode. I can't fault him in that. It's hard to put two punches together when a guy grabs you after you land one. He beat him worse than Trinidad beat him."

The main concern for Steward and the rest of Team De La Hoya was that De La Hoya still wasn't throwing the same kind of thunder he used to. The unspoken fear: As he traveled up in weight, what passed for overwhelming power in the lighter divisions would just be fast punches as a welterweight or above. His hands were fast and deadly accurate, but he no longer seemed to be able to rock the heavier fighters. Was he just a normal puncher at welterweight?

Steward, in the days before he was fired, said no way.

"He throws the right hand, and before he lands it, he's drawing it back and throwing another punch," Steward said. "He doesn't let it vibrate, as I call it, to get the full power effect of it. That was just some bad habits that he got into with Rivero. I don't think he's changed them. One of my main problems is he's gotten into this habit of getting down and bobbing and weaving . . . because that was the Willie Pep move that the old man had taught him. I said, 'You're five-eleven . . . you're as tall as Ray Robinson was. You should stay on the outside.' I wanted to start teaching him more tricks that would've been more advantageous."

But the plots, paranoia, and intrigue were once again about to take down a De La Hoya trainer—far faster than Rivero. Steward guessed that Alcazar was scheming against him, but what could he do about it? All he could do was trust the fighter. Alcazar wanted total control of De La Hoya's training—and reported back to Joel Sr. everything he thought Steward was doing wrong.

Too much off time, he told Joel Sr. Too much screwing around. Too much talk about Lennox Lewis. Too little sparring work. Emanuel Steward, he told Joel Sr., isn't taking Oscar's training seriously. He told him that Oscar was out of shape.

But Steward's street smarts were too keen for subterfuge. He had temporarily moved his whole operation from Detroit to the San Bernardino Mountains—brought Detroit fighters to this mountain resort, brought a heavyweight champion—and they were plotting against him?

"I could feel it coming," Steward said. "You know . . . you can tell, you could just see little things. You could feel things. And I could feel Alcazar on the phone, steadily lying, really, with Oscar's daddy. You could feel it. I'd see him, 'How are you doing, *que pasa.* . . .' And he'd smile. But you could see it in his eyes. You could see it all coming. Then we'd have the meetings, supposedly all of us. And the father would never look me in the eye, that type of stuff. You could see it all coming."

After Camacho, De La Hoya went up for the training camp to prepare for a December fight against Wilfredo Rivera with Stewart still on board. Early in the camp, Steward invited his friend and boxing aficionado Robert Shapiro up to Big Bear to watch De La Hoya train. Shapiro, the O.J. Simpson lawyer, got up to De La Hoya's compound, rang the bell at the driveway fence, and Steward let him in.

But as Shapiro watched, one of De La Hoya's bodyguards pulled Steward aside and spoke bluntly.

"We don't want him around up here around Oscar," the bodyguard said, indicating he had gotten his orders from Mike Hernandez.

"Bob is a personal friend of mine and he's a big fan of Oscar," Steward replied.

"Well, he may try and be his lawyer," the bodyguard said.

Steward recounted the story with exasperation and exhaustion. That was the way they were going to get rid of him—Arum and Hernandez feared that Steward was bringing people up to meet Oscar so Steward could steal the fighter away.

"I told Shapiro," Steward said, "and Bob said, 'Just fuck it, then I won't ever be around again. I just came up because I like the kid. I wasn't trying to be no damn lawyer for him. I like boxing.'"

It was coming—but the final trigger wasn't pulled yet.

Any other fighter would have packed it in for the year, been pleased with four fights since February and hit the links for a while. De La Hoya would have loved to do that, but Arum already had him booked for the hard-hitting Rivera, who made his name in two tough losses against Whitaker. How better to upstage Whitaker than not to fight him, and beat one of his old foes instead?

Though Rivera had very little chance to win the fight, the event was slightly energized by the fact that one of Rivera's agents was none other than Robert Mittleman, the old De La Hoya comanager.

"Listen, this kid is one of the most spoiled, little creepy guys you'd ever want to meet," Mittleman said. "And he knows it. And everyone who knows him knows it. Has success gone to his head? I think so. Not publicly. He's wonderful with the public. He's terrific, don't you think?

Beautiful smile, nice looking. I think that high voice will preclude him from the acting thing. I have nothing against him. But I would love to see my guy beat his ass. He deserves it."

De La Hoya, who pocketed $6 million for the pay-per-view fight, his first fight in Atlantic City, New Jersey, said he didn't mind the presence of Mittleman. He had been through it with Finkel and Duva, so Mittleman was old hat.

"It's . . . interesting," De La Hoya said. "But you know what, there's no friction whatsoever. Hey, he was trying to do his job. I did my job, and things didn't work out, we went our own ways. It was like a divorce, you know? The lawsuits have been dropped, and thank God everything is behind me. But of course there's motivation there. There's great motivation to beat Rivera because of Mittleman."

With Steward, De La Hoya was in a talking mood at Big Bear. He wanted to talk business, and he figured Steward was the best man around to dispense some advice. Lately, he and Hernandez were scrapping with Arum over purse sizes and opponent choices. De La Hoya almost walked away from the Kamau fight when he was upset about the purse. De La Hoya had balked a little at the Rivera purse. They were beginning to believe that Arum was getting too much of the gold mine. They were getting tired of Arum. Who else was out there? De La Hoya asked Steward.

"There was another world that he had questions about—he wanted to talk about this other world that was beyond Las Vegas and Mexico and California," Steward said. "One day he wanted me to drive down the mountain with him. He says, 'Emanuel, what is Don King like?' I said 'Well, Don King is the greatest promoter of all time. But you are damn sure much better off to stay with Bob Arum. You could have never become what you've become if you were Don King's.' He said, 'Why? Didn't he make Mike Tyson?' I said, 'He didn't make Mike Tyson.' I always told him the facts of life. Then he says, 'Well, look at all the money he makes.' I said, 'You know, Mike Tyson was big before Don King came into the picture.'"

De La Hoya was curious. And when the Holyfield-Moorer rematch came around in early November, he was eager to go. Interestingly, De La Hoya had never attended a big heavyweight fight in Las Vegas and ached to be a part of the mingling crowd. Steward was already going as part of the Showtime pay-per-view telecast, and Oscar wanted to come with him. It was a Don King card, and Arum wanted De La Hoya nowhere near King. Ever.

Steward didn't get tickets for De La Hoya. But when Arum heard De La Hoya was going, he was furious—at Steward. He was sure Steward was bringing him there to meet King—whom De La Hoya had never met—and bargain for a piece of De La Hoya's management. Hernandez was worried, too. The fact that De La Hoya apparently lost about $400,000 at the crap tables that night did little to calm down the situation.

Arum and Hernandez immediately blamed Steward, and suspected he was tearing De La Hoya away from them—plying him with drinks and women and luring him to King.

"First of all, I didn't bring Oscar anywhere," Steward said later. "How can you blame somebody for what *he* did? He said he always wanted to go to a big heavyweight fight, so he did. I didn't want him to come. He came in on his own. I didn't see him. I was busy doing TV for CNN and for the pay-per-view. When I was up there doing my broadcast, Oscar came up and he said hello. He said, 'Don't worry, Alcazar's with me and Rich Rose [from Caesars].' I said just go out and have some fun. And he said, 'I'm going back tomorrow, anyway.'

"And that's all I saw of Oscar. So if I can be blamed for some of that stuff, I've got a problem," Steward said. "And I heard that Alcazar was gambling with him. That was a totally unfair rap. I've never seen Oscar gamble. I don't gamble. I don't encourage it. Once when he had a meeting, Bob Arum was telling Oscar that you shouldn't do that . . . because you can win once, but you're never going to beat them all the time. All of that is something I had no idea about. . . . I talked to him maybe two minutes, I put the earphones back on, and Oscar went right back down and I didn't see him again. I had my own job to do."

As soon as De La Hoya was back in Big Bear—and word filtered back that he'd lost all that money—Arum and Hernandez immediately convened an emergency meeting.

"How much money did Don King offer you? How much was it?" Arum grilled De La Hoya, who denied he had even spoken to King.

Three times Arum asked the same question, and all three times De La Hoya denied it. Just tell us how Steward tried to do it, Arum said. De La Hoya said that Steward had nothing to do with anything, and nothing happened, anyway.

But there was a decision that already had been made by Arum and Hernandez and Joel Sr.: Steward was gone. Fired.

Steward said he didn't even try to fight it. "I told Oscar, 'Look, I'm packing up my stuff, brother, I'm getting out of here,'" Steward said. "'There's too much stress that you're going to have to go through.' He says, 'Why are they doing this? You never say nothing but good stuff about Bob.' ... Bob should be thanking me. The best thing Bob could've had was me with the fighter. Because I supported everything he did, 100 percent.

"They were trying to find any reason to get rid of me. Everybody became uncomfortable with me—except for Oscar. Well, the rest of the kids around, they liked me. Mike Hernandez has been a gentleman all along. But he's a big moneymaking machine and everybody was intimidated by this kid liking anyone."

In his own nonconfrontational way, De La Hoya tried to support Steward after the firing—but made it clear that he wasn't going to overrule his father or Arum or Hernandez on the matter. De La Hoya said it was all about his father's discomfort with Steward's training style: the days off, the relaxation, the whispers from Alcazar.

"I felt comfortable with Emanuel Steward," De La Hoya said days before the Rivera fight. "He trained me good. He brought life into the training camp. He made it fun for me. He really understood the power I possess. With Don Jesus, it was all hard work. Emanuel gave me the confidence that he was teaching me, but he kept it fun. If it had been solely up to me, yes, of course, he would still be here."

So if the fighter liked him and wanted him to stay, why was Steward gone?

"I hate arguing with my father," De La Hoya said. "I didn't want my family destroyed over this little situation. I don't want anything between us. Blood is thicker than water. . . . My father had a hunch that Emanuel was not spending enough time with me. I love Emanuel Steward, but my father didn't agree with my opinion and I went with his decision. There's been other times when I wouldn't budge."

Steward didn't quite know what to make of the departure. De La Hoya said he wanted Steward to be his trainer. He said his father was the main one pushing for Steward to be dumped. And he had told Steward that he tried to avoid his father at all costs.

Joel Sr. was still calling the shots for such an important decision? Emanuel Steward, from Detroit and the high-level boxing world, couldn't hope to understand the hidden corners of the relationship between Oscar and his father. You'd have to go back years to understand that, back to when Oscar was six and his father put gloves on his hands for the first time.

"The strange thing is," Steward recalled, "him and his daddy don't really like each other. That's the weirdest shit. Here's a perfect example: After we had a meeting in Mike's office, I was going to leave and Oscar says, 'No, no, come on, we've got to go get something to eat.' We go to the restaurant, and you could tell the tension with him and his dad. They never talk too much. I sit down and Oscar sits right next to me. So the dad sits on the other side of Oscar. And then there's Bob Arum, there's [Arum's matchmaker] Bruce Trampler, Mike Hernandez, Mike's wife . . . that was it.

"So we're sitting and the dad hasn't said nothing in all this time to Oscar. Then he waits and he looks at him and he says, 'You know, you weren't in fucking shape for that last fight.' And Oscar says, 'What the fuck are you talking about? The Camacho fight?'

"So Oscar looked at him, and just put his head on the table. He was so fucking mad. And he just looked at me and said, 'He never says nothing good.' He just kind of walked away from the table, walked around for a little bit. He came and sat down and for the rest of the time they never said anything to each other. This is the shit that's not even me. These are things that's just them. It's been going on for years."

Once, when he fired Mittleman and Nelson, De La Hoya thought he could escape the cycle. And with Rivero and Veronica, he was halfway out. But his father never got fired. Oscar could never quite dare to walk away completely.

And what was left was a rich and motherless son, wishing that he could be free, but unable to summon the will to separate himself from the father who made him a star, and who drove him crazy.

"My dad never tells me I did great," De La Hoya once said. "He may tell me what I did good, but he'd never say, 'My son did great.' He thinks my head would swell."

Said Joel Sr.: "I would never say he is perfect. No, no. I think he is great looking, sometimes, but if I say he is perfect, he will think, 'I *am* perfect.' He knows I don't say that kind of thing. . . . I am proud of him, but not because he is a boxing star. I am proud because he is my son. He is my blood."

Alcazar was back as the undisputed No. 1 trainer, and to help him talk to the media and maybe offer some advice between rounds, Arum brought in veteran New York trainer Gil Clancy.

De La Hoya knocked down Rivera in the fourth, but did not come close to a knockout. He sliced up his face with blazing combinations, winning on an eighth-round technical knockout when blood poured over Rivera's face from multiple cuts.

But there were more troubles coming in the De La Hoya camp.

Conditioner Andy Shumway was a genial former running back from Wisconsin who had been part of a team hired a year earlier to help De La Hoya with his conditioning and weight training when he needed to bulk up from 135 pounds eventually to 147.

Early in the process, after the Chavez fight, Dominique Paris, one member of the conditioning team who had grown close to De La Hoya at Big Bear, tried to cut out the rest of the team and offered his services as the sole conditioner. When the rest of the team found out, Paris was fired. But De La Hoya brooded about the move and the absence of Paris.

"He misses Dominique, I think," Hernandez said obliquely. "He wants to chase all over France to find him."

But the situation was settled when Shumway took over for Paris up at Big Bear for the Whitaker camp and beyond. Then, when Hernandez maneuvered to send Pajar off the mountain, Shumway became the camp coordinator, responsible for De La Hoya's schedule and the general camp administration. Not surprisingly, De La Hoya bonded with Shumway, too, and loved it when Shumway brought his baby daughter up to camp.

For the Rivera fight, De La Hoya wanted Shumway to maintain his administrative role, but this time Alcazar was back and not interested in anybody else having responsibilities he himself could handle. The tension, once again, was thick. Soon enough, Shumway was let go, too.

"Alcazar and I had a little rift," Shumway said. "The common denominator always seems to be Robert's insecurity on his grasp on Oscar. There's nothing I can do about that. I'm a dogmatic person. It's all kind of a pecking order. And Robert had been spanked down a couple of times by bringing in Rivero and Manny. . . . He just felt he needed to be in control as much as he could. He wanted to control everything that was going on, so after the Camacho fight, he insisted I not be involved up in the camp.

"Alcazar and I had one flare-up. It took about two seconds. And he said, 'We'll see.' And it took a while, but he proved it. Oscar and I always got along real well, but who knows? Oscar is as good as the last person that talks to him. He's really influenced greatly by the people who have the closest proximity. And when you're not around, there's nothing you can do. I think Oscar's the type of guy that doesn't like to rustle anybody's feathers. And he wants to pretty much stay away from any controversy or anything like that . . . as far as who's running camp. He doesn't want to deal with it. He lets everybody else around him kind of deal with it."

The man who always maintained the closest proximity was Alcazar. "He doesn't want to lose any of the credit," Shumway said. "He wants to be the guy who guided Oscar through. He doesn't want to have to share that with anybody. He doesn't want anybody to be known to have been any help at all."

After Rivera, De La Hoya was tired again and wanted time off. He was scheduled in February to defend his title against the WBC's No. 1 contender, an unheralded fighter from France by the name of Patrick Charpentier. But De La Hoya wanted no part of a February fight, and, quite conveniently, discovered a wrist injury that postponed the fight until March. A few weeks later, De La Hoya postponed it again, moving it all the way to June.

Whispers spread—not exactly discouraged by De La Hoya insiders—that De La Hoya was sitting out as a protest against Arum, that he was toying with the promoter, using the injury, which was actually not that serious, as a ploy to keep Arum guessing. Steward said he'd heard that King had set up a meeting with Joel Sr., though all sides denied it. De La Hoya's contract with Arum ran through 2002, but several sources said that Hernandez was looking into ways to break it. Other sources said Hernandez was just floating the rumor to make Arum shiver and renegotiate their present deal.

As usual, when De La Hoya took time away from boxing, uncertainty was the dominant emotion of those around him.

"When you look what goes on in that camp," said Steve Nelson, the former comanager, "the history is people just don't have a way of lasting with him. For whatever reason. There's so many different factions pulling at him and the whole idea of loyalty seems to not be there at all. Most guys, you're going to have your ups and downs and generally work things out. But in Oscar's camp, it doesn't work that way. In Oscar's camp, you're there one day and gone the next. It's not just us— Shelly Finkel, Robert Alcazar, Rivero, Manny Steward. . . ."

And will it ever stop?

"I have been told that they're not thrilled with Arum," said Nelson, who says he still talks with Mike Hernandez. "I know for a fact there's been conversations, how to get out of his contract. And to me, Arum's done a great job for him. How do you satisfy someone like this? Making that kind of money, he should be a very happy guy. And to be unhappy, there's something not quite right there. I think he should be a very happy kid. I don't know how he is. But whenever you see so much change, it strikes me funny. I don't know if he could ever be truly happy, in anything. . . . I'll tell you, if he can't be happy today, with what he's taking home and his lifestyle, how can you make him happy?

"There's no question, Bob Arum's not quite an angel. And if there's any chance to gain an edge for himself, to get more than maybe he should be getting, he's going to take it. And I'm sure he's going to do it. I know they've asked for accounting, and they have not gotten it. Bob's got a Don King–like deal with Oscar. We know that because we still have periodic conversations with Mike Hernandez. On top of his promotional fees, Arum gets 25 percent of Oscar's purses. Which is a little bit of a Don King deal, which is kind of amazing to me.

"I know he doesn't pay Mike Hernandez, although Mike makes money off of him on all kinds of side deals. He's been real smart that way. I know for a fact that Mike is his landlord for his fan club, and I know the rent he's paying is so far above what it should be. And I know Mike has gotten other deals through Oscar."

Eventually, De La Hoya declared himself healthy, and the Charpentier fight was set for June, in El Paso's Sun Bowl. The reaction there was even greater than the rush of San Antonio. The day the tickets went on sale, twenty thousand were sold, for a nothing fight against a fighter nobody had ever heard of before or probably would ever think about again.

By the time of the fight, forty-three thousand screaming fans jammed into the Sun Bowl on a windy day. Nothing more was asked of De La Hoya than to vanquish an unworthy foe and wink at the crowd like a movie star in the middle of a love scene.

In the stands, a sign held by two girls asked: HOW ABOUT IT, WILL YOU MARRY US? Another sign: OSCAR, I WANT TO HAVE YOUR BABY! And: OSCAR, I WON'T ASK FOR CHILD SUPPORT!

Said HBO's Larry Merchant: "I don't know if it's Leonardo DiCaprio or Michael Jordan or some combination of the both of them."

In appreciation of the crowd response (and also as an indication of how little he thought of Charpentier), De La Hoya pulled off his first ring-entrance stunt, walking out in a shimmering gold-lined pancho and wearing a huge black sombrero.

That would be the highlight of the night, because Charpentier was nowhere near up to even competing with a world-class fighter. By the time he was put on his back for the third time in the third round, and out, Charpentier had landed only five punches. De La Hoya landed eighty in the fight.

And the girls yelped for him even louder.

But the ridiculous ease with which he won the fight opened De La Hoya to hard questions: When was he going to fight somebody serious? When was he going to test himself? It had been over a year since he had fought Whitaker, and even Whitaker was thirty-three years old. When would De La Hoya fight the other young champions in his divisions? Was he scared to risk it against Felix Trinidad or Ike Quartey? Even to give a rematch to Whitaker?

De La Hoya soaked up the libidinous air and gave a wry smile.

"There's no hurry," he said. "We have an agenda. There's no rush."

There wasn't, and the heat of El Paso told him so. They would buy him doing anything, fighting anybody, as long as he smiled, and they could see him.

In the *El Paso Times* that week, columnist Maribel Villalva gave a burbling voice to the phenomenon: "When Oscar De La Hoya blows kisses, something happens. The sky starts spinning, and the pavement starts shaking. When Oscar De La Hoya smiles, the world just stops in its tracks.... Women adore Oscar, and El Paso women practically wrote the book on how to love him.... But what's so wonderful about this twenty-five-year-old Aquarius is that he takes it all in stride. Yes, he knows he has enough sex appeal to last him until he's eighty, but he's never let it get in the way of him and his fans.... So was I nervous? Yes, but I did manage to pay attention to some important details. Here are some: He had a five o'clock shadow; he's left-handed; he likes to lick his lips before smiling; he crosses his hands over his chest and under his arms. Standing next to him, I reached only his neck. And just in case anyone has ever wondered, he smells incredible—not necessarily like cologne, just clean and fresh."

After the Oscar-mania in El Paso, De La Hoya turned his attention to a slightly more serious, remarkably more lucrative, and only marginally more risky undertaking: facing Julio Cesar Chavez in a September 18 rematch back in Las Vegas, more than two years after the first debacle. With a swirl of prime fighters milling about the welterweight division waiting for their shot at De La Hoya, who still had never knocked out a true welterweight, the decision to grant Chavez a rematch answered every cynic's supposition.

De La Hoya had never given anybody a rematch before, why Chavez? Why now? De La Hoya said this was strictly his personal choice, a matter of ending Chavez's claims that the first fight was marred by the cut. It was closure, at $9 million guaranteed, without much chance of an upset. That was the cynical part. De La Hoya hadn't fought a risky fight since Whitaker in April 1997, and Chavez, at age thirty-six, was just another version of Camacho: washed-up, undersized, and valuable only because of name recognition. One last milking of the Mexican audience, one last box-office (if not artistic) bonanza. This fight would be at the 147-pound welterweight limit, or seven pounds more than the last time—and even that time Chavez was woefully undersized. This is the fight Mike Hernandez wanted more than any other.

The Chavez rematch, however, turned out to be surprising for what it revealed. Not about Chavez, who charged determinedly forward, pounded it out with De La Hoya for eight hard rounds, then quit on his stool after the eighth to give De La Hoya the knockout victory. This was Chavez, the Oldie Tour: It looked okay on the surface, but it lacked all snap and crackle. It was to be expected. It was not surprising. Also not surprisingly, the fight did excellent pay-per-view business: Those who missed the first bout because of the closed-circuit showing could see this one at home, and it was estimated that there were about 600,000 pay-per-view sales, for a gross of about $28 million.

But what the fight exposed was De La Hoya's fraying technique and lack of any real boxing teacher or stylistic focus. Yes, he tore up Chavez again, cut his eye open again, and ripped a long, jagged piece out of Chavez's bottom lip. But De La Hoya got hit harder and more often by the little Chavez (De La Hoya outweighed him by almost twenty pounds on the night of the fight, twenty-four hours after the official weigh-in), and apparently had no fight plan, or willingness to adhere to one. De La Hoya was just a big, fast counterpuncher again, just like he was when he was twenty-one—and when he got knocked down twice by smaller fighters.

If Chavez could lean in, absorb the punishment, and rock De La Hoya back on his heels at least two or three times, what would a legitimate welterweight hammer-hitter do to De La Hoya? What could Felix Trinidad do with openings like De La Hoya suddenly was offering? Or Ike Quartey, who was signed to meet De La Hoya in November? Why were De La Hoya's arms down at his waist for most of the fight? What happened to the jab that enabled him to blast Chavez in the first fight without fear of getting hit in return?

What happened to the stylist of two or three years before? He was gone, gone with Rivero, gone with Steward, gone with all the former trainers who were whisped away by Mike Hernandez when he feared their growing influence over De La Hoya. All that was left was Alcazar, and, only for fight night, Gil Glancy. Which meant that really, all that was left was De La Hoya's will to survive, his still-staggering talent, and his lucky star. After all these years, and all that money, he was still the overflowing talent, and the intrigue still was to see his struggle to fulfill his boxing destiny—or watch it wither away, overcooked by nervous handlers and the multimillionaire's lifestyle.

De La Hoya, in his more reflective moments, seemed to guess at the consequences of his particular genius. When he wrote his love letter to Peralta, he hinted at the wounds below the surface, injuries that were covered up now by screaming girls and nights of beer and dice. He wondered if he ever had a choice, if there was ever any chance that he wouldn't become a fighter, and succeed, and earn millions, and sit up on the mountaintop, peering down at the normal people living normal lives down below.

It's not that he yearned to be poor again, or to lose. But he felt directed sometimes, pushed toward an inevitability that was impossible to elude. His greatest mistakes never seemed to cripple him. His failures were always miniature. His accidents were always harmless. The people he loved most—the ones who might have drawn him to another, fuller life—were always pulled away from him. All things pointed him ceaselessly to the mountaintop. . . .

Veronica, who came the closest to loving him as his mother did, looked at him and saw a lost boy.

"I think he's in a very self-destructive mode," Peralta said. "I think his life has come to a point where he has everything. He's got girls falling at his feet left and right. Not only girls, he's got men falling at his feet. Everybody wants to do business with him. Everybody wants a piece of Oscar De La Hoya, and that's wonderful.

"But he does not have a sense of identity because he has had everybody control his life or manipulate him. . . . He's allowed them to do that. Because it's the easiest way to go when you're young and you're becoming a millionaire. He didn't acquire a sense of identity prior to being a millionaire. So now that he's a millionaire, it's made him so much more insecure because he doesn't know who he is, where he stands, what he represents. He doesn't know where he's going. All he knows is he has tons of money."

Was every tragedy and triumph, every argument with his father and every negotiation with Bob Arum and every trainer and every firing and every knockout and every critic's word ... was it all part of something deeper than he could grasp? It was all easier to swallow this way, he said. He walked away from people, because they no longer served his greater purpose. The more he fought, and the greater the distance he put between himself and even the best fighters gathered to beat him, the more he understood: He was not only made for boxing, in a very real sense, the sport was created for his glory. There was no other answer.

"I think boxing has always been my destiny," he said once, in the dark, staring out onto his putting green from his wood porch. "When I first stepped inside that ring, I loved it. I would turn into this different person even as a kid, when I first started. I was brought to this world to fight. Not for free, but fight for money. I've never fought on the streets. Never ever got into a brawl. Never. Never. Only when I would be forced to fight. ... This is all my dad's creation. He created me."

Then he thought about his mother, lost so long ago. Was she part of the invisible hand?

"I just went to the grave a few days ago, actually," he said quietly. "I talk to her all the time. I sometimes tell her, you know, 'Thank you....' I know that she's looking down and taking care of me. Because everything I do always turns out good. Everything. And I thanked her for letting me keep on winning and guiding me. I just go there and sometimes just get angry. 'Why isn't she here? Why?' I still to this day, I can't explain. Why isn't she here?"

And what would she think of her tall young son now? What would she say to Oscar De La Hoya, about his career, about his estrangement from his and her hometown, about his life. ... What would Cecilia De La Hoya think?

"She was more concerned with me as a person," Oscar said. "I think if she was here now, she probably would've wanted me to be married and happy, with eight little kids. ... She knew that boxing made me happy, but Mom always wants to see her sons happy, no matter what. But my personal life is not really too good. If she was here, I would've been married. She would've pushed me to do that, that's for sure. I can hear her, *'I want grandchildren!'*"

A few months after that elegiac discussion, on February 18, 1998, De La Hoya's son, Jacob, was born. After he demolished Charpentier in El Paso, De La Hoya was approached by an HBO camera and an interviewer. And the new father grabbed the microphone.

"This fight here meant a lot to me. There was just one focus on my mind today. This fight is dedicated to my little boy, Jacob. He's three months, and I miss him. This is for you!" he said, wild enough and loud enough to be heard in heaven.

Oscar De La Hoya's Professional Ring Record

Born: February 4, 1973

1992	Nov. 23	Lamar Williams	Inglewood, CA	KO 1 (Pro Debut)
	Dec. 12	Cliff Hicks	Phoenix, AZ	KO 1 (2–0, 2 KOs)

1993	Jan. 3	Paris Alexander	Hollywood, CA	KO 2 (3–0, 3 KOs)
	Feb. 6	Curtis Strong	San Diego, CA	KO 4 (4–0, 4 KOs)
	Mar. 13	Jeff Mayweather	Las Vegas, NV	KO 4 (5–0, 5 KOs)
	Apr. 6	Mike Grable	Rochester, NY	Win/DEC 8 (6–0, 5 KOs)
	May 8	Frankie Avelar	Stateline, NV	KO 4 (7–0, 6 KOs)
	June 7	Troy Dorsey	Las Vegas, NV	KO 1 (8–0, 7 KOs)
	Aug. 14	Renaldo Carter	Bay St. Louis, MS	KO 6 (9–0, 8 KOs)
	Aug. 27	Angelo Nuñez	Beverly Hills, CA	KO 4 (10–0, 9 KOs)
	Oct. 30	Narciso Valenzuela	Phoenix, AZ	KO 1 (11–0, 10 KOs)

1994	Mar. 5	Jimmi Bredahl	Los Angeles, CA	KO 10 (12–0, 11 KOs) Win WBO 130 title
	May 27	Giorgio Campanella	Las Vegas, NV	KO 3 (13–0, 12 KOs) Retain WBO 130
	July 29	Jorge Paez	Las Vegas, NV	KO 2 (14–0, 13 KOs) Win WBO 135
	Nov. 18	Carl Griffith	Las Vegas, NV	KO 3 (15–0, 14 KOs) Retain WBO 135
	Dec. 10	John Avila	Los Angeles, CA	KO 9 (16–0, 15 KOs) Retain WBO 135

1995	Feb. 18	John John Molina	Las Vegas, NV	Win/DEC 12 (17–0, 15 KOs) Retain WBO 135
	May 6	Rafael Ruelas	Las Vegas, NV	KO 2 (18–0, 16 KOs) Retain WBO/Win IBF 135
	Sept. 9	Genaro Hernandez	Las Vegas, NV	KO 6 (19–0, 17 KOs) Retain WBO 135
	Dec. 15	Jesse James Leija	New York, NY	KO 2 (20–0, 18 KOs) Retain WBO 135
1996	Feb. 9	Darryl Tyson	Las Vegas, NV	KO 2 (21–0, 19 KOs)
	June 7	Julio Cesar Chavez	Las Vegas, NV	KO 4 (22–0, 20 KOs) Win WBC 140
1997	Jan. 18	Miguel Angel Gonzalez	Las Vegas, NV	Win/DEC 12 (23–0, 20 KOs) Retain WBC 140
	Apr. 12	Pernell Whitaker	Las Vegas, NV	Win/DEC 12 (24–0, 20 KOs) Win WBC 147
	June 14	David Kamau	San Antonio, TX	KO 2 (25–0, 21 KOs) Retain WBC 147
	Sept. 13	Hector Camacho	Las Vegas, NV	Win/DEC 12 (26–0, 21 KOs) Retain WBC 147
	Dec. 6	Wilfredo Rivera	Atlantic City, NJ	KO 8 (27–0, 22 KOs) Retain WBC 147
1998	June 13	Patrick Charpentier	El Paso, TX	KO 3 (28-0, 23 KOs) Retain WBC 147
	Sept. 18	Julio Cesar Chavez	Las Vegas, NV	KO 8 (29-0, 24 KOs) Retain WBC 147

About the Author

Tim Kawakami is a sportswriter with the *Los Angeles Times* and covered boxing for the paper for four years. He also has covered UCLA basketball and the Los Angeles Rams, and currently covers the Los Angeles Lakers. He lives in Redondo Beach, California.